Policy transfer and
criminal justice

Policy transfer and criminal justice

Exploring US influence over British crime control policy

Trevor Jones and Tim Newburn

Open University Press

Open University Press
McGraw-Hill Education
McGraw-Hill House
Shoppenhangers Road
Maidenhead
Berkshire
England
SL6 2QL

email: enquiries@openup.co.uk
world wide web: www.openup.co.uk

and Two Penn Plaza, New York, NY 10121-2289, USA

First published 2007

A catalogue record of this book is available from the British Library

ISBN-10: 0 335 21668 4 (pb) 0 335 21669 2 (hb)
ISBN-13: 978 0 335 21668 0 (pb) 978 0 335 21669 7 (hb)

Library of Congress Cataloging-in-Publication Data
CIP data applied for

Typeset by RefineCatch Limited, Bungay, Suffolk
Printed in Poland EU by OZGraf. S.A.
www.polskabook.pl

The *McGraw-Hill* Companies

Contents

Acknowledgements

The research which forms the basis for this book was generously supported by the ESRC (Grant no. L216252035) and was part of the Future Governance research programme. It was a pleasure to be part of the programme and we owe a particular debt of thanks to Professor Ed Page, its Director, for his friendship, support and advice over a number of years. It is increasingly difficult in modern university life to find sustained time in which to write and Trevor Jones would like to thank Cardiff School of Social Sciences for a period of study leave in 2005/06 during which time this book was completed. A very large number of people gave up time to be interviewed as part of this study and we thank them all. They are too numerous to list in full. Early in the study we benefited from the research assistance of Peter Hall and our thanks go to him. At the outset of our work in the USA we were given significant help by the staff of the British Embassy in Washington DC, and we would like to thank Bob Peirce, Jamila Burke and particularly Olivia Mcleod. Finally, in relation to the US element of this study, we would be remiss if we failed to acknowledge the important support provided by Sam Adams, patriot and brewer.

Presentations based on elements of this research were given at: the British Criminology Conferences in Keele in 2002, Bangor in 2003, Portsmouth in 2004 and Leeds in 2005; the American Society of Criminology meetings in Atlanta in 2001, Chicago in 2002, Nashville in 2004, and Toronto in 2005; the 2001 Political Studies Association conference in Manchester and at the American Political Science Association Annual Meeting in San Francisco in 2001, and at Queen's Belfast, University College Dublin, LSE and Leeds, Oxford, and Cambridge universities. We are grateful to the organizers and participants at all these events for the feedback we received. A number of colleagues have commented on work that has gone into this book and we thank them for that. David Faulkner and Paul Rock read the manuscript in full and helped improve it in a number of important ways. We have drawn on a number of already published articles and we gratefully acknowledge the permission of the publisher and editors of the following journals to reproduce elements from this work: 'Policy convergence and crime control in the US and UK', *Criminal Justice*, 2(2): 173–204, 2002 (Sage Publications); 'Comparative criminal justice policy-making in the US and UK: the case of private prisons', *British Journal of Criminology*, 45(1): 58–80, 2004 (Oxford University Press); 'Symbolic politics and penal populism: the long shadow of Willie

Horton', *Crime, Media, Culture*, 1(1): 72–87, 2005 (Sage Publications); and 'Three strikes and you're out: exploring symbol and substance in American and British crime control politics', *British Journal of Criminology*, 46(3): 781–802, 2006 (Oxford University Press).

1 Convergence and Divergence in Crime Control

Introduction

The focus of this book is on what some British political scientists are increasingly coming to refer to as 'policy transfer' (Wolman 1992; Dolowitz et al. 2000). This relates to a growing perception that, over the past two decades, social policy in the UK has increasingly involved the importation of ideas from abroad, particularly from the United States. Of course, policy transfer is only one way of understanding the movement of political ideas and policies. Moreover, the movement of policies between societies is not a new development nor, importantly, does it occur in one direction only. Thus, Rodgers (1998) shows in great detail how the 'classic' era in American social politics before the Second World War, an era characterized by huge developments in urban planning, rural regeneration, the design and organization of public housing and social insurance, was profoundly influenced by models and experiments derived from Europe.

Nonetheless, there is a very clear perception that the United States has been either the direct source of, or at least the inspiration for, a number of the policy developments in Britain over the past 20 years. Indeed, the list is long, and includes: 'welfare to work' (Dolowitz 1997; King and Wickham-Jones 1999); the introduction of the internal market in the health service (O'Neill 2000); the child support agency (Dolowitz 2000c); the adoption of Sure Start and related early intervention models; reforms to both further and higher education (Hulme 2000); independence for the Bank of England (along the lines of the Federal Reserve); elected mayors; and the language of the 'new deal'. Our concern in this book is with the somewhat under-explored subject of policy transfer in the area of crime control (though see Nellis 2000; Wacquant 1999c; and the contributions in Newburn and Sparks 2004b) and, more particularly, on transfer between the United States and the UK. Again, this is an area in which many observers believe the United States has been a significant influence on the nature and trajectory of British policy. Jock Young (2003: 40–1), for example, has noted how

> Via [John] DiIulio and James Q. Wilson Labour adopted the metaphor of the war against crime and against drugs, and incarceration as the key weapon in this war. From Wilson, it took the concept of zero-tolerance . . . I am not suggesting that either Tony Blair or the Home Secretary at the time, Jack Straw, have any direct acquaintance with these commentators. Merely that it is the ideas of such thinkers filtered through the lenses of policy advisers and speech-writers that have greatly influenced New Labour's policy on law and order.

In a similar vein, not long after his appointment as Director of Public Prosecutions in 2003, Ken Macdonald made a widely reported speech in which he castigated the government for following a tough US agenda and for importing 'prison works'.[1] We should reiterate at this point that we are not arguing that this is the only, or even the most important, area of possible policy transfer in criminal justice in recent times. It has merely been the particular focus of our concerns. We could just as easily have looked at the influence of ideas, policies and practices such as restorative justice that would appear to have originated in part from Australia and New Zealand. However, it is on the possibility of the transfer eastwards across the Atlantic that we focus in this book.

The American historian Denis Rothman has remarked that 'the least controversial observation about American criminal justice today is that it is remarkably ineffective, absurdly expensive, grossly inhumane, and riddled with discrimination' (1995: 29). Had he been an observer from the UK, however, he might have added to this list, with a due sense of irony, that, despite its alleged faults, American criminal justice also appears to be enormously politically attractive. Thus, paradoxically, despite the highest incarceration rate in the world, together with levels of lethal violence that dwarf our own (Zimring and Hawkins 1997), somehow our politicians find 'Made in the USA' (Wacquant 1999b) crime control policies strangely seductive.

Thus, in recent times we have seen the emergence of a strong private corrections industry in the UK, initially at least involving American corporations offering to build, manage and staff private prisons, and to manufacture and oversee the use of electronic tags. During the 1990s a number of apparently American slogans found their way to these shores and were used by politicians to frame new policy ideas such as mandatory sentencing ('three strikes and you're out'), restrictions on early release ('honesty in sentencing'), and strategies for dealing with disorder ('zero tolerance policing'). Albeit briefly, a 'Drugs Tsar' was introduced to oversee government drugs policy, curfews have been introduced in response to anti-social behaviour by young people, and a variety of other apparently US-inspired initiatives – drugs courts, community courts and, indeed, the more general 'what works' approach – have been visible on the criminal justice landscape at some point during the last decade. Indeed, such developments are by no means confined to the USA and Britain, with apparently similar shifts in policy taking place in continental Europe (De Maillard and Roche 2004; Pakes 2004; Punch *et al.* 2005) and, to a lesser degree, Australia (Frase 2001; O'Malley 2004) and Canada (Doob and Cesaroni 2004). A generalized shift toward a more punitive culture of control has received widespread criminological attention, and it is to some of this work on convergence in criminal justice systems that we turn next.

Convergence and divergence in crime control

Criminologists have traditionally focused more upon the content and consequences than upon the *genesis* of criminal justice and penal policy. In recent years, however, a number of highly influential writers have addressed the question 'what shapes criminal justice and penal policy?' Two main perspectives have emerged in recent work that attempts to answer this question.

A substantial body of recent writing on this matter suggests that crime control and penal policy continue to be strongly influenced by national, and sub-national, political institutions, cultures and historical traditions. A number of authors have focused particularly upon what appear to be continuing contrasts and divergences between penal policies in different nation states. For example, Tonry (1999a, 2001) stresses the striking differences in penal policy interventions between countries with different historical and cultural traditions. As he argues: 'The world increasingly may be a global community . . . but explanations of penal policy remain curiously local' (2001: 518). In his more recent analysis of British and American penal cultures (2004a, 2004b) Tonry develops this theme and explores some of the significant continuing differences between jurisdictions. He argues that until the early 1990s, criminal justice and penal policy in the UK had more in common with other Western European nations than the USA. However, since this time he perceives a growing tendency for British policy to emulate that in parts of the USA, much of which he links to the Labour Party's changed position on crime and punishment. Although ultimately Tonry believes this to be the product of political choice and the strategic decision-making of senior Labour politicians, he argues that these policy outcomes were made more likely by three cultural characteristics that he believes are not shared by other European countries such as France or Germany. First, he suggests that the population in Britain have become peculiarly risk-averse regarding crime, a condition he relates to growing government emphasis on crime prevention in recent decades which has had the perverse effect of actually exacerbating fear of crime and disorder. Second, he draws upon the work of Whitman (2003) – discussed in more detail below – to suggest that the British have developed a particular cultural taste for the debasement of offenders. Finally, he argues that people in Britain have a more acute sense of 'self righteousness and punitiveness' about deviance and deviants than exists in other European countries (Tonry 2004a: 55–66). Thus, Tonry's arguments place strong emphasis on the importance of particular national political cultures and institutions as key shapers of crime control and penal policy.

In a similar vein, Melossi has argued that '[p]unishment is deeply embedded in the national/cultural specificity of the environment which produces it' (2004: 407). His work has highlighted the striking differences over time between penal systems in the US and in Italy, and how this relates to deep-seated cultural attitudes that are associated with Protestant and Catholic religious traditions. The work of Pat O'Malley (2004) has examined the resistance to the 'war on drugs' and to the emergence of 'actuarial justice' in Australia and New Zealand. His explanation lies not in exploring the differing ways in which particular political jurisdictions respond to neo-liberalism but, rather, rests on the argument that different forms of neo-liberalism have been at work in these jurisdictions. These distinctive forms, and the ways in which they 'reflect the filtering and translating effects of national politics' have been critical in the development of an inclusive and social-democratic mode of institutionalizing risk in Australasia compared with the more exclusive, conservative neo-liberal mode in the United States (2004: 218).

Recent discussions have focused in particular upon the distinctiveness (or otherwise) of crime control and penal policy in the USA when compared with other Western democracies (Poveda 2000; Garland 2005). This draws upon a substantial body of work on 'American exceptionalism' that highlights a number of apparently distinctive features of the USA that set it apart from other Western democracies. These include such things as the persistence of a strong form of individualism, suspicion of the state and government generally, the lack of influence of socialist political parties and organized labour, and continued high levels of religious observance (Lipset 1996). A number of authors have suggested that penal policies in the USA are qualitatively distinct from those in other countries because of particular cultural and historical features of US society.

For example, an interesting historical analysis of national differences in approach to crime control has recently been provided by James Whitman. Contrasting the penal histories of France and Germany with America, Whitman explores why 'over the last quarter century, America has shown a systematic drive toward increased harshness by most measures, while continental Europe has not' (2003: 57). In part, his answer lies in the extent to which penal policy-making has remained relatively insulated from punitive public demands in France and Germany – particularly when compared with the febrile penal atmosphere in the United States. In northern continental European countries, criminal justice is traditionally strongly influenced by trained bureaucrats, whereas in most parts of the USA it is far more open to the vicissitudes of popular opinion. Whitman's analysis of the differences between these jurisdictions, however, lies partly in attitudes toward the state, and partly in how differences in status hierarchy became translated into very different attitudes toward punishment. Whitman's thesis then contrasts public attitudes towards central state institutions in the USA with European countries. For example, historically there has been widespread public acceptance of the strong state bureaucracies that exist in Germany and France when compared with the significantly more circumscribed, and distrusted, apparatus in the USA. In relation to status hierarchy and punishment, Whitman describes how in France and Germany there was a process of levelling-up in which, gradually, all prisoners were accorded respect and treated moderately. By contrast, American punishment has been, and remains, degrading. Zimring (2003) links the persistence of capital punishment in the USA (in stark contrast to European nations) to long-established historical traditions and distinctive cultural traits that are particularly associated with parts of the USA (what he terms 'the vigilante tradition'). Linking all this work is a focus upon explaining contrasts between penal policies in different jurisdictions, a strong theme within which is the particular distinctiveness of the USA.

The attempts by Whitman and others to explain differences and divergences in contemporary systems of control have much to commend them. However, these approaches have their limitations. For example, it may be argued that they overplay evidence about difference between countries and overlook some highly important globalizing elements in policy change. A further limitation is that some of this literature underplays the role of political agency and presents a rather deterministic view of policy change (Garland 2005). For example, if we put too much weight upon the cultural embeddedness of penal systems and the legacy of historical path-dependencies, then we risk suggesting that national criminal justice systems are almost impervious to radical change, whether brought about by global influences, domestic pressures or a combination of the two. Finally, there is a danger of placing too much emphasis on the national level. Arguments that focus upon differences between nation states, and in particular how national political cultures and institutions resist and rework transnational policy ideas, may present a rather one-dimensional and top-down view of policy change. Many policy innovations arise at the sub-national level before moving up to the national level (Stenson and Edwards 2004), and others travel between regions in different jurisdictions without necessarily emerging as national policies (Edwards and Hughes 2005).

By contrast, a focus upon similarity and convergence between the USA and other Western democracies has characterized another highly influential body of work that has emerged in recent years. For example, Nils Christie

(2000) has explored the growth of incarceration in many countries during the latter part of the twentieth century. He highlights a number of structural and cultural changes associated with these developments. For example, he suggests that changes in social organization in capitalist societies have led both to a decline of informal social controls and to an increased tendency to report incidents for formal processing by the police. Public demands for harsher punishments have also been encouraged by a generalized sense of insecurity arising from structural and cultural developments in capitalist societies. At the same time, the commodification of crime control in capitalist societies and the growing commercial corrections market have been a key factor fuelling the expansion of prison populations. Christie argues that penal policy in many industrialized countries is increasingly influenced by what he terms the 'prison-industrial complex', an international alliance of commercial penal and industrial interests that profits from expansionist penal policies. These developments should not be regarded as irrational or in any sense extraordinary. On the contrary, they are the 'natural outgrowth of our type of society, not an exception to it' (2000: 178).

Similar, but broader themes are developed in the work of David Garland (2001a) who has highlighted the emergence of a 'culture of control' in the UK and the USA. Garland argues that the style and substance of penal policy in the UK and the USA have become increasingly similar in recent years. This is explained by fundamental shifts of social structures and cultural configurations visible, to a greater or lesser degree, across many late modern capitalist societies. Garland argues that, in both the USA and the UK, two kinds of contrasting policy strategies have been introduced (first and more vigorously in the USA but later followed by the UK). The first type involves the introduction of pragmatic or 'adaptive' approaches to the crime problem, such as the introduction of private sector management techniques to the criminal justice systems, the promotion of management reforms and privatization, rigorous systems of performance measurement, diversion from the criminal justice system, the pragmatic redefinition of the goals of criminal justice agencies, and the active 'responsibilization' of a range of private, voluntary and community agents in the field of crime control. The second involves the simultaneous (and paradoxical) adoption of policies of 'denial'. That is, in both the USA and the UK, governments have responded to the growing awareness of their instrumental limitations in the crime control arena by adopting primarily expressive law enforcement and sentencing policies, in some respects representing a return to a system resonant of the eighteenth-century amalgam of weak enforcement and draconian punishment. The object of such policies is 'to denounce the crime and reassure the public' (2001a: 133), rather than aiming to reduce levels of crime. The key to understanding policy convergence, therefore, is to analyse fundamental structural and cultural developments in capitalist societies. Garland accepts that '[p]olitics and policy always involve choice and decision-making and the possibility of acting otherwise' (2001a: 139). However, the broader focus of this approach downplays the importance of conscious political agency as a shaper of policy outcomes. The political choices that have been made reflect deeper changes in social structures and cultural sensibilities.

Thus, there is a significant body of work whose primary focus is the convergence of penal policy across different national contexts. A number of criticisms have been made of this approach. In particular, it has been argued that it places too much emphasis on convergence, and overlooks substantial differences in policy between different nations. Zedner (2002: 341), for example, has suggested that 'the more "volatile and contradictory" the philosophies, policies and practices of punishment appear to be, the greater the drive among penal theorists to give an account capable of rendering them, if not coherent, then at least comprehensible'. Relatedly, it can be argued that convergence theories underplay the importance of political agency and the mediating influences of contrasting national and sub-national political and legal institutions and cultures. Arguably, they also downplay the increasingly important role played by supranational bodies such as the United Nations, the European Union and the Council of Europe, each of which has an explicit harmonizing role in respect of particular policy areas across specific groups of nation states. Finally, of necessity because of its broad focus, such work is relatively unconcerned with the essentially contested and unpredictable nature of public policy-making process and, as a consequence, albeit unintentionally, has a somewhat deterministic flavour. Convergence theories tend to give the impression that the direction of policy is inevitable and irreversible.

Recent overarching studies of convergence have been hugely important in developing criminological scholarship and have made a significant contribution to our understanding of current trends in penal policy. At the same time, scholars who have provided more focused and detailed policy histories that identify and explain regional and national differences have enhanced our comprehension of the ways in which local political cultures and the activities of key political actors serve to initiate, reshape, mediate or resist policy ideas and innovations that travel across jurisdictional boundaries. It is important to note that we do not suggest that authors whose work falls into either of these broad approaches are presenting a picture of total convergence on the one hand, or complete national/local autonomy on the other. Indeed, most authors writing in this field clearly recognize the simultaneous existence of elements of convergence and divergence between nations and regions, and accept that policy outcomes arise from a complex interplay between local, national and international forces. As David Garland has observed, the different emphases of these distinct approaches are, in a sense, irreconcilable because they relate to the 'unavoidable tension between broad generalization and the specification of empirical particulars' (2001a: vi). However, although we would concur with this on one level, we do think that it is possible to develop further the focus upon both similarity and difference between national penal systems, drawing upon the important insights of both the 'broad generalization' approaches that Garland refers to, and those which concentrate more upon the 'empirical particulars'. Inevitably, the current work leans more towards the latter approach, in that its focus is upon the development of specific policies at particular times and places. However, in exploring the ways in which specific policies are formed at given points in time within the context of distinctive political institutions and cultures, it is important to remain mindful of the degree to which broader social and cultural trends shape (and are themselves shaped by) these developments. Therefore, we believe that it is both possible and useful to attempt to reconcile the insights provided by studies coming from the broad global/convergence and local/ divergence vantage points, and the study that led to this book is an attempt to begin to do so.

Crime control in the USA

As we have explained, our primary focus in this book is policy transfer in the arena of crime control and, in particular, transfers between the USA and Britain. Before moving on, it is worth taking a brief look at the current state of crime control in the USA. This inevitably will involve a generalizing overview that obscures significant differences within and between different states of the USA (Newburn 2006). A number of authors have been critical of the tendency to treat crime control in the USA as if it were a single, monolithic system (Tonry 2001; Garland 2005). In practice, of course, there are some very significant variations in the ways in which criminal justice and penal policy is organized across the 50 states of the US, yet this remains largely unstudied (Newburn 2006). However, having said this, it remains the case that there seem to be certain features of dominant approaches to crime control in the USA that distinguish it from many other countries. This is now well-trawled territory for scholars around the world, not just the United States. As noted above, there is a substantial body of work that highlights particular features of the USA and arguably renders it distinct from a range of other Western democracies in a number of important ways. This idea of 'American exceptionalism' has also emerged in the field of criminal justice and penal policy, and has been the subject of strong debate (Poveda 2000; Garland 2005; Whitman 2005; Zimring 2005). It is thus important to note that this debate has focused upon some of the key features of criminal justice and penal policy in the USA that may, in some way at least, be considered to differentiate it from many European countries.

The easiest and the logical place to start is with the prison population, for this is perhaps the most extraordinary feature not only of the American penal landscape but arguably of any liberal democracy in the late twentieth century. The first important point to note is the extent and pace of change that have taken place in the past 30 years. For most of the twentieth century the incarceration rate in the USA, though on the high side internationally, remained relatively stable between 100 and 120 per 100,000 population. It started to rise steadily in the 1970s and by 1995 had reached 600 per 100,000. By comparison, in 1995 the rate per 100,000 in Japan was 37, in Germany and Italy 85 and around 100 in England and Wales. Only Russia had a higher incarceration rate than America. The incarceration rate in the USA is now over 700 per 100,000. Whereas in 1972 there were less than 200,000 Americans in prison, there are now, a little over 30 years later, over two million. Whichever way one looks at it, the change is truly staggering.

There is not the time here to explore the reasons for this explosion in any detail. However, before moving on, some of the features of this carceral experiment require a little further consideration. The first is crime rates. Undoubtedly, most people on being told that the US prison population had grown tenfold in the past 30 years would assume that this was a product of rising crime rates. By and large, however, they would be wrong (Tonry 1999b). Crime rates, though they are now higher than they were in the early 1970s, have in general remained remarkably stable in the USA. Crime rates rose in the 1970s, declined in the first half of the 1980s, increased again until the early 1990s, and have been generally in decline since. Throughout these rises and falls the use of the prison has increased. When crime went up, so did the prison population, but it continued to do so even when crime went down (Greenberg 2001).

What then of the possibility that it is precisely the increased use of punishment generally, and custody particularly, that has inhibited what would have otherwise been much more significant rises in crime (Downes 2001)? There is clearly, at least, some form of historical association with the stemming of the rise in crime in the USA and the growth of the use of mass incarceration. There is, however, little evidence to suggest that this relationship is a causal one, and there are also both a sufficient number of potential mediating factors and also counter-examples from other countries to cast significant doubt on such a notion (Greenberg 2001). The most robust research suggests that the prison build-up was responsible for about one quarter of the overall crime drop during this period, though it may well have had a more significant impact on violent crime (Spelman 2000). Nevertheless, as a single factor it does not come close to explaining the crime drop in the USA.

As is now well documented (see, for example, Beckett 1997; Currie 1998), what we have witnessed since the early 1970s has been a highly politicized experiment in crime control. Beginning in 1964 with Barry Goldwater, the then Republican challenger to President Lyndon Johnson, politicians have increasingly talked tough on crime-related issues. It was during Richard Nixon's term of office, however, that the two issues that are arguably most important in understanding the last 25 years of law and order politics in the USA began clearly to emerge in political rhetoric: race and drugs. Nixon appealed 'to voters' fears of social unrest and violent crime . . . especially on white fear of black street crime' (Chambliss 1999: 19). The 'war on crime' declared by Nixon was followed by a full-scale 'war on drugs' declared by Ronald Reagan in 1982, and heightened by his successor, George Bush. In his first television address to the nation on 5 September 1989, President Bush said, 'All of us agree that the gravest domestic threat facing our nation today is drugs.' He called for 'an assault on every front' and urged Americans to 'face this evil as a nation united' (Bertram *et al.* 1996: 114). He went on: 'The rules have changed: if you sell drugs, you will be caught; and when you're caught, you will be prosecuted; and once you're convicted, you will do time. Caught, prosecuted, punished . . . American cocaine users need to understand that our nation has zero tolerance for casual drug use' (1996: 114). Between 1981 and 1993 the federal budget for drug law enforcement surged from $855 million to $7.8 billion (1996: 110).

Law enforcement rather than treatment has, not surprisingly, been the major tool employed in the war on drugs. Billions of dollars have been spent on the three main components of this war: source country efforts (attacking drug production abroad), interdiction (seizing drugs on their way to the USA), and domestic law enforcement (arresting and incarcerating sellers and buyers). Domestically, the law enforcement effort involved high levels of arrests and, crucially, the introduction of 'three strikes' laws and increased determinate sentencing. Put crudely, 'three strikes' and related determinate sentencing practices have two major consequences. First, they increase the proportion of arrested drug offenders sentenced to prison and, second, they increase the length of time served (Mauer 1999a).

These highly racialized strategies have had a highly disproportionate impact on African-American communities. Thus, African Americans, who constitute approximately 13 per cent of the US population, accounted for 21 per cent of drug possession arrests nationally in 1980. By 1992 this had risen to 36 per cent – all against a background of data that show that roughly similar proportions of whites and blacks use drugs in the USA (Mauer 1999b). There was very nearly a 500 per cent increase in the number of drug offenders in prison between 1985 and 1995. Very substantial proportions of these were African American. The starkest contrast can be seen in lifetime likelihood of imprisonment. Young, black males born in 1991 have an extraordinary 29 per cent chance of being imprisoned at some point in their life. The chance lowers to 16 per cent for Hispanic males and 4 per cent for whites (Mauer 1999a). The consequence of the racialized 'wars' on crime and drugs in the United States is that over half of all prisoners now are African American and almost a further fifth are Hispanic. The situation is even starker if one looks at young men only. According to the Washington DC-based Sentencing Project, over one-third of black males in the United States aged 20–29 are either in prison, jail, or on probation or parole on any given day. So serious is this situation that at least one academic commentator has referred to it as a process of 'ethnic cleansing' (Chambliss 1999).

Massive increases in prison populations, and sentencing policies that underpin such trends, have thus become strongly associated with notion of US 'exceptionalism'. However, recent influential work has demonstrated that similar (if much less marked) trends are visible in Europe (Christie 2000). One area where US criminal justice has shown an indisputable divergence from other Western democracies in recent years, however, is in the use of capital punishment. Whereas over the past three decades, European countries have abolished the use of capital punishment, since the late 1970s its use has increased in the USA. This divergence has accelerated during the 1990s. As David Garland has observed:

> In a period when many nations completely abolished the death penalty, international conventions outlawed it, and Europe finally became a death penalty-free zone, the USA moved rapidly in the opposite direction, increasing its annual number of executions (from one or two per year at the start of the 1980s to a peak of 98 in 1999), passing new capital punishment legislation, reducing the level of judicial review and regulation and consolidating an increasingly bipartisan political support for the institution.
>
> (2005: 348–9)

This apparent departure from European trends has been understood and explained in very different ways. Zimring (2003) relates it to longer-standing traditions in cultures and social practices in certain parts of the USA, whereas Garland (2005) sees it arising from a more recent (and contingent) constellation of forces that have emerged during the past three decades. Whatever the outcome of this debate, it is clear that there are current features of US criminal justice which, although there is wide disagreement about their root causes, are still generally considered as remarkable in comparison to other Western democracies.

In many senses, approaches to criminal justice and penal policy in the USA do not on the surface appear to be an obvious candidate for lesson-drawing for politicians from other jurisdictions. Indeed, one does not have to delve too far into the past to find senior figures in the British Labour Party castigating US approaches in criminal justice. Perhaps the most startling example of this can be found with reference to comments of the current UK Prime Minister made while in Opposition:

> The Shadow Home Secretary, Tony Blair, said that the idea of using America as a model for Britain was 'one of the most alarming and misguided notions of modern times that will be greeted with disbelief by anybody with experience of the American penal system'.
>
> (Travis 1993)

Yet, at several points in recent years it has appeared as if British politicians, in both major parties, have remained in thrall to American crime control ideas – much more so than policies and practices that might be developing in other parts of the world. In addition to asking questions about the nature of lesson-drawing in criminal justice, one of our concerns in this book is *why* America should continue to be an apparent source of inspiration. One possible answer to this conundrum lies in the global reach and power of North American industry, media and culture. Indeed, their collective power and reach have sometimes led to something of an elision of ideas of 'Americanization' and 'globalization'. In addition, the existence of a common language clearly helps facilitate the transfer of ideas between nations. Perhaps as importantly, the existence of multiple criminal justice systems within the federal USA aids and abets experimentation, making it a fertile ground for politicians searching for inspiration. Though there is undoubtedly more to globalization than the spread of US products, policies and practices, it is to the idea of Americanization that we turn next.

Americanization

Ever since the Second World War, the subject (or, for some, the threat) of Americanization has been a significant theme in British public life. The term 'Americanization' has been particularly associated with the field of cultural studies, where it has been used to denote the process 'of transfer of goods and symbols from the United States to other countries' (Fehrenbach and Poiger 2000: xiv). There have been a large number of studies of cultural exports from the USA, in particular in the spheres of film, music and the broadcast media (see, for example, Epitropoulos and Roudometof 1998). Post-war affluence and optimism, the spread of mass media, emerging youth subcultures and youth markets, together with changes in the moral climate – often referred to as 'permissiveness' (Newburn 1992) – were all in some way associated with what was believed to be the growing influence of American culture. Americanization has been used in ways that have both positive and negative connotations. From one viewpoint, post-war American influence in Europe can be seen as 'a benign and beneficial combination of political mandate, economic stimulus, and consumer practice' (Fehrenbach and Poiger 2000: xx). On the other hand, a significant body of work since the 1970s has presented American influence in an entirely negative light, highlighting a perceived American 'cultural imperialism' (Schiller 1992), and presenting the process of Americanization and resistance to it as 'homogenizing evil empire versus the charmingly diversified world' (Fehrenbach and Poiger 2000: xix). In the words of Pells (1997: 189), 'Since the beginning of the twentieth century, the word "Americanization" had summoned up a sense of danger – a feeling that the US was imposing its economic and cultural will, either unconsciously or with sinister intent, on Europe.' Such polarized views, however, oversimplify the complex processes of cultural interaction and dialogue, and arguably underplay the role of agency and choice.

More recently, growing attention has been paid to the alleged Americanization of social policies in many Western countries, with particular attention paid to labour market and welfare policies (Walker 1998). Dolowitz (1997), for example, demonstrates that there is a long history of connection between 'workfare' policies that developed in the USA and the UK. Early links between the Thatcher and Reagan administrations were later developed and consolidated during the leadership of Blair and Clinton (Deacon 1999). Peck and Theodore (2001) provide interview evidence suggesting that, in terms of the search for policy ideas, Labour Party officials switched their attention from continental Europe to the USA during the period immediately prior to their return to office in 1997.

Though this period – the rise of New Labour and the first two New Labour governments – is the primary focus of much of the discussion in this book, it would be misleading if this were presented as something of a radical break with the immediate political past. Thus, while it is unusual for Labour administrations to have such close ties with their US counterparts, this is arguably less the case with Conservative administrations. That said, the nature of the relationship between the Thatcher and Reagan administrations in the 1980s was unusually warm even by Conservative–Republican standards. Hugo Young (1991: 249) suggests that 'The Reagan–Thatcher axis was the most enduring personal alliance throughout the 1980s. From Moscow to Pretoria, from Tripoli to Buenos Aires, no theatre of global conflict failed to feel its effects. It eclipsed, where it did not determine, many of the details of Mrs Thatcher's performance in the diplomatic field.'

Though the personal relationship between Bill Clinton and Tony Blair never rivalled the Reagan–Thatcher friendship, it is nevertheless clear that the rise of Clinton in the American political scene had a number of very important effects on the British Labour Party. Among these, undoubtedly the most important was the way in which the Democratic Party provided the template for the Labour Party's transformation into 'New Labour'. The lengthy political dominance of Republicanism in the USA and Conservatism in the UK in the 1980s led to vociferous debates within both the Democratic and Labour Parties over the possible sources of electoral success in what were clearly changed times. The process by which the Democrats and Labour became 'New Democrats' and 'New Labour' has been broadly characterized as one of 'modernization' (see Newman 2001) and, centrally, involved a broad process of policy reformulation and image redesign. In policy terms, modernization, according to advocates, meant an attempt to find a 'third way' – a means of transcending old dichotomies and, in particular, that of old-style social democracy on the one hand and neo-liberalism on the other (Le Grand 1998). It also involved giving considerable thought to the public image of the two parties and in due course, in the eyes of some at least, a process of rebranding or image overhaul. It also meant paying particularly close attention to the importance of symbolic politics, not least in the area of crime.

By the early 1990s Labour had been in opposition for well over a decade and serious commentators had begun to speculate whether it would ever be possible for the Labour Party to win another general election. For some in the Labour Party, the breakthrough came with the election of Bill Clinton in 1992. The Labour Party in the UK was a close observer of the 1992 Presidential election (Rentoul 1995, Sopel 1995, Gould 1998). Those that were sympathetic to what had happened to the Democratic Party in the USA sought both to learn and to apply the lessons. A number of Labour Party politicians and advisers were involved in this act of electoral lesson-drawing. Indeed, this process of lesson-drawing occurred in both directions. Senior Democrat strategists were keen to learn lessons from the UK Labour Party's unsuccessful election campaign in 1992. Dave Hill, the Labour Party Head of Communications, was seconded to the Clinton campaign team, accompanied by a number of other Labour Party associates (Dolowitz *et al.* 2000). One of these, who has written most explicitly of his experience, was Philip Gould who spent a number of weeks working with the Clinton campaign team in Little Rock giving advice on tactics, particularly regarding the crucial last week of the campaign (the point at which it was generally suggested that Labour lost the 1992 election). Although we cannot be certain about the degree of influence of lessons from the UK Labour Party, it is clear that the Democrat campaign was significantly different from any of its predecessors:

> The Democrats pursued a strategy which emphasised modern marketing and advertising techniques and used information technology to its upmost. They also used consultants with specialised knowledge of political advertising, techniques such as telephone surveying and stratified public opinion polling. In addition, sophisticated focus group technology became the core of the campaign strategy.
>
> (Dolowitz *et al.* 1999: 720)

Philip Gould returned to the UK and wrote a series of papers for the then Labour Party leader, John Smith, on the lessons for Labour (Butler and

Kavanagh 1997). According to Gould (1998), 'Bill Clinton's election in 1992 showed the world that the left could win, and it showed the left how it could win'. In relation to the how, Gould says three things were central: the rebranding of the party to become 'New Democrats', shifting the political focus towards so-called 'middle America' (then referred to as the 'working middle class') and, in narrower campaigning terms, the use of 'rapid rebuttal'. These lessons were directly drawn from the Democratic Party and, more particularly, a Democratic Party particularly affected by the 1988 election. As Gould (1998: 162) noted:

> After the defeat of Michael Dukakis in 1988, I visited the United States to talk to people who had been involved in the campaign, all of whom were feeling terribly the burden of defeat. It was quite clear where they had gone wrong: they had capitulated to the awesome Republican attack and they had failed to connect to the great American middle class.

Just as the defeat of Dukakis and Bentsen in 1988 convinced many Democrats that a new strategy was required, so successive election defeats in the 1980s and 1990s convinced some in the Labour Party that the same was true for them: 'The trauma of four successive election defeats was scorched across the soul of the Labour Party, and burnt deep into the small group who had seized its commanding heights in the name of modernisation' (Rawnsley 2000: 3). On both sides of the Atlantic, the parties, and their leadership candidates, were successfully portrayed as 'liberal' and ineffectual. Writing in 1990, pollster Stanley Greenberg (1995: 151) suggested that Dukakis:

> . . . did not articulate any set of principles, offered no special perspective, and invoked no deeply resonant historical experience. The public was left, by default, with Lee Atwater's savage caricature: a Democratic Party short on patriotism, weak on defense, soft on criminals and minorities, indifferent to work, values, and family, and, inexplicably, infatuated with taxes.

As Labour Party pollster, Philip Gould, noted later (1998: 173), 'Greenberg was describing Michael Dukakis and the Democratic Party, but he may as well have been describing Neil Kinnock and the Labour Party in 1992.' Whether either Greenberg's portrayal of the Dukakis campaign, or Gould's implication that it is equally applicable to Labour under Kinnock, are accurate is, on one level, relatively unimportant. The crucial factor is that key advisers – and it is clear that Greenberg did have an influence on the Clinton Democrats (Baer 2000) and that both Greenberg and Gould were influential voices in the design of New Labour – believed the messages of the past to be clear and the implications for future directions to be equally transparent. These lessons were to be applied to all the areas in which the party could be portrayed as liberal and out of touch. For both Democrats and Labour one of these was to be crime (Downes and Morgan 2002).

In this regard, one of the very clear lessons learned by the New Democrats, subsequently passed on to New Labour, was the power and importance of symbolic politics; of using a phrase or an action to convey something more powerful and significant. As two influential New Labour architects put it in the early 1990s, 'The lessons which the British left can learn [from the USA] are not so much about *content* – although there is valuable intellectual exchange already underway – as about *process'* (Hewitt and Gould 1993). They might have gone on to note that in addition to learning lessons about process, they learnt at least as much about style. From the rebranding of the party, through the adoption of a new form of political language (Fairclough 2000), and the use of spin and soundbite, New Labour consciously adopted much from the New Democrats, and involved key Democratic Party strategists in its own election campaign (Hewitt and Gould 1993). Indeed, the Americanization, or for some the *Clintonization*, of the Labour Party has led to accusations that the very nature of the British parliamentary system is being changed, not least in the emergence of a more 'Presidential' style of governing by the Prime Minister (Foley 2000).

Beyond personal and political relationships, there are clearly a number of other factors that may ostensibly have played some part in making the United States an attractive source of policy ideas. These include the existence of a common language (providing a strong incentive to look at written documents from other English-speaking nations and have discussions with them), shared ideologies (from the 1980s New Right agenda to the persistence of neo-liberalism under New Labour and the New Democrats), timing (the USA had started down some roads earlier than the UK, particularly in terms of labour market and welfare reforms), and links between think tanks and policy entrepreneurs (Denham and Garnett 1999).

Stone (1996, 2000) argues that think tanks have provided a crucial link between the USA and the UK since the early 1980s. These organizations were central in promoting the ideas of privatization and market liberalization that gained currency, in particular in the UK and the USA, during the 1980s. In Britain, a number of think tanks were involved in promoting neo-liberal ideas including the Institute for Economic Affairs, the Centre for Policy Studies, the Adam Smith Institute and the David Hulme Institute. In the USA, although the federal programme of privatization was more limited, think tanks were also important, including the Heritage Foundation, the American Enterprise Institute (AEI) and the Hoover Institution. Stone's conclusion is that the main impact of think tanks is 'in the construction of legitimacy for certain policies and in agenda setting' (2000: 67). The details of policy, however, remain in the hands of government officials. Thus, think tanks can 'strengthen the necessary conditions of transfer, but cannot by themselves constitute sufficient conditions, nor are they a causal force for transfer' (2000: 67).

Is policy transfer important?

Clearly, then, there are a large number of connections between the USA and the UK, politically, culturally and socially. In the arena of crime control, as David Garland has argued convincingly, there are a number of very important parallels between developments on both sides of the Atlantic suggesting a degree of policy convergence. Indeed, he makes a very strong case for viewing developments in America and Britain as being more *similar* than *different*. There are clear convergences, shared styles of governing, policies and practices that have the same nomenclature and appear to be driven by similar concerns and objectives. To the extent that similar *cultures of control* have and are developing in America and Britain, Garland locates the sources of these developments in the social and cultural changes associated with the coming of late modernity. This is essentially a structuralist explanation which, though it does not rule out the possibility that there may have been some 'political imitation and policy transfer' (Garland 2001a: viii), sees these as relatively minor concerns compared with the broader and deeper changes argued to be at work.

This is not a position with which we disagree. Nothing in what follows is intended to suggest that political imitation or policy diffusion or transfer are the most significant factors in explaining any shared characteristics in the cultures of control in America and Britain. Nevertheless, there are a number of reasons why we believe the study of policy transfer within criminal justice to be important. First, in comparison with some other areas of public policy, it is clearly under-researched. The reason for this is almost certainly the same reason that the study of policy-making more generally in this area is also relatively rare: by and large, such work has been left to political scientists and social/public policy scholars, and none of these groups has hitherto shown a great deal of interest in crime and criminal justice. The empirical study of policy transfer allows for detailed examination of particular areas, to examine first, the nature and the degree of policy convergence in specific fields, and second, how far and in what ways active policy transfers (rather than, say, a coincidence in domestic social and economic forces) have contributed to this.

Second, it is our view that where criminologists do talk about policy and policy-making, they tend to underplay or under-emphasize the role of political agency and the influence of particular, political and legal institutions. Paul Rock's work (see, for example, Rock 2004) would be an important exception to this observation. However, Rock's work aside, in much criminological work there is a tendency to assume that the intentions of policy-makers are contiguous with policy outcomes: policy instruments frequently being read as a straightforward representation of policy-makers' aims and objectives. In practice, and we return to this in slightly more detail in the following chapter, it is rare that policy-making assumes such a rational form. Rather, as we will argue, and later show, it is often the messy result of unintended consequences, serendipity and chance. The study of policy transfer is one way in which the issue and significance of political agency in policy-making can be explored empirically and for this reason we consider it to be of importance.

The third reason for believing the study of policy diffusion and transfer to be important is the issue of convergence and divergence. As we have said, a number of authors have made strong, indeed convincing, cases that there is much in the cultures of control in the developed economies of the 'West' that appears to be common. In certain respects there appears to be growing similarity or convergence between criminal justice and penal systems – and, indeed, the broader institutional structures for responding to crime and the threat of crime. However, there are clearly also important differences and divergences. And, it is here, again, that we think the study of policy transfer comes into play. The study of policy transfer requires particular attention to be paid to the aetiology of policy. Centrally it is, of course, concerned with examining the extent to which ostensibly similar policies in different jurisdictions really are similar. In this way, such work is as alive to the existence of divergences as it is to commonalities and convergences.

Finally, and linked with the previous points, the final reason we would offer here in defence of the study of policy transfer is that it brings to the fore the possibilities of alternatives. In her critique of David Garland's (2001a) *The Culture of Control*, Lucia Zedner suggests that one of the dangers of what she describes as the 'dystopian' elements of his account is that they may serve to reinforce the feeling that the changes described are not only happening, but are inevitable. The risk, she argues, is that such work 'will further entrench a culture which penal theorists might properly think they have a duty to resist' (2002: 363). Whether or not she is accurate in this suggestion, it does seem clear to us that there has developed in recent times a sense of pessimism in social science regarding the possibility of a future very different from the circumstances we find ourselves in now. This is particularly characteristic of the work of some of the 'globalization' theorists (for a critique of such work, see Bourdieu 1999; Harvey 2000). In this context, in our view, any social scientific endeavour which allows human agency to reappear as an important element in explanation, which sees contemporary developments as being in part the product of the conscious decisions and actions of political actors, and which allows for the possibility, therefore, that particular policies may be refashioned or resisted, holds some promise – however limited. It is here that the study of policy transfer has some value for, as Garland (2001a: 201) notes, contemporary crime control policies are not inevitable. Rather, 'they are the outcome (partly planned, partly unintended) of political and cultural and policy choices – choices that could have been different and that can still be rethought and reversed'.

2 Policy-making and policy transfer

A key objective of this book is to address the relative dearth of empirical studies of the policy-making process in the sphere of criminal justice and penal policy. As noted earlier, to date, the primary focus of empirical research by criminologists has tended to be the content and impact of policy rather than its origins. Political scientists, unsurprisingly, have shown greater interest in the details of the policy-making process. They have undertaken detailed studies of the process of policy formulation in a number of different spheres ranging from agricultural policy to telecommunications deregulation. However, to date, there has been remarkably little interest shown by political scientists in the sphere of crime policy. In a similar way, criminologists have paid relatively little attention to the processes of policy-making, though the work of Paul Rock (1990, 1998, 2004) stands out as an important exception. In this chapter we develop a framework for the rest of the book by providing an overview of relevant literature on policy-making and policy transfer. The chapter is divided into three broad sections. We begin by examining the notion of 'policy' in some detail, focusing in particular on the distinction between 'levels' of policy and the 'processes' via which it comes about. The second section reviews the literature on policy transfer and related concepts such as convergence, lesson-drawing and learning. The third section provides a brief overview of the methods employed in this study of policy transfer. We conclude by developing from this discussion a more specific framework of analysis for the specific policy areas that we consider in subsequent chapters.

Exploring 'policy' and 'policy-making'

We have outlined elsewhere the need to avoid taking the term policy as given (Jones and Newburn 2002b). In particular, it is important to draw a distinction between two key dimensions of policy concerned with 'process' and 'substance' respectively. First, it is important to emphasize that policy-making can be represented as a set of processes involving a number of analytically distinct stages or streams. The structure of these streams, and the way in which they interact with one another, have an important influence on the second dimension – policy 'substance' – our central concern here. Thus, policy may also be considered substantively at a number of different levels ranging from the more symbolic elements such as ideas and rhetoric on the one hand to the more concrete manifestations such as policy instruments and practices on the other.

Policy process

It is important to recognize that public policy represents the outcome of a set of processes, rather than an event in itself. One tradition within the study of policy-making has been the systems analysis approach (Easton 1965). This presents policy as emerging from a distinct set of problem-solving processes: problem definition, formulation of alternative solutions, weighing up the implications of alternatives, and experimentation with the preferred choice. In this model, decision-making proceeds in a logical, comprehensive and purposeful manner. Stone (1988) criticizes such approaches as overly mechanistic, and argues that it assumes implicitly a 'rationality project' in its sequential model of the policy-making process. The content of policies is negotiated continuously in the problem definition, legislation, regulation and court decisions, and again in the decisions made by street-level bureaucrats. The various stages of the policy process outlined above are not distinct, and there are participants and events that cross stages. Furthermore, policy outcomes may be an unintended by-product, or may emerge very gradually (Hill 1997). Notwithstanding these limitations, breaking the policy-making cycle into distinct stages, while not necessarily reflecting the real world, has provided political scientists with a useful analytical tool for empirical exploration of the processes involved.

One model which pays due attention to the complex and fluid nature of the policy process, yet provides a systematic approach to its analysis, is Kingdon's (1995) general theory of public policy-making. He identifies three distinct 'process streams' that can be identified within the system. The 'problem stream' concerns the process of generation of problems requiring attention by policy-makers. The 'policy stream' involves the generation of policy ideas and proposals. Finally, the 'political stream' comprises such things as the outcome of elections, developments in the 'public mood', interest group campaigning and other central elements of the political context within which problems and policies circulate. Kingdon suggests that although the three streams usually operate more or less independently of one another, the three converge at critical times whereby 'solutions become joined to problems and both of them are joined to favourable political forces' (1995: 20). From time to time, 'policy windows' (in the form of opportunities for promotion of particular proposals or conceptions of a problem) are opened by developments in the political stream (such as elections, political scandals, or international crises) or the emergence of particularly compelling problems. These windows provide opportunities for what Kingdon calls 'policy entrepreneurs' to push their pet proposals and problems. Such people, according to Kingdon, may be found at multiple points within a policy community. They might be in or outside government, in professional organizations, pressure groups and so on. 'But their defining characteristic, much as in the case of a business entre-preneur, is their willingness to invest their resources – time, energy, reputa-tion, and sometimes money – in the hope of future return' (1995: 122). They work to facilitate the linkage of problems and proposed solutions to the polit-ical stream. The success of policy entrepreneurs depends upon their ability to respond quickly to these windows of opportunity, before other solutions become favoured. Although a good part of this is down to the skill of the policy entrepreneur, crucially, there is also a substantial element of luck involved. Central to his model is the recognition of the contingent and emergent nature of policy, highlighting the often unanticipated and unexpected nature of pol-icy formation and outcome. For Kingdon, a significant development in policy is most likely when problems, policy proposals and politics are linked together into a clear package. Although applying these concepts and ideas to policies that originated a decade ago or more poses a number of problems, the current study still found Kingdon's general approach to be of great value in helping to make sense of the uncertainty of the public policy-making process.

Policy levels

Empirical research into policy formulation inevitably tends to focus upon the more concrete manifestations of policy in the form of published policy statements, legislation, regulations or court rulings. In this vein authors such as Bernstein and Cashore have argued that empirical studies need to focus upon formal policy decisions such as statutes, regulations and statements, because these manifestations of policy capture the 'actual choices of govern-ment' (2000: 70). However, others have identified a number of distinct ele-ments of policy including: policy content (statutes, administrative rules and regulations), policy instruments (institutional tools to achieve goals such as regulatory, administrative, judicial tools) and policy style (consensual, con-frontational or incremental) (see Bennett 1991). Similarly, Dolowitz and Marsh (2000) outline various different elements of policy including policy goals, content, instruments, programmes, institutions, ideologies, ideas and attitudes. Pollitt (2001) draws upon the work of Brunsson (1989), who argues that it is important not to 'make the mistake of supposing that organiza-tional statements and decisions agree with organizational actions' (1989: 231).

Similarly, Pollitt (2001: 938–40) suggests that understanding the complexity of public policy requires us to consider the analytically distinct levels of 'talk' (political rhetoric and symbolism), 'decisions' (written policy statements, specific legislation, programmes, etc.) and 'action' (the actual implementation of such policies on the ground). He notes that, in practice, there are often significant gaps and contrasts between these different dimensions of policy. This book draws distinctions between three levels of policy. First, at the broadest level, *policy ideas, symbols and rhetoric;* second, the more concrete manifestations of policy in terms of *policy content and instruments;* and finally, the more practical applications of policy in terms of its *implementation* by practitioners and professionals.

Policy convergence and policy transfer

It is clear that the domestic public policy process is increasingly open to the influence of individuals, institutions and economic forces operating beyond the borders of nation states (Bernstein and Cashore 2000). This is related to a number of developments, such as an increasingly globalized economic system, rapid improvements in communications technology, and the growing influence of supra-national institutions (Dolowitz 2000b). Such developments have been reflected in a growing interest in the concept of policy transfer between different jurisdictions (Dolowitz and Marsh 1996, 2000; Stone 1999). There is now a substantial literature within political science exploring policy transfer and related concepts, including 'lesson-drawing' (Rose 1993), 'policy convergence' (Bennett 1991), and 'policy diffusion' (Eyestone 1977). This section provides an overview of this body of research and writing with the broad aim of developing a framework within which we can explore some specific developments in crime control policy in later chapters. We begin with a discussion of what are perhaps the broader concepts of convergence and diffusion that now have quite a long history within the field of political studies.

Policy diffusion and convergence

Although policy transfer has come to be treated as the master concept in some of the literature, it should be distinguished from the broader concepts of policy convergence and diffusion. As outlined in more detail below, what links various types of policy transfer is an element of purposive action. Even where policy transfer is coerced, the idea of policy transfer suggests that political agents are aware that they are drawing upon knowledge and experiences of other jurisdictions. The terms policy diffusion or convergence clearly go beyond straightforward policy transfer. That is to say, policy transfer is not a necessary prerequisite for policy convergence (Stone 1999). Notions of convergence and diffusion go beyond the intentional actions of political actors, and include analysis of the broader structural and cultural shifts associated with globalization. As Deacon (1999) points out, in his analysis of similarities between US and UK welfare policy, policy-makers in different countries may arrive independently at the same conclusions, without any conscious process of transfer or any influence between them: 'A convergence of ideas does not necessarily imply that one thinker has influenced the other' (1999: 13). Many of the studies of the diffusion of particular policies and convergence between jurisdictions have focused upon the macro level and explored variables such as the influence of industrialization, the spread of democratic institutions, and broader social and economic forces that over time work to shape social structures, political processes and public policies in the same mould. In this sense, such studies resonate with the broader analysis of international developments in penal policy discussed in the previous chapter (Christie 2000; Garland 2001a).

Discussions about convergence between the political structures, economic systems and social arrangements of different countries have a considerable history, much of which has focused on the apparently homogenizing processes of industrialization and modernity (Kerr *et al.* 1973; Inkeles 1981). Kerr (1983: 3) defines policy convergence in this sense as 'the tendency of societies to grow more alike, to develop similarities in structures, processes and performances'. During the 1960s and 1970s, social scientists explored the broad similarities and differences between nations and examined whether or not such societies were becoming more alike over time. Many of these studies took the form of cross-national comparisons of aggregate macro socio-economic variables, comparing nations in terms of indices such as rates of economic growth; percentage of workforce employed in agriculture; percentage of GDP spent on health, education and welfare; average life expectancy, and many others. Such approaches attempted to correlate broad measures of economic development with various indices of public policy. From the 1960s onward, debate emerged between those who argued that convergence was an inevitable outcome of the processes of modernization and industrialization (for example, Wilensky 1975) and others who argued that national institutions and cultures remained distinct in many important ways (Castles and McKinlay 1979; Goldthorpe 1984). With the focus on this broad notion of societal convergence, Kerr (1983) argued that the statistical evidence suggested that there was substantial convergence between industrial societies in terms of content of knowledge, mobilization of the resources of production, the organization of production, patterns of work, lifestyle patterns and the distribution of economic rewards. However, he also argued that there was little evidence of significant convergence along other dimensions, including economic structures, political institutions and arrangements and patterns of belief. A significant literature on the subject of policy diffusion also grew from the 1960s onwards. An important strand within this work focused upon the speed at which, and the ways in which, particular policy interventions appeared to spread between different state jurisdictions in the USA (Eyestone 1977). Much of this work was based on statistical comparisons between different states, with scholars attempting to isolate the influence of exogenous variables (including the active selling of policies by 'leader states') and endogenous variables (covering such factors as socio-economic, political and ideological conditions within particular states that render the adoption of particular policies more likely). This literature highlighted the particular institutional settings that appear to promote the diffusion of policy innovations between jurisdictions, in particular, levels of functional interdependence between states and also the existence of networks that bring together policy actors from different jurisdictions (Walker 1969; Mintrom 1997). It is possible to draw parallels between this kind of work and the general approach of those influential works discussed in Chapter 1 that have focused upon broad trends of convergence in penal policy (Christie 2000; Garland 2001a).

More recently, Pollitt (2001) has explored the notion of convergence in the context of the apparent global spread of discourses and practices associated with 'New Public Management'. He disagrees that global economic pressures have led to a strong degree of convergence, at least in terms of actual management practices, and argues that there is much evidence of 'extensive diversity, variety and historical continuity in national reform trajectories' (2001: 936). He suggests that in the sphere of public sector management, at least, convergence has been far more visible in the spheres of 'talk' and, to an extent, 'decisions' than in terms of 'action' in the form of substantive policy practices or outcomes. In this way, '[f]ashionable labels are thus frequently borrowed – because of their legitimating power – but are then stuck onto a range of products, some of whose contents are far more limited and conventional than the founding texts envisaged' (2001: 944). As we will see later in the book, this observation resonates strongly with what we have found in some areas of criminal justice and penal policy. Pollitt concludes that convergence in talk and decisions in this sphere operates as a 'useful myth' that works to the advantage of key policy actors including academics, consultants, civil servants, politicians and public sector managers:

> Thus, 'real' policy convergence may be more story than fact, but, if so, it is a myth that will support careers, enhance images and boost the incomes of those who purvey its signs and symbols.
>
> (Pollitt 2001: 945)

Bennett (1991) cautions against inferring too much from evidence about cross-national similarities, either in terms of assuming policy transfer has taken place, or in terms of deterministic assumptions about the influence of transnational forces. As he observes, 'the analyst must avoid the pitfall of inferring from a transnational similarity of public policy that a transnational explanation must be at work' (1991: 23). He goes on to identify four key routes via which policy convergence may come about: 'emulation', 'elite networking', 'harmonization', and 'penetration':

- *Emulation.* This denotes a voluntary form of policy transfer involving the utilization of evidence about a policy programme in another jurisdiction and a deliberate drawing of lessons from that experience (Rose 1993). Emulation involves an intentional imitation of policy developments and programmes in other countries. Recent suggested examples of such emulation of American policies by British policy-makers would be 'welfare to work' and the granting of independence to the Bank of England (along the lines of the Federal Reserve) (Dolowitz *et al.* 2000).
- *Elite networking.* This is concerned with policy transfers via trans-national groups of actors sharing expertise and information about a common problem. There has been increasing evidence of growth of coherent networks of professionals in different spheres, engaging in regular interaction at the supra-national level. Bennett argues that policy transfer of this sort initially develops outside the realm of formal domestic politics, with the development of an international policy culture. Once consensus among these transnational policy communities about particular policy interventions is achieved, participants then actively promote particular policies domestically.
- *Harmonization.* Harmonization refers to those situations in which policy transfer is driven by formal intergovernmental organizations and structures established as a result of national interdependence. These developments are often referred to using the language of globalization and transnationalization and have applied across a range of policy areas. Recent examples affecting the UK would be the introduction of the Social Chapter setting out European standards for employment conditions, and the introduction of a common currency: the 'Euro' (Radaelli 2000).
- *Penetration.* In contrast to the above three routes to policy convergence, Bennett's notion of penetration involves a significant element of coercion. It is via this route that nation states are forced to conform to particular policy developments driven by other nations or external organizations or structures. Key examples include the application of monetarist economic policies to third world countries as a condition of aid or loans from the World Bank or the IMF, and the terms negotiated by major transnational corporations to secure inward investment in particular areas/countries.

Although earlier work on diffusion/convergence focused on macro socio-economic variables, Bennett's examination of the various routes through which convergence may occur concentrates more upon agent-driven factors associated with intentional, or at least conscious, forms of policy transfer. Thus, Bennett's approach is also open to the criticism that it makes assumptions concerning the basic rationality of the policy process (seeing policy-making as a purposive and systematic sequence) and that it does not sufficiently allow for the impact of chance events, unintended effects and the structural and cultural context. However, the model does provide a useful starting point for the empirical examination of transfer in particular policy arenas.

As one of the earlier writers in the field observed, the idea of convergence refers to 'directions of movement' and not to 'existing conditions at a moment in time' (Kerr 1983: 3). This makes the important point that we cannot infer policy convergence from the mere fact of similarity between jurisdictions at one time or another: 'Convergence should also be seen as a process of "becoming" rather than a condition of "being" more alike' (Bennett 1991: 219). This highlights an important feature of the current study. While much of the focus of this book is upon similarities and differences between the USA and the UK in terms of criminal justice and penal policy, this cannot tell us anything conclusively about overall convergence/divergence between the two countries. This would require a much more ambitious study involving a more systematic comparison of the two countries' trajectories over time. What we do wish to address, however, is the more modest aim of exploring some particular processes that may contribute to a broader picture of convergence or divergence. This focuses our gaze much more specifically on the specific ideas associated with policy transfer.

Policy transfer and lesson-drawing

The concept of policy transfer is defined as 'the process by which knowledge of policies, administrative arrangements, institutions and ideas in one political system (past or present) is used in the development of policies, administrative arrangements, institutions and ideas in another political system' (Dolowitz 2000b: 3). This definition covers the voluntary and consensual forms of transfer implied by such terms as 'lesson-drawing', and the less voluntary forms covered by concepts such as 'direct coercive transfer'. Dolowitz and Marsh (2000) argue that it is helpful to think of policy transfer on a continuum, with lesson-drawing under conditions of perfect information and rationality at the one end (completely voluntary) and direct imposition on the other (completely coerced). Most forms of transfer will fall between these two extremes, and it is important to understand that most forms of policy transfer will arise from a mix of coercive and voluntary pressures (Dolowitz and Marsh 2000).

For example, European Union directives may be coerced in the sense of being compulsory, although voluntary, in the sense that individual nation states have voluntarily chosen to be part of the EU.

Dolowitz and Marsh (2000) highlight seven key questions that can helpfully frame the study of policy transfer, and these provide a useful starting point for our consideration of transfer in the realm of criminal justice and penal policy. These key questions are:

- *Who are the key actors involved in the process?* Dolowitz and Marsh suggest that key actors could include elected officials, political parties, civil servants, pressure groups, policy entrepreneurs, transnational corporations, think tanks, supra-national governmental bodies and NGOs, and consultants.
- *Why do actors engage in policy transfer?* Policy transfer may simply be a rational way of informing policy development in the domestic environment, looking beyond national boundaries for policy ideas and evidence about implementation. Foreign evidence may also be used in a post-hoc manner to justify decisions already taken. As noted above, actors may have little choice in cases of coerced transfer where external forces mean that certain policies are pressed upon jurisdictions.
- *What is transferred?* This question relates to our earlier discussion of distinct policy levels. Eight categories are identified by Dolowitz and Marsh: policy goals, contents, instruments, programmes, institutions, ideologies, ideas and attitudes, and negative lessons.
- *From where are lessons drawn?* Of course, lessons can be drawn from a range of different sources including the sub-national levels of localities and regions, the level of the nation state, and also from the international stage.
- *What are the different degrees of transfer?* Dolowitz and Marsh highlight a range of degrees, including copying (complete and direct transfer); emulation (transfer of ideas behind a particular policy or programme); combinations (mixtures of different policies); and inspiration (where policy in another jurisdiction inspires change in a particular direction but the final outcome does not draw directly upon the original).
- *What constrains or facilitates the policy transfer process?* It appears that copying, i.e. complete and total transfer of policies between jurisdictions, is rather rare, and this can be related to a number of constraints within the policy process, including contextual factors (such as differences in political structures and organizational cultures) and the existence of significant political opposition to transfer of certain policies.
- *How is the process related to the 'success' or 'failure' of policies?* Dolowitz

and Marsh identify three possible forms of 'failed' transfer including: uninformed transfer (when the borrowing country has incomplete information about the policy and how it works in the country of origin); incomplete transfer (where the elements that made the policy a success in the country of origin are not all transferred), and inappropriate transfer (insufficient attention paid to social, economic, political and cultural context).

The seventh question raises a number of difficulties. These primarily relate to the fact that it seems to concern particularly subjective issues, and the authors themselves note the difficulty in defining and establishing policy 'failure' or 'success'. It implies a very particular (and we would argue rare) form of policy transfer, one in which politicians or policy-makers set out clear aims and the policy-making process follows a highly rational and predictable trajectory. As we have already discussed, this tends not to be the case in public policy-making. However, the first six of these questions do provide a particularly useful way of framing the study of policy transfer within the field of criminal justice and penal policy. In different ways, we apply versions of these questions to our particular areas of interest in Chapters 3–5. However, we should remain wary of the danger of focusing overly on the actions of individual policy actors and also over-emphasizing the degree of rationality in the policy-making process. This point is further developed below in our discussion of the limitations of the policy transfer literature. For current purposes, however, it does seem that there is an important missing element in the seven questions posed by Dolowitz and Marsh. By starting with the 'why' question, they proceed from the assumption that policy transfer has actually taken place when, as outlined below, it is not always straightforward to establish this empirically. Furthermore, their focus is primarily concentrated on the rationales adopted by particular actors for engaging in policy transfer. What is ignored by this question is the broader organizational and structural imperatives that may be equally, if not more, important as an impetus to policy transfer.

Picking up on this theme, Radaelli (2000) suggests that the policy transfer approach can be enhanced by the concepts of organizational analysis, and draws upon the concept of 'isomorphism' developed by DiMaggio and Powell (1983). Organizational theory has outlined how the emergence and structuration of an organizational field lead to the homogenization of organizations included in the field, and in the appearance of new entrants. DiMaggio and Powell outlined two kinds of isomorphism. First, there is 'institutional isomorphism', in which institutions compete not just for resources and for customers, but also for political power and institutional legitimacy. In this sense, copying others' organizational structures is not a process driven by efficiency considerations, but is a way of securing legitimacy. Second, there is 'competitive isomorphism', in which competitive markets lead to the emergence and diffusion of the most rational and efficient solutions to environmental challenges. Radaelli focuses upon the first of these – isomorphic changes that are not primarily related to attempted efficiency gains. He discusses three sources of isomorphic change highlighted by DiMaggio and Powell: coercive (due to dependence on key organizations or government mandate); mimetic (triggered by uncertainty so that organizations mimic others perceived to be more successful or legitimate); and normative (pressures resulting from professionalization, in which common education and socialization pressures produce a common cognitive base). Radaelli applies these concepts to developments within the European Union regarding approaches to monetary policy, taxation and media ownership. However, in our view there is every reason to suppose that the concept of institutional isomorphism is equally helpful in thinking about transfer in the criminal justice field, and we will return to this in later chapters. However, in brief, it appears, for example, that mimetic and normative change applies quite well to police organizations adopting 'zero tolerance' ideas (in particular, the mimetic dimension). In sum, this work highlights the need to combine the study of policy transfer with analysis of legitimacy mechanisms, and offers schema in which actors follow rules, shared interpretations, symbols and meanings which develop in the background, as part of the taken for granted part of political life.

As noted above, it is important not to simply assume that policy transfer has occurred. Evans and Davies (1999) argue that there is a tendency to make exaggerated claims about the existence of policy transfer, which is too often simply assumed from similarities in policy rhetoric, instruments or outcomes. They propose a set of questions that they argue constitute criteria for a more rigorous empirical demonstration that policy transfer has occurred. These are worth quoting in some detail, since, in conjunction with some of the questions outlined by Dolowitz and Marsh, they help to inform the development of a framework for the study outlined in this book:

- *What is the subject of analysis?* Any study of policy transfer must be clear about the subject being studied and, in particular, whether the study is about facilitating policy transfer, studying the transfer process as it is occurring, or making a claim that transfer has occurred in the past. The current study is retrospective and therefore falls into the latter category. This has important implications for the methodological approaches for the study, which we discuss at the end of this chapter.
- *Who/what are the agents of transfer?* Studies need to clearly identify the agents of transfer, why they engage in such activity, and how they go about it.
- *Is there evidence of non-transfer?* 'Non-transfer' would include elements

of a policy programme that have been taken from domestic antecedents or that are genuinely innovative. In addition, the term also includes parts of an original idea or programme that are filtered out during the policy development process.

- *How good is the evidence provided to support a claim of policy transfer?* This can include the views and perceptions of the recipient subjects, detailed similarities between the concrete policy content in different jurisdictions, and implementation analysis to look at the wider outcomes of policy.
- *What conclusions can be drawn about the nature/extent of policy transfer?* This includes overall conclusions about whether policy transfer has or has not occurred, the degree of policy transfer, and what has actually been transferred. Evans and Davies make the useful distinction between 'soft' transfers (including ideas, concepts and attitudes) and 'hard' transfers (including actual policy programmes and implementation) (Evans and Davies 1999: 382–3).

Smith (2004) provides an analysis of the part played by policy transfer in the development of UK climate policy. From the existing literature, he outlines a three-part test for empirically confirming whether policy transfer has occurred:

- demonstration of significant similarities in policy between jurisdictions;
- identification of agents who have transferred knowledge about policies in other jurisdictions and made policy-makers aware of them;
- compelling evidence that policy-makers actually utilized such knowledge in policy development.

(Smith 2004: 81)

Smith goes on to highlight the difficulties in separating external influences, such as policy transfer, from endogenous policy development. In climate policy at least, Smith found a continuous process of cross-fertilization between exogenous and domestic influences during policy development, that makes the isolation of an independent policy transfer effect extremely difficult. As we outline in Chapters 3–5, in each of the particular policy areas we explored, although there was some evidence of initial transfer of elements of policy from the USA, it is clear that subsequent domestic (and other) influences worked to resist and in some cases reform the imports. Despite such difficulties, it is clear that the study of policy transfer can be a fruitful if complicated area of inquiry. Nevertheless, there are a number of other shortcomings in the extant literature in this area that it is important to mention briefly before we move on.

Problems with policy transfer

The policy transfer literature has to date displayed a number of important limitations. Stone (1999), for example, has outlined how the policy transfer literature needs to be informed by the perspectives of other bodies of work, and in particular work on policy networks. This is partly because, as Dolowitz and Marsh (1996) note, much of the earlier policy transfer literature over-emphasized the role of formal political institutions connected with the state, and in particular the importance of the intended actions of politicians and civil servants. Another problem concerns the extent to which claims about policy transfer are supported by rigorous empirical evidence. In fact, one leading expert in the field has argued that there is a 'paucity of systematic research that can convincingly make the case that cross-national policy learning has had a determining influence on policy choice' (Bennett 1997: 214). This lack of detailed empirical research applies especially in the field of criminal justice and penal policy. A common problem within the literature is the tendency to produce what amounts to informed journalistic narratives, which are vague about the nature of evidence to support policy transfer. One example of this is Dolowitz *et al.* (1999), who discuss the idea of policy transfer from the USA in terms of electoral strategies and social policy. Defining policy transfer in a broad sense (to include non-voluntary aspects), the authors argue that a demonstration of policy transfer requires evidence that UK policy-makers were actively searching for a policy in the area considered, that ministers and/or civil servants visited the USA to examine particular programmes, and that key elements of these programmes were incorporated into the UK strategy. This overlooks the possibility of policy-makers having decided upon a particular course of action independently of any US influence. Visits to the USA may simply serve to confirm an already decided approach, or the US example may be used as a tool for legitimizing decisions that had already been made.

Another important limitation of some of the transfer literature (in common with a broader range of policy studies research) concerns the inherent assumption of rationality that we outlined earlier in the chapter. Hill (1997: 9) has argued that policy claims may be 'rationalizations after the event, to try to convince us that chance events or events that actors did not really control were planned'. In studies of transfer, this is particularly important in that we may be tempted to assume that one country directly influenced another simply on the basis of the apparent similarity of policies adopted in each. As Bennett cautions: 'Emulation should not be inferred from the successive adoption of similar policies by different states in the absence of any empirical evidence of conscious copying, lesson-drawing or adaptation' (1991: 220). Thus, policies may become similar in different national contexts in the absence of any conscious process of policy transfer at all. As Deacon

(1999) points out, two people may independently arrive at the same idea without any contact or transfer of information between them. Similarly, countries may face comparable problems that give rise to similar policy solutions, and thus convergence does not necessarily imply that policy transfer has occurred.

Evans and Davies (1999) highlight a number of important limitations of the policy transfer literature, and suggest some possible ways forward. They define policy transfer as 'an action-oriented intentional activity' (1999: 366), and argue that policy transfer should not be presented as an explanatory theory. On this view, theory is concerned with precise causal explanation and prediction, and consists of systematically related law-like generalizations that can be tested empirically. Rather, the policy transfer approach should be viewed as an 'analogical model' which is helpful in furthering our understanding of a particular field, allowing for novel hypotheses to be developed and suggesting new lines of enquiry. While Evans and Davies pay tribute to the work of Dolowitz and Marsh for giving coherence and clarity to a rather fragmented and multidisciplinary literature, they highlight four specific limitations with the policy transfer literature to date. First, at the transnational level, the current literature provides little evidence about 'to what extent and why policy transfer has become widespread throughout western democracies' in recent decades (1999: 365). Second, at the level of domestic structures, research has insufficiently developed the relationship between state structures and political agency. Third, there has not been enough attention paid to inter-organizational relationships and their role in policy transfer. In particular, the authors suggest the utilization of network analysis and more focus upon the role of knowledge elites as agents of policy transfer (as suggested by the literature on 'epistemic communities'). Finally, much of the literature has suggested that transfer in some form or other has become a pervasive part of the policy process. As noted above, it is difficult to isolate the specific processes of policy transfer from the broader policy development process.

Evans and Davies (1999) argue that policy transfer provides a useful meso level concept. By this, they mean that it can provide an intermediate link between studies at the micro level that focus upon the specific processes surrounding particular policy decisions, and those macro studies that look at wider structural questions concerning broader trends in contemporary societies. As they point out, '[m]acro-level theories are often abstract and frequently applied to concrete situations with little attention to mediating processes, while micro-level theories tend to ignore the impact of broader structural factors on microdecision-making settings' (Evans and Davies 1999: 363). Evans and Davies's work thus begins to provide a more conceptually sophisticated approach towards utilizing the concept of policy transfer. In particular, they argue that we need to develop a 'multi-level' and 'multi-layered' approach to analysing policy transfer. In sum, we need to develop an approach that 'recognizes the importance of global, international, transnational and domestic structures and their ability to constrain and/or facilitate policy development and also understands that policy transfer may be the result of inter-organizational politics' (1999: 367). In our view, the study of policy transfer therefore provides a promising way forward in attempting to integrate the important insights provided by the contrasting approaches towards studying convergence/divergence in crime control and penal policy that we discussed in the opening chapter.

Researching policy transfer

So far in this chapter we have talked about the meaning of the term policy transfer and have discussed approaches taken in the literature to interrogating the processes and outcomes of attempts at policy transfer, together with some of the problems evident in such work. In this final section we draw upon the relevant literature to develop a framework for the analysis of policy transfer in criminal justice between the USA and the UK. The starting point is the widespread perception that policy transfers between US and UK policy have been increasing in importance in recent years. As we discussed briefly in the last chapter, on the surface at least, there appear to be key similarities in some high-profile policy developments in both countries during recent decades. However, it is far from clear that a process of policy transfer was involved in the emergence of these policy changes. The empirical question of *precisely* what, if any, the role of political imitation and policy transfer has been remains to date rather under-explored. To this end, the aim of the study upon which this book is based was to undertake a detailed empirical examination of the processes of policy formation on both sides of the Atlantic and an exploration of the possible links between the two. Our specific focus in this book is upon processes of policy transfer and diffusion from the United States to Britain.

The study was based on the premise that the best way of exploring the realities of the process of policy transfer is to examine concrete examples of policy change. As noted above, we concentrated primarily on three high-profile developments in British crime control and penal policy during the 1990s: the privatization of corrections; mandatory minimum sentencing ('two' and 'three strikes'); and 'zero tolerance' policing strategies. As with all case study-based research there are limitations to which the data collected can viewed as representative, and can be used as the basis for prediction or generalization (Bryman 2002). Had other areas of policy been chosen as the basis for our study, then it is possible, indeed likely, that different insights about the nature and extent of policy transfer might have arisen. However, within the inevitable limitations of time and budget, these three case studies provide important insights into the policy process and the impact of policy transfer upon it. A number of factors influenced our particular choice of case study areas, but in particular we wished to explore three areas from different parts of the criminal justice system (policing, sentencing and corrections), each of which was strongly perceived to have been based upon developments in the USA. This choice of three apparent *prima facie* cases of American imports was, far from being a limitation, a deliberate strategy. Our aim has been to examine the degree to which policy outcomes in the USA and the UK were indeed convergent; and then, to the extent that they were, to explore how far and in what ways processes of active policy transfer contributed to this. This study is the first empirical examination of policy transfer in crime control. As such, it was not intended to go beyond these three areas, nor beyond transfers between the USA and the UK. The role of transfer in shaping outcomes in other areas of criminal justice and penal policy, and the impact of influences emanating from Europe and other parts of the world, could not be the focus of this work. These issues, as we make clear in the final chapter, are a matter for a broader programme of future research.

The primary foci of the study were, first, the apparent transfer of *policy ideas/symbols/rhetoric, policy content*, and *policy instruments*, and second, the various *processes* by which such transfer comes about (or is constrained). Within the three specific areas we focused on the perceptions of, and strategic actions taken by, key policy actors, including elected officials, political parties, civil servants, pressure groups, senior practitioners within criminal justice agencies, and 'policy entrepreneurs/experts'. This approach was also informed by a detailed review of the political science literature on such concepts as policy networks, policy transfer and related issues, and approaches to studying the policy-making process. Research was then undertaken on both sides of the Atlantic, involving two key elements. The first stage of the study was primarily devoted to conducting a detailed review of the literature and available documentary evidence concerning the three particular areas. The main aim of this stage of the research was to produce a series of detailed narratives of how policy changed in the three specific areas under consideration (according to the documentary evidence) *prior* to the collection of any interview data. These narratives have formed the basis of work published elsewhere on comparative criminal justice policy-making in the USA and the UK (Jones and Newburn 2005, 2006). These narratives were subsequently used as a framework to inform the selection of interviewees and the content of topic guides. The second stage of the research comprised a series of interviews with key participants in (and those with an informed view about) the policy process in both the USA and the UK.

Documentary analysis

The first major element of the research is the collation and content analysis of relevant documentary material. Key documentary sources included the following:

- Government and opposition publications – in the UK this includes Green and White Papers, Acts of Parliament, discussion/consultation documents, Home Office circulars, manifestos and (Shadow) Ministerial speeches; in the USA: federal and state legislation, consultation documents, and speeches by leading senators and congressmen; we did not have access to internal government papers which might, of course, have altered our accounts significantly.
- Parliamentary/congressional debates and reports – in the UK using *Hansard*; Home Affairs Select Committee Reports. In the USA, analysis of Senate and Congressional Debates, collation and analysis of relevant Congressional/Senate committee reports.
- Newspapers – we examined the development of each of the policy initiatives described via reporting in a range of broadsheet newspapers.
- Pressure group and think tank publications – in the UK including the Institute for Economic Affairs, the Adam Smith Institute and others; collation and analysis of publications by comparable organizations in the USA including the Heritage Foundation, the Manhattan Institute, the Drug Policy Alliance, the Cato Institute and the American Legislative Exchange Council.

Interviews

The second stage of this study involved a series of semi-structured interviews with key actors in the policy-making process. These interviews were used to explore further the key events and time frames of policy development and to provide a richer understanding and explanation of the perceptions and involvement of key actors. A key objective here was to obtain access to senior people who could provide first-hand accounts of the particular policy developments in which we were interested. In the event, the well-developed links of the research team with the current British government, with the major pressure groups and think tanks involved in criminal justice, as well as with all the main home affairs correspondents in the UK, helped to overcome most access problems, although unfortunately a number of senior politicians declined to be interviewed. Some key players in the particular policy stories in which we were interested were deemed to be unapproachable given their current position in high office. In particular, we have had to rely on second-hand accounts of the central roles played by Jack Straw and Tony

Blair in the development of the specific policy areas under consideration here. In general though, we were extremely pleased with the degree of access provided by key players in the policy process on both sides of the Atlantic. Already established links with the US Department of Justice, the National Institute of Justice in Washington and academic criminologists and political scientists in the USA successfully opened doors on the other side of the Atlantic. Although, as noted, some key players declined to be interviewed, many of those approached were more than happy to cooperate with the study. In general, therefore, we were very successful in gaining access to senior politicians and policy-makers as well as others significantly involved in policy development and campaigning, and felt that we were able to obtain detailed and rich first-hand accounts of the policy process in particular areas of change.

The interviews examined both British and American perspectives on the relationship between US and UK crime control and penal policy during the relevant period, and the influence of one on the other. All interviews were recorded and transcribed, and then systematically analysed via thematic grids. Most interviews were 'on the record', in that the interviewees were happy for us to identify them in our published work. A small number of interviewees, although happy for us to use their comments, asked that we disguise their identity in any publications. Those interviewed in the UK and the USA fell into eight main categories:

- politicians involved in the selected policy areas;
- political and policy advisers to the Clinton administrations in the USA and the Thatcher, Major and Blair administrations in the UK; the office of the Mayor of New York City;
- civil/public servants in relevant departments (e.g. Department of Justice, Office of National Drug Control Policy in the USA; Home Office, Prison Service, Prisons Ombudsman, etc. in the UK);
- senior criminal justice professionals working in the police, prison and probation services;
- pressure group and think tank representatives – (including Cato Institute, American Legislative Exchange Council, Drug Policy Alliance, Justice Policy Institute, Sentencing Project, Western Prison Project, the ACLU in the USA; and the Prison Reform Trust, NACRO, the Adam Smith Institute, the Institute for Economic Affairs, the Howard League in the UK);
- home affairs and political correspondents of broadsheet newspapers;
- members of the other key organizations involved – Prison Governors' Association, Prison Officers' Association, Association of Chief Police Officers, HMIC, and the private corrections industry in the UK; the American Bar Association, the National Institute of Justice, the

Police Foundation, the RAND Corporation, National District Attorneys' Association and others in the USA; and

- academic experts in the main case study areas.

Clearly, there are a number of issues to consider in assessing and ordering the accounts provided by participants in the policy process, including difficulties with accurate recall years after the events under consideration. The best answer to such problems, ideally, would be to undertake contemporaneous research that observed the emergence of particular policies as they happened. This has been the approach of the foremost criminological scholar of the policy process, Paul Rock, who has provided a fascinating and detailed analysis of the development of victim policy in the UK by studying policy-making, in his words, '*in situ*' (Rock 2004). This approach requires a more concentrated focus upon a single and more recent, preferably current, area of policy development. Given our aim was to focus upon key areas where US influence was generally assumed and also to obtain examples of policy-making from different sectors of criminal justice (police, corrections and sentencing), this highly focused approach was not appropriate for the current study. It was possible, however, to address to some degree the limitations that a broader and more historical approach brought with it. As far as possible, we tried to compare various different sources against each other. Thus, the accounts of key actors, placed at different vantage points within and outside the formal institutions of policy-making, were balanced against each other, and these in turn were compared with the findings of the documentary analysis. Ultimately, of course, the 'true' picture of how or why things happened cannot be uncovered, and any study relying to a great degree on policy actors' accounts requires a considerable degree of informed, but nevertheless subjective, judgement by the researchers. In this sense, we need to provide a health warning at the start, and accept that readers may in some cases have a very different interpretation from ours of how and why things developed in the way they did. However, despite the gaps and the other inevitable limitations of a study such as this one, we remain confident that we obtained some extremely interesting insights into the policy-making process in a key area of public policy, and the role of transfer within this.

Conclusion

The following three chapters explore particular areas of policy change in the USA and the UK. The starting point, in each case study, is to try to ascertain to what extent, if at all, policy developments in the UK were the result of a process of policy transfer as outlined in the literature. In order to do this, we focused our analysis on a framework that was shaped by the existing work on policy transfer that has been reviewed in this chapter. In particular, we drew upon the key questions about policy transfer raised by Dolowitz and Marsh (2000) and Evans and Davies (1999), the three-point test for the empirical verification of policy transfer developed by Smith (2004), and the different processes; of policy convergence outlined by Bennett (1991). Thus, in each particular policy area, we first explore evidence for transfer in terms of an appropriate difference in timing of policy development in the USA and the UK, and the existence of sufficient similarities in policy ideas and content to be consistent with a picture of policy transfer. We then seek to identify key policy actors who operated as agents of transfer and explore their strategies and motivations. Third, we examine the nature and the processes of policy transfer, and within this assess the evidence that knowledge about one jurisdiction was used in policy development in another. Finally, in each case, we explore the limitations of transfer and the ways in which initial policy ideas were resisted, reformed or supplemented by domestic influences and other factors. In short, we argue that elements of policy transfer, in differing ways and to differing degrees, were visible in all three specific policy areas under consideration. Of course, this focus is not meant to suggest that we think policy transfer was the only, or even *the major*, influence at work; merely that there are plausible reasons to believe that some form of policy transfer may have been at work and, thus far, there has been little empirical attempt to document the extent and nature of such activity.

3 Privatizing punishment

This chapter focuses upon two key aspects of the growing involvement of commercial companies in the delivery of punishment in the UK: contracting out of management (and eventually the design and building) of prisons and remand centres, and the provision of electronic tagging in the criminal justice system.[1] The chapter begins with an historical account of the emergence and development of the commercial corrections sector in the UK. The remainder of the chapter is framed around four key issues concerning policy transfer. The first three of these broadly correspond to the three questions highlighted by Smith (2004) as an empirical test that policy transfer has occurred (see Chapter 2). First, we argue that similarity in policy ideas and content between the USA and the UK, and the timescale of developments in each country, suggest a degree of policy convergence and are consistent with the hypothesis that policy transfer contributed to this in some way. Second, we identify the key individuals and organizations acting as 'transfer agents' and examine their activities and motivations. Third, we outline the evidence that knowledge from one jurisdiction was used in policy development in another by exploring in more detail the processes of policy transfer. The fourth section examines constraints on policy transfer and, in particular, how the original policy idea was subsequently shaped by domestic influences. The chapter ends with some general conclusions about the extent and nature of policy transfer in the sphere of privatized corrections.

The re-emergence of commercial corrections in the UK

Contracting out of prisons

The commercial provision of prisons and correctional services (such as transportation) has a long history in the UK (McConville 1981; Cavadino and Dignan 2002; Zimring 2002). However, from the mid-nineteenth century onwards, the prison system became an increasingly centralized public bureaucracy. The rebirth of commercial provision of prisons began in the early 1970s, when the Home Office contracted the private security firm Securicor to manage detention centres (and associated escort services) for suspected illegal immigrants at the four main English airports (Ryan and Ward 1989; Ryan 1996).

The policy of contracting out of prisons and remand centres to commercial providers was first mooted in 1984 by the free-market think tank, the Adam Smith Institute (ASI) (Adam Smith Institute 1984). Although initially not taken seriously in mainstream political circles, the ASI continued to promote the idea, publishing a further report on the subject in 1987. This described in positive terms a number of commercially run correctional institutions in the USA, and argued that these developments demonstrated that the establishment of commercially run prisons would be a desirable policy in the UK (Young 1987). In between the publication of the two ASI reports, the first signs of official interest in contracting out of prisons began to emerge. In 1986, the Home Affairs Select Committee (HAC) of the House of Commons began an inquiry into the state of prisons in England and Wales. The chairman of the Committee, who was to play a crucial role in later developments, was the Conservative MP, the late Sir Edward Gardner. During the course of the inquiry, committee members visited a number of US correctional facilities, including several institutions operated by Corrections Corporation of America (CCA). Although not part of its original brief (which was a much broader inquiry into the problems faced by the prison system in England and Wales), the subject of commercially run prisons subsequently came to dominate media discussions of the Committee's deliberations. Differences emerged along party lines, with Labour members strongly objecting to the support for contracting out of prisons expressed by some leading Conservatives (including Sir Edward Gardner and another senior Tory member, Sir John Wheeler). Because agreement could not be reached, the issue was not discussed in the main committee report, but rather dealt with in a separate short report (Home Affairs Committee 1987). This report recommended that the government conduct an experiment in the commercial contracting of a remand institution.

At about the same time, the junior Home Office minister Lord Windlesham began to lobby the Prime Minister to consider the development of a separate, commercially contracted remand sector (Windlesham 1993). Though the PM's initial response was not positive, it seemed that commercial contracting out of prisons and remand centres remained at least on the margins of the government's agenda. The Home Office minister Lord Caithness visited the United States to examine the evidence on prison privatization, and on his return he reported positively on what he had seen (Rutherford 1990). During this period a consortium called UK Detention Services was formed, comprising the US company CCA and two British construction companies, John Mowlem and Sir Robert McAlpine and Sons Ltd (Prison Reform Trust 1994). Not long after this came the publication of the Green Paper, *Private Sector Involvement in the Remand System* in July 1988 (Home Office 1988a). Commercial lobbying was now developing rapidly, with various consortia forming to respond to possible opportunities in the penal sphere. The company Contract Prisons was established with the former HAC chairman Sir Edward Gardner as chief executive. In addition, the commercial security providers Group 4 Securitas and Securicor set up subsidiaries specializing in the provision of detention services.

By the late 1980s, however, the remand population was falling quite significantly, and it appeared that the Home Office remained inclined against including provision for contracting out in the forthcoming Criminal Justice Bill. However, pressure from the Number 10 Policy Unit (and, by implication, the PM herself) resulted in a clause being included that would allow for the contracting out of new facilities in the remand sector (Windlesham 1993). The Criminal Justice Bill introduced in the autumn of 1990 included a provision to allow for contracting out of *newly constructed* facilities for *remand* prisoners. Amendments introduced at the committee stage, orchestrated by Conservative backbenchers and Home Office junior ministers (Windlesham 1993; Cavadino and Dignan 2002), extended the power to contract out to facilities for sentenced prisoners, and also to existing prisons and remand centres.[2] During 1991, contract details were announced for two privately contracted penal establishments. The first of these was the Wolds Remand Centre in Humberside, awarded to the security company Group 4 (due to open in Spring 1992). Despite strong criticism from opposition MPs, privatization continued to gather pace, and the contract for a second privately managed prison (Blakenhurst) was signed with UK Detention Services in December 1992. In September 1993, Home Secretary Michael Howard announced that the government planned to contract out about 10 per cent of the prison system in England and Wales, although he did not make clear whether this was 10 per cent of prison establishments or of the prison population. In February of the following year, the company Premier Prison Services[3] was awarded the contract for a third privately managed prison, in Doncaster.

The government's commitment to the policy of contracting out was confirmed in August 1994 with the publication of a shortlist of 20 prisons to be 'market tested'. This was, however, quickly shelved after a complaint by the Prison Officers' Association (POA) to the Central Arbitration Committee about a lack of prior consultation. In addition, under the European Commission's Acquired Rights Directive, commercial contractors had to maintain existing jobs and conditions in respect of any new contracts that they won, which reduced the potential savings to be made from contracting out (Cavadino and Dignan 2002: 232). Despite these obstacles, the policy of contracting out continued and extended beyond its original scope, which had restricted it to new facilities for remand prisoners. Another privately run prison, Buckley Hall, managed by Group 4,[4] opened in 1994, and in June 1995, a consortium including Tarmac and Group 4 won the contract to build and manage a 600-cell category B prison at Fazakerley, Liverpool. A consortium comprising Costain and Securicor was contracted to build and manage the 880-place Parc Prison at Bridgend in South Wales. These were the first of six new penal institutions planned under the government's Private Finance Initiative (PFI). The government published a White Paper in 1996 that outlined plans to privately finance, design and build a further 12 prisons from 2001–02, with the aim of providing 9600 new prisoner places.

In March 1997, the Home Affairs Committee of the House of Commons published the report of another extensive inquiry into the prison service in England and Wales. This considered the subject of commercially contracted prisons in far more depth than had the 1987 inquiry. It also considered written and oral evidence presented by representatives of a number of commercial corrections companies (including Group 4 Prison Services Ltd, Premier Prison Services Ltd and UK Detention Services Ltd). In addition, six members of the committee (including the chairman, Sir Ivan Lawrence) visited a range of publicly run and commercially contracted prisons in the USA (in California and Texas). The Committee also received written evidence on commercially run prisons from the Australian States of Queensland, New South Wales and Victoria. Unsurprisingly, representatives of the commercial corrections sector presented a highly positive view of developments since contracting out. Against this, the Howard League, the Prison Reform Trust and the POA presented robust critiques of contracting out of prisons. In its final report, the Committee reported overwhelmingly favourably on the English and Welsh experience with contracting out of prisons. It concluded that many of the initial concerns about the principle of contracting out prisons to commercial providers had 'not proved justified' and that the 'idea of privately managed prisons is undoubtedly now more generally accepted, and should be allowed to develop further' (Home Affairs Committee 1997: xxx). The Committee also drew positive conclusions about the quality of performance of commercially managed prisons, about the level of financial savings delivered to the prison service, and about the positive effect of competition upon standards and efficiency in the public sector. It was argued that 'there needs to be a continued expansion of the private sector if the full benefits of competition are to be obtained' and recommended the resumption of a market-testing programme within the prison service (Home Affairs Committee 1997: xxxi).

May 1997 saw the election of a Labour government that, in opposition, had strongly criticized the policy of contracting out prisons. However, this position was to change quickly. In June 1997, the Home Secretary Jack Straw renewed the UK Detention Services management contract for Blakenhurst prison, and confirmed arrangements for two new privately financed, designed, built and run prisons. In November of the same year, the first commercial contract for a prison in Scotland was announced. Kilmarnock Prison Services Ltd[5] signed a contract with the Scottish Office to design, construct, finance and manage HMP Kilmarnock. This prison became operational in 1999.

In 1998, in a speech to the (POA conference, Jack Straw announced that in future all new prisons in England and Wales would be privately constructed and run (although the Prison Service was now also to be allowed to tender for the contracts when current contracts expired). Contracting out was also to be used to promote reform in 'under-performing' public prisons. For example, in July 1999, the prisons minister announced that Brixton prison was to be market tested with a view to contracting out. By late 2006, there was a total of 11 prison service establishments in England and Wales, plus one in Scotland, being run by commercial companies. This situation is some way off the commercial sector of 20–30 prisons envisaged by representatives of commercial prisons companies in evidence to the 1997 Home Affairs Committee Inquiry (see above). In addition, despite the strong conclusions of the Committee that private prisons had become an accepted part of the penal landscape, penal reform groups continued to campaign strongly against them. In early 2005, the Prison Reform Trust raised concerns about the ethical principles of contracting out, as well as questioning the alleged efficiency improvements brought about by the policy (Prison Reform Trust 2005). However, it is true to say that contracting out of prisons has not become a major area of public controversy, and it is difficult to disagree with Cavadino and Dignan's earlier assessment that 'the policy of encouraging private sector involvement in the design, construction, financing and operation of prisons in England and Wales now appears unassailable' (2002: 234).

Privatization, probation and electronic monitoring

Although commercial prisons have dominated most of the discussion about privatization of punishment, the electronic monitoring (EM) of offenders, or tagging, played an important role on both sides of the Atlantic in establishing private contractors as legitimate providers within criminal justice in recent times. EM did not become a significant policy option in England and Wales until the late 1980s. Credit for promoting the idea of EM to government is generally given to Tom Stacey, a journalist who had been jailed while working in Kashmir for the *Sunday Times*, and who had 'developed a deep animosity toward incarceration' (Nellis 2000: 103). Stacey formed a small pressure group in 1982, the Offender Tag Association (OTA), and began a campaign for the use of EM as an alternative to custody. Despite his efforts it took some considerable time before government began to show any real interest in EM. In 1986, the House of Commons Home Affairs Committee's inquiry into the prison system of England and Wales outlined above also examined the possible potential of EM. Its main report recommended that the Home Office study EM

(Home Affairs Committee 1987; Richardson 1999) and Lord Caithness, a junior Home Office minister at the time, and John Wheeler MP, a member of the HAC, went on a 'fact-finding tour to the US' (Nellis 2000). Also in the late 1980s a conference was held at what was then Leicester Polytechnic, exploring the experience of EM, including in the USA, and debating its potential for the UK and elsewhere. Correctional staff from the USA participated in the conference, together with representatives of three American companies (BI Incorporated, Correction Services Incorporated and Digital Products).

The 1988 Green Paper, *Punishment, Custody and the Community*, proposed pilot work with EM (Home Office 1988b). The first trials began in Nottingham in August 1989, North Tyneside in September 1989 and Tower Bridge Court, London, in October 1989, with the contracts going to Marconi in the first two and Chubb in London. There were a number of differences between the US and UK programmes. In the UK, for example, EM could only be used on a non-statutory basis as new legislation had not been passed. It could not be used as a sentence of the court, therefore, but only as a condition of bail for unconvicted defendants or unsentenced offenders as an alternative to custody (Richardson 1999). The Home Office expected that at least 150 offenders would be tagged within the six-month experimental period. The reality was that in total only 50 orders were made and in January 1990 the trial was stopped.

Despite the problems with the pilots, curfew monitoring was positively mentioned in the 1990 White Paper, *Crime, Justice and Protecting the Public* (Home Office 1990) and the Criminal Justice Act 1991 set provisions for a second attempt at EM. All was abandoned, however, in the rightward lurch in penal politics fairly soon after the passage of the 1991 Act. The Criminal Justice and Public Order Act 1994 introduced the curfew order as a community sentence in its own right, and was followed by a second set of trials in 1995. The new pilot project was launched in three sites – Norfolk, the City of Manchester and Reading. On this occasion, the contracts went to Geographix in Norfolk and to Securicor (in Manchester and Reading), the latter using equipment supplied by a subsidiary of a US corporation. The trials were slow to develop and were extended by the Home Office on three occasions. Although evaluation suggested that curfew orders were a practical possibility, it questioned whether it was realistic to imagine that it might have anything other than a marginal impact as a sentence (Mair and Mortimer 1996). The experiment did, however, appear to lead to something of a softening of attitude towards electronic monitoring by the probation service (Mair 1997).

Following the change of government in 1997, New Labour embraced EM with even greater fervour than its Conservative predecessors. The use of electronic monitoring was extended by the Crime (Sentences) Act 1997 – legislation begun under the Tories but introduced by the New Labour government – to include offenders under the age of 16. Four new areas were added to those already operating in 1998 (Cambridge, Suffolk, Middlesex and West Yorkshire).

The Crime and Disorder Act, 1998 introduced the home detention curfew scheme (HDC), the first time that EM was to be used as an early release scheme. This came into operation at the end of January 1999, was made available nationwide and marked the beginning of EM services to cover the whole of England and Wales.

Future developments

Most recently, governmental commitment to involving the private sector (and other bodies) in the provision of criminal justice services has been highlighted by the official endorsement of the concept of 'contestability'. This term – taken by critics as shorthand for 'privatization' – was first used in a major review of sentencing and the penal system published in 2003 (Carter 2003). This recommended, among other things, combining the prisons and probation services to provide an integrated system of managing offenders, both within prison and after release. It also recommended the application of contestability to correctional criminal justice services in order to deliver the most cost effective custodial and community services. The government's response to this report endorsed many of its major recommendations, and a new National Offender Management Service (NOMS) is currently being established. The government argued that, following what it saw as a positive experience with competition in the prisons sector, contestability was to be further applied within the new system of offender management:

> We intend therefore to encourage the private and 'not for profit' sectors to compete to manage more prisons and private and voluntary sector organizations to compete to manage offenders in the community. We want to encourage partnerships between public and private sector providers and the voluntary and community sectors which harness their respective strengths. As a market develops, offender managers will be able to buy custodial places or community interventions from providers, from whatever sector, based only on their cost effectiveness in reducing re-offending.
>
> (Home Office 2004: 14)

Thus, the clear commitment by the government to the concept of competition among providers from the public, private and voluntary sectors in the provision of correctional services indicates that this area is likely to be a significant opportunity for future growth in commercial provision.

Timing and policy similarity

In this section, we explore the empirical evidence for policy transfer in the arena of privatized corrections. An important precondition for any argument that transfer has occurred is that developments in the supposed 'importer' country came later than those in the 'exporter', and that there is a sufficient degree of similarity between the policies in each to be consistent with a picture of transfer. In broad terms, we argue that the contracting out of prisons and the use of electronic tagging both meet these conditions.

Timing

In the field of commercial prisons, it is clear that the emergence of initial ideas and then the substantive manifestations of policy took place first in the USA with the UK following some time later (Jones and Newburn 2005). Criminal justice systems in both countries faced similar problems during the 1980s, including rapidly expanding prison populations (albeit on very different scales), and faced the difficulty of meeting demand for places within the constraints of traditional public sector procurement procedures. The first mainstream prison to be run on commercial lines in the USA opened in 1984 in Houston, Texas, run by the Corrections Corporation of American (CCA). Further establishments were opened in the following year, during which CCA made an unsuccessful bid to run the entire Tennessee state prison system.[6] During the mid- to late 1980s, other private corrections corporations, such as the United States Corrections Corporation and Wackenhut, also entered the market at state and the local county level, mainly in the southern states (Jones and Newburn 2005). The early to mid-1990s saw continued growth in the private corrections sector, although this was unevenly spread across the country (Mattera and Khan 2001). By the late 1990s, the private prison sector remained concentrated in 23 western and southern states. High-use states included Texas, Oklahoma, Florida, Louisiana, Tennessee, California, Colorado, Mississippi, and Washington DC (McDonald et al. 1998). More recent figures show that 19 states in total have no prisoners held in private facilities (US Department of Justice 2001). The late 1990s saw significant slowdown in the US private corrections market. The confidence of institutional investors in companies like CCA was shaken by high-profile scandals involving mismanagement, escapes, and mistreatment of prisoners (Greene 2001). In early 2002, the Sentencing Project (2002: 3) observed that '[s]ince 2000, no states have negotiated new private prison contracts, and several states have curtailed their relationship with the private prison industry'. In addition to a slowing down of private contracts, some private corrections facilities have been brought under public sector control.[7] Although state governments have been a shrinking source of private corrections contracts, the federal government has become an increasing source of demand for the commercial corrections industry, and by 1997 the Federal Bureau of Prisons was the primary customer for commercially provided prison places (McDonald *et al.* 1998; Sentencing Project 2002). As we have seen above, the first commercially run penal establishment in the UK did not open until 1992, some eight years after the appearance of commercially run prisons in the USA.

Regarding electronic monitoring, Nellis (2000: 100) has argued, 'on the surface at least, electronic monitoring provides a particularly sharp example of policy transfer'. Nellis demonstrates that electronic monitoring was operational in the USA for six years before it became operational anywhere else. An experiment involving the monitoring of psychiatric patients using radio transmitters in the late 1960s clearly shows that the core ideas originated in America before emerging in other countries. 'Tagging' was first discussed as a method for tracking psychiatric patients in the USA in the 1960s, with the first trials taking place in Massachusetts in 1967. Despite early experiments, therefore, it took the best part of a further 20 years before EM emerged within the American corrections system. Now virtually all states have a system of EM (Prison Reform Trust 1997). The first coherent programme was set up in Palm Beach, Florida, and began in 1984. Within a two-year period there were 30 programmes monitoring a total of 1000 offenders. By 1988, Michigan, Illinois and Florida were key users of EM and between them had an average daily tagging caseload of 3000 offenders. By 1991 the Bureau of Justice Statistics estimated that there were approximately 400 separate schemes in operation monitoring 12,000 offenders, but with a rapidly increasing incarceration rate the search for alternatives continued. The National Institute of Justice in Washington DC estimated in 1998 there were approximately 1500 schemes with 95,000 EM units in use (National Institute of Justice 1999). However, despite what on the surface looks like a steady and consistent period of growth, Whitfield counsels a degree of caution in this regard, noting the number of problems that beset early programmes and that, in practice, far fewer offenders were subject to such supervision than was indicated in NIJ estimates. Dick Whitfield, perhaps the other closest observer of the development of EM in recent times, concurs with Nellis's view, arguing that 'in practical terms, the electronic monitoring of offenders started in the United States of America in 1984' (Whitfield 1997: 9).

Policy similarities

In terms of the policies themselves, there is sufficient similarity between the US and UK experience of contracting out of prisons to support the proposition that policy transfer did contribute to UK developments. This was most important at the level of broader ideas and issues of principle concerning commercial involvement in the provision of prisons. However, similarities are also apparent in terms of the more substantive levels of policy, policy content and instruments.[8] In both the USA and the UK, legislative action was required to confirm the legality of the contracting out of prison management. For much of the recent period in the USA, the most important legislation has been passed at the state level (see Cummins 2000 for a discussion of developments in Texas). However, since the late 1990s there has been a growth in federal use of private prison facilities (Jones and Newburn 2005). The policy instruments that were used to implement the policy of contracting out were also broadly similar in the UK and the USA. Each country subsequently experienced a growth in the number of contracts between governmental/state authorities and private sector companies for the provision of correctional services. Furthermore, some of the key players in the UK market were part owned by major US corrections corporations, suggesting the possibility of a broadly similar approach to delivering correctional services. At the same time, of course, there have been important divergences in the experiences of contracting out in different jurisdictions in the USA and the UK, many of which can be related to the particular cultural, legal and political circumstances within which the policy developed (Jones and Newburn 2005). We consider these differences in more detail below, but for current purposes we would argue that there is sufficient similarity – in broad terms – for the hypothesis of policy transfer to remain viable.

Regarding general principles, the basic notion that offenders (or suspected offenders on bail) can be monitored and restricted via electronic monitoring was the same on both sides of the Atlantic. In terms of more specific policy content and instruments, the comparison becomes more difficult because of the large number of different models that developed in the USA. However, notwithstanding differences in application (and in the nature of the technology used) that later emerged, the fact that in both the USA and the UK EM has been used as a condition of bail, a sentence of court (both in its own right and in conjunction with other community sentences), and as a method of securing early release of prisoners, suggests sufficient policy similarity to be consistent with some degree of policy transfer.

Policy transfer agents

We can identify a number of key policy transfer agents who drew explicitly upon US exemplars to promote policy change in the UK in both areas of commercial involvement in corrections discussed here. Documentary analysis of the historical development of contracting out of prisons highlights a number of key players, many of whom were interviewed during this study. The main agents of transfer in the arena of contracting out of prisons fall into three categories. The first includes 'policy entrepreneurs' (see Chapter 2), and in particular free market think tanks such as the ASI and the campaigning organization, the OTA, were central. The second category of key agents included a number of politicians, including Conservative members of the House of Commons Home Affairs Committee in the late 1980s (in particular Sir Edward Gardner and Sir John Wheeler) and a number of other senior politicians including Lords Caithness and Windlesham. The third category, vitally important in the development of EM in the UK, consisted of a small number of key Home Office officials tasked with implementing the policy. Finally, the role of commercial consortia including US corrections corporations was vital in the initial lobbying for change and subsequent winning of contracts in the prison system.

Policy entrepreneurs

As discussed above, the ASI was the source of the first advocacy of contracting out of prisons in the UK in its reports in 1984 and 1987. These reports explicitly referred to developments in the USA as exemplars of what might take place in the UK. A key figure in both reports was Peter Young, the one-time Head of Research at the ASI who also was based in the ASI's office in Washington, DC between 1985 and 1987. In interview, he made it clear that the ASI made a deliberate attempt to draw upon US experiences:

> [C]ertainly the Institute always consciously looked for practical examples of how a policy would work in some other part of the world ... the Institute focused on trying to make practical policy recommendations as opposed to outlining the philosophical case for something or other. And if you're making practical policy recommendations by far the strongest, most effective way of doing so is by identifying where the policy or a variant of it operates successfully somewhere else and saying 'Look, it works there, why couldn't it work here?'
>
> (Peter Young, personal interview)

Young went on to argue that the USA was a rich source of practical policy ideas and innovations, because of the sheer size of the country and the number of different jurisdictions. Another motivation for looking to US experience concerned close contacts between the ASI and similar-minded think tanks and policy institutes in the USA (in particular, the Heritage Foundation, but also the Cato Institute and Reason Foundation). The importance of personal and institutional links between such organizations has been noted extensively elsewhere (Stone 2000; Jones and Newburn 2002a). While based in the USA, Young reported that he drew upon what US evidence there was, in particular, studies by the Reason Foundation (among others), to develop the ASI's recommendations regarding commercially run prisons. These ideas were subsequently promoted in the UK via briefings with sympathetic politicians (see below), and more generally in gaining media coverage for what, Young accepted, was initially considered (in his own words) to be something of a 'joke as opposed to a serious policy proposal'. In interview, the Director of the ASI, Dr Madsen Pirie, confirmed Young's account and stressed that the fundamental motivation behind the ASI's support for private prisons was a general ideological belief in the importance of promoting radical market-based reforms. A key selling point for the policy of contracting out was the promise of cost savings to government in conjunction with the possibility of undermining the power of the POA. However, it should also be noted that the ASI also argued on the basis of what appear to be genuinely held beliefs that the policy would lead to improved standards in prisons, and better regimes for the rehabilitation of offenders.

Although the ASI was clearly important in initially raising the idea of privately contracted prisons, its influence on subsequent developments was limited. It is significant that all the politicians and Home Office officials with whom we spoke downplayed the influence of the ASI and could not recall a great deal of contact with the organization. For example, David Mellor made a point of strongly denying that the thinking of Home Office ministers or officials was influenced by free market think tanks at this time. The Home Secretary at the time of the Criminal Justice Bill that became the 1991 Act, David (now Lord) Waddington, told us: 'I cannot recall the work of the Adam Smith Institute at that time.' Although it is possible to raise questions about accuracy of recall, or indeed raise issues about the tendency of politicians to deliberately downplay external influences, these accounts do appear convincing and are consistent with the findings of other studies. For example, Stone (2000) has highlighted the close personal and institutional links between neo-liberal think tanks on both sides of the Atlantic. She argues that although such organizations were clearly influential in promoting certain ideas and programmes within criminal justice (as in other fields), we should be cautious about assuming substantial direct policy influence of think tanks. Other studies have questioned the ASI's claims of significant direct influence over Conservative administrations of the 1980s. It is suggested that such claims are based upon the tenuous assumption that if the government introduced a policy previously recommended by the ASI, this was evidence of direct influence (Denham and Garnett 1999). However, the authors argue that a very large number of policies promoted by the ASI were *not* adopted by governments, and note that the ASI's 'direct influence on policy during the 1980s was far less than its role in creating and maintaining a Thatcherite ethos'. Nevertheless, we would argue that the ASI was an important influence promoting the initial idea of commercially contracted prisons, and the US inspiration for this is quite explicit in both documentary and interview evidence.

Similar themes can be seen in the story of the transfer of EM. Here, however, the key policy entrepreneur was Tom Stacey, who established the Offender Tag Association (OTA) in 1982 to campaign for the introduction of electronic tagging in the UK. In 1981, Stacey had first explored the idea of using electronic monitoring of offenders with a friend at the University of Kent, and lobbied the Home Office Prisons Department, but with no apparent result. In autumn 1982, he wrote a letter to *The Times* suggesting the development of EM. This occurred at about the same time as the use of EM in the USA began to be reported in the UK press, although Stacey argues that he was not aware of US developments at the time. During the mid-1980s, the OTA undertook press and media interviews to promote EM, and organized a number of conferences (including some at the then Leicester Polytechnic) that included delegates from US firms providing EM services to criminal justice systems in the USA. Stacey himself reported that much of his early efforts were subject to ridicule, and other respondents reported that he was viewed as a charming eccentric rather than somebody to be taken seriously. However, it is difficult to disagree that Stacey (and the OTA) played a vital role in the early genesis of the policy of EM in the UK, in terms of placing the idea on the margins of the policy-making agenda. In terms of the US influence, Stacey's account is interesting. He suggests that he was unaware of early developments in the USA, and came to the idea independently himself. However, given that some developments had already occurred in the USA, it is clear that Stacey and the OTA acted as early 'transfer agents' in that they facilitated the contribution of US delegates to the conferences on EM during the 1980s.

Thus, in both contracting out of prisons, and the emergence of EM, policy entrepreneurs played a key role in helping the broad policy ideas 'rise to the top of the policy soup' (Kingdon 1995). To differing extents, they both actively drew upon US exemplars, and promoted their ideas within the media and, where possible, directly to politicians and policy-makers. In terms of the next phase of policy development, however, it was other categories of transfer agent that were to play a vital role.

Politicians

From the historical account above, there were a number of politicians who began actively to promote the policy to government and can therefore also be regarded as key transfer agents. In both the development of EM and contracting out of prisons, the central influence was exerted by Conservative members of the HAC in the late 1980s, and in particular the chairmen at the time, the late Sir Edward Gardner and his successor, Sir John Wheeler. Although in interview Sir John Wheeler argued that it was the general climate of the times, rather than US experiences in particular, that was the 'trigger for change' in this policy area, he accepted the importance of the US lessons in the development of contracting out of prisons. He was a young MP at the time, seeking to make his mark, at a time when the governments of Margaret Thatcher were implementing a programme of radical free-market reforms within which policies of contracting out and privatization loomed large. He argued that the key motivation for promoting reform in the prison service was to improve the state of the prison system, then, in his view, displaying all the negative characteristics of large, union-dominated, centralized and inefficient public bureaucracies. Sir John did accept, however, that within these broader cultural shifts, the visit of HAC members to view particular developments in the USA was important:

> Now I do recall that we did one piece of work which took us to the United States of America . . . And in the course of that visit we did pick up some experiences, almost indirectly since they were not the principal purpose of the visit in some ways, but I do recall that with the help of the British Embassy saying 'Oh, by the way, you might be interested to know that X was taking place' in one particular establishment, and we went to see it.
>
> (Sir John Wheeler, personal interview)

Sir John outlined how both he and the late Sir Edward Gardner were 'immensely influenced' by what they saw in the USA, although he emphasized that these experiences confirmed views that they already held about ways forward in prison reform, rather than introducing them to completely new ideas. Nevertheless, the importance of the US exemplars remains clear:

> I remember then, too, going to see a prison in Florida which had been handed over quite imaginatively to the private sector, in the early days of this experiment 20 years ago, and the warden, we call them governors, who'd been a prison professional manager all his life, all his working career, said to me . . . 'Do you know, the first time in my career I've actually wardened an institution properly . . . I have the money, I hold the budget, the staff are accountable to me not to a union, but to me. I have a board and I am accountable. Then there is a contract, this is a profit-making organization, we know all about that, but we have to deliver a service effectively.' And I went round this prison, I noticed that the staff weren't in uniforms, so beloved of so many prison institutions the world over, no jangling keys, no great big boots, shiny toe caps, crew cuts, all the crap that you're accustomed to seeing.
>
> (Sir John Wheeler, personal interview)

We interviewed other former members of the Home Affairs Committee who also took part in the visit to the USA. The former Conservative MP Janet Fooks (now Baroness Fooks) provided an account that strongly resonated with that of Sir John Wheeler, and reported how impressed they had been with the facilities and conditions of the US privately run prisons, in contrast to the state-run institutions. The Labour MP Gerry Bermingham also visited the USA, and confirmed that Committee members had been impressed by what they saw. However, he reported that he was far more sceptical about how representative of CCA establishments this was, and was also aware that they were being clearly courted by the company (who flew them around the USA on a CCA private jet). Bermingham reported that with hindsight, though he did not perceive it at the time, he came to the view that the HAC inquiry had been cleverly 'hijacked' by supporters of the contracting out of prisons.

The account of Sir John Wheeler and other former members of the HAC is consistent with the recollections of Lord Windlesham (see above) about the importance of these politicians in promoting this particular reform. Former Home Secretary Lord Waddington confirmed the important influence of the Home Affairs Committee in this area: 'We did attach considerable importance to the recommendation in the Home Affairs Committee's Report.' Nevertheless, supporters of contracting out of prisons still faced a significant degree of initial scepticism from Home Office officials and a number of senior Conservative politicians from the left of the Party, such as Douglas Hurd. Furthermore, a number of informants also confirmed that leading members of the Thatcherite wing of the Conservative Party also looked on such proposals with suspicion. Sir John Wheeler himself noted that 'at the time even Margaret herself looked me up and down in a rather scathing way'. This general picture was supported by the recollections of David Mellor, then Prisons Minister in the Home Office, and David Lidington MP (then political adviser to Douglas Hurd), and Lord Waddington (as David Waddington, successor as Home Secretary to Douglas Hurd). Lord Waddington, for example, confirmed to us that he was initially disinclined to include a clause in the Criminal Justice Bill that would allow for the contracting out of remand centres. He said that this 'was the product of native caution'. He reported that 'officials were perhaps even more cautious but they were far from obstructive' (Lord Waddington, personal communication). At the same time, Lord Waddington was not aware of any major interest from the Prime Minister: 'It was not one of the issues in which the Prime Minister was taking a big interest; I cannot remember her raising the matter with me at any of our regular private meetings.'

Thus, in contracting out of prisons we have a fascinating example of a major shift in penal policy that almost came out of the blue, promoted not by civil servants or as part of an official political programme, but rather by a small group of committed backbenchers. This was in the face of considerable caution from senior Home Office civil servants, and a good degree of cautiousness from government ministers, including Home Secretaries Douglas Hurd and David Waddington, as well as the Prime Minister herself. The motivations of these reformers were both ideological and pragmatic. Key players such as Sir John Wheeler were open about their general beliefs in the role of commercial pressures and competition in improving public services. However, he also expressed a more pragmatic and humanistic desire to improve conditions in the prison system and to promote better treatment of prisoners. Although their more senior opponents within the Conservative Party may have shared some of these beliefs, there was a strong sense that 'law and order' issues should remain within the state sector, and a concern about provoking a major industrial dispute with the POA. A combination of these issues for some time kept any serious discussion of the policy on the margins. In fact David Mellor, who was Prisons Minister at a crucial period (autumn 1989 to summer 1990) told us that during this time 'I have no recollection of any private sector involvement being seriously discussed and I would be very surprised if it was' (David Mellor, personal interview).

Thus, what amounted to a significant change in penal policy emerged almost as an afterthought, following a change of mind from the No. 10 Policy Unit and, by implication, the Prime Minister herself. The decision to incorporate a clause in the 1991 Criminal Justice Act that would open the way to experiment with a commercially contracted remand centre was primarily driven by the symbolic need to appear radical. Windlesham (1993: 421–2) argues that the decision was taken by the Prime Minister 'because of her conviction of the need for radical reform outside the prevailing consensus; not for any reasons of penological principle or administrative practice', and the decision 'was a symbol as well as an experiment' (1993: 307). For Margaret Thatcher, the decision symbolized her independence, her radical nature and her belief that her government should be perceived as a 'conviction government' (Jenkins, 1987: 183). David Lidington MP perhaps best summarizes the way in which this policy emerged, while giving due significance to the 'effective lobbying' of backbench Conservative MPs, as an idea that simply arose at the right time:

> Private prisons was an idea that met the need on a number of fronts, in that they appeared to offer a way of, first of all, getting new institutions . . . up and running quickly. Secondly, of delivering, if you looked at the American experience, rather better regimes than we seemed to be doing in this country, and also separating remand from sentenced prisoners.
>
> (David Lidington MP, personal interview)

Thus, US influence was clearly important in the initial stages of policy development, during the early years of contracting out of prisons in the UK. After this time, US experience continued to be a source of lessons. In interview,

Michael Howard reported that officials continued to undertake visits to the USA during his tenure at the Home Office, in order to inform the development of this policy:

> [T]he decision to privatize prisons had been taken by . . . my predecessor but I had to implement it and so obviously we were very interested in how privately operated prisons operated elsewhere.
>
> (Michael Howard, personal interview)

Politicians were also important transfer agents in the promotion of EM in the UK. Many of the key figures in the contracting prisons story reappear here. In particular, Sir John Wheeler and other members of the HAC were impressed by the EM schemes they saw in the USA during the 1986 visit discussed above, and the final report of this inquiry recommended that the Home Office introduce some experiments with tagging (see above). However, although the influential HAC's support no doubt helped the cause of EM in the UK, there is little evidence, either from documentary sources or from interviews with members, that they expended a great deal of energy in further promoting the policy (compared, for example, to active lobbying of government ministers for the contracting out of prisons). In addition, Home Office minister Lord Caithness, who visited in the late 1980s, also reported positively on the idea of EM. Nellis argues that it is not clear how important the Caithness/Wheeler tours of the USA were in stimulating eventual Home Office support, but hypothesizes that both Caithness and the then Home Secretary, Douglas Hurd, may both have been influenced by positive reports from American schemes and American companies.[9] It was, however, a later Home Secretary, Michael Howard, who was to play a key role in the development of EM in England and Wales. Though the aim of reducing the prison population was no longer an acceptable criminal justice goal at this time, Nellis argues that the Home Secretary, Michael Howard, was intrigued by the potential of EM as a standalone punishment – effectively 'home confinement'. This view is supported by our interviews with key respondents in the policy network at the time. According to Hugh Marriage, Deputy Head of the Probation Unit of the Home Office at that time, Howard faced considerable opposition to his promotion of EM from many of his officials:

> And Michael Howard came in and said he wanted tagging. And frankly a whole host, a raft of official advice said the American experience is that tagging doesn't work, and if it doesn't work in America, it won't work here, it's going to be expensive, it's going to cost us an arm and a leg, it's going to rile the probation service, and you should steer clear of it . . . And I was about the only person of fairly senior rank who had not been involved at all in advising ministers.

Eventually Michael Howard lost his temper, ran out of patience, one should say, and said, 'I'm sorry, I want it.' And at that point the Home Office did what it always did, which was to make sure that the person who implemented it had not had any hand in saying that it was impossible, that it wouldn't work.

(Hugh Marriage, personal interview)

Not only was Michael Howard keen on the idea of EM but, according to Marriage, he also had clear ideas about how it should be brought about:

Also, part of this message was Michael Howard saying 'I want a private sector correctional thing – non-custodial alternative. We've privatized the prisons and we want this to be a private sector one, and the final bit is that I want you to implement this without any contact with the probation service. I do not want the probation service sabotaging this scheme.' So those were the requirements.

(Hugh Marriage, personal interview)

Marriage himself was the civil servant nominated to lead on the work, and by his own account (and those of others), he shared some of Michael Howard's views about the probation service. In Hugh Marriage's own words, he wanted to 'challenge the culture in the UK', particularly 'the old style unreformed probation service, the sacred cow that's existed in this country since I think probably the mid-sixties and I regard as a complete bane of my professional life. They're very nice people but they're wholly ineffective.' Michael Howard's Criminal Justice and Public Order Act 1994 introduced the curfew order as a community sentence in its own right and Nellis (2000) argues that the provision in the Act, Schedule 9 (para. 41) draws directly upon the American model. Marriage and his team were to play a key role in implementing EM according to Howard's wishes, sometimes in the face of considerable resistance (from other parts of the Home Office, the courts, penal reform groups and, not least, the probation service), as outlined below. For present purposes it is sufficient to underline the central role of a politician, Michael Howard, in driving change. A number of respondents highlighted the fact that he takes a close personal interest in US developments, and it is reasonable to suggest that he was aware of developments in EM in the USA, and inclined to view them as a positive lesson to be learned for Britain. Although politicians did not provide the original impetus to the development of policy in this area, clearly, some politicians played a vital role in later developments. A former senior member of the Association of Chief Officers of Probation, Dick Whitfield, provided an interesting insight as to why ministers were open to developments in EM, even in the face of equivocal (to say the least) research evidence as to whether it actually worked. In his words:

> I don't think ministers . . . beyond needing a lot of column inches and
> a feeling that they were doing something, started with any great belief
> that tagging was going to change the world . . . But it's a very sexy
> thing in many ways, it's very visual, it's got quite a powerful message
> and there's the excitement of new technology that's added onto it.
> And it's a very good thing for ministers to talk about . . . Symbolism is
> enormously important; it would be daft to pretend that it wasn't a big
> issue all the way along the line.
>
> (Dick Whitfield, personal interview)

Symbolic politics was thus crucial to the role played by politicians in the story of EM, as in many other areas of crime policy. The aim was to convey a tough message, that something was being done, and electronic tagging provided a useful way of convincing the public that community sentences were not a soft option. However, there were also more specific motivations in the attraction of EM to Michael Howard. First, as noted above, Howard was keen to develop commercial sector involvement in the provision of community penalties and this provided a way forward. In addition, a related advantage would be to undermine the power of NAPO and pave the way for more radical reform of the probation service. Thus, key politicians with clear motivations played an important role in the development of EM, and a degree of US influence on their motivations was visible. However, the detailed way in which EM developed in the UK was primarily influenced by some key officials in the Home Office, not least one already mentioned, Hugh Marriage.

Civil servants

As the above account makes clear, there was considerable resistance among Home Office officials to the initial proposals to increase private sector involvement in the provision of prisons, and in EM. Reservations about the contracting out of prisons were shared by senior government ministers, as evidenced in the accounts of David Mellor and Lord Windlesham (to take two key examples of respondents who served as Home Office ministers during the crucial time). The policy change was eventually introduced at the somewhat sudden behest of the Prime Minister, who clearly changed her mind. In the case of EM, however, there was a more protracted process of negotiation and promotion within and outside the Home Office within which the implementation team (appointed when Howard insisted that EM be taken forward), led by Hugh Marriage, was absolutely vital.

Marriage confirmed this, and confirmed the importance of US lessons in this process. He reported that having recruited a scientist and an administrative officer to work with him on the task of introducing EM, the next thing he organized was for all three of them to visit schemes in Michigan and Florida. A number of US contacts for these visits were set up via a colleague in the form of a former Chief Inspector of Probation, described by Marriage as 'a real American buff', who regularly visited the USA for leisure and had an extensive network of acquaintances working there. Marriage's account of change suggests that American experience was paradoxically both used as a source of resistance and as a stimulus to policy transfer. As both Dick Whitfield and Marriage reported, the general conclusion of US research evidence was rather negative regarding the potential of EM, and this had been used by Home Office officials as an argument against its development in the UK. However, the fact that there were practical examples of tagging in operation in the USA meant that, for Marriage and his team, faced with a short implementation deadline, this was the natural place to visit. Marriage made it clear that there was no attempt simply to copy US schemes, but rather to develop a hybrid model drawing on positive elements from different states, as well as trying to avoid some of the perceived pitfalls of the US system.

> . . . certainly after – it was only about a week – I knew what tagging looked like, which was a great help. And I got from Michigan and from Florida and the various schemes a decent understanding of what tagging could do, and that's good for the technical specifications.
>
> (Hugh Marriage, personal interview)

Marriage reported that on their return from the USA they drew up a specification which was 'a sort of dream ticket of all the American available tags . . . and we stuck that out for tender'. However, they also attempted to tailor the UK specification appropriately, which led to what Marriage described as 'an entirely new English tagging system'. One example of this concerned the basic size of the tag itself. In the USA these tended to be very large, deliberately in order to stigmatize the offender. Marriage felt that US schemes in general used EM in an overly punitive way, and thus sought to develop a smaller tag that could be worn on the leg or wrist and hidden from public view.

Hugh Marriage made it clear that he was strongly in favour of tagging and that he pursued his task with what he called 'a missionary zeal'. This supports other respondents' accounts of the key role he personally played in policy development. Dick Whitfield, for example, argued how important it was for certain policies to have a 'champion' in the Home Office who would see them through. Marriage's strategy was to 'sell' EM to various constituencies in different ways. For example, he highlighted to ministers the possibilities of EM being portrayed as a tough policy, and also portrayed it to reluctant magistrates as 'pure punishment'. However, in what were sometimes strained dealings with NAPO representatives, possibilities for reducing the prison population and more rehabilitative elements of EM were emphasized.

Commercial corporations

A third key set of agents of policy transfer were the commercial corrections corporations themselves. Evidence here is harder to come by, for a number of reasons including issues of commercial confidentiality, and the potential controversies connected with concerns about undue commercial influence over political decision-making. In the USA, there is strong evidence of commercial corrections corporations intervening directly in the legislative process, providing political contributions to sympathetic candidates, and lobbying effectively for legislation both to introduce contracting out in the first instance, and also to promote harsher sentencing policies in order to expand market opportunities for commercial providers (Jones and Newburn 2005). We should state that our study found no evidence at all of commercial companies influencing, or even attempting to influence, sentencing policies in the UK (though clearly that is not to say that this does not, or could not, happen). However, there is significant evidence of the involvement of commercial corporations in promoting the initial move to contracting out in the late 1980s and early 1990s, and in the subsequent development of this policy.

Although Sir John Wheeler argued that commercial companies had 'no influence at all' on the policy decisions leading to the implementation of contracting out, the accounts of Windlesham and others provide plentiful examples of the importance of the lobbying effort. As noted above, it seems clear that an important impetus to the promotion of the initial ideas of prison contracting was the visits to US institutions run by US-based multinational corporations such as CCA and Wackenhut. Second, there was clear US influence in so far as these companies formed consortia with UK companies to lobby for change at the early stages, and later to win contracts to run (and eventually build) remand centres and prisons. This influence has arguably since declined, as a result of sell-offs and mergers, but nevertheless formed an important impetus to change at the time. The involvement of US corporations is not surprising, given the lack of any British (or other) companies with experience of running correctional institutions. As a senior representative of the Home Office Contracts and Competition Group told us, there simply was nowhere else to turn other than the experience of US companies at this time, because the US model was the only one in existence. Something that became the subject of considerable controversy was the close personal links between some politicians and the commercial security/corrections industry, with both Sir Edward Gardner and Sir John Wheeler prominent in these links (see above). Finally, the appendices of evidence of the second report of the HAC to consider commercial contracting out of prisons provide extensive documentary evidence of the lobbying efforts of the commercial sector to continue to influence change (although we should note that the commercial prisons sector has still not expanded to the extent that they have argued for).

Overall, therefore, there is clear evidence of the influence of US-based corporations on UK policy in this area, although it is difficult to establish the extent and nature of such influence. On the surface, it seems far less than has been the case in the USA. We found no evidence at all of commercial companies lobbying in order to attempt to influence sentencing policy, as has been the case in certain parts of the USA. Stephen Shaw, former head of the Prison Reform Trust and one-time campaigner against contracted prisons, strongly supported this view. In interview, Shaw expressed the view that although commercial corrections corporations clearly have an interest in penal expansion and that this may be an incentive for them to try to influence public policy, this does not seem to have happened in the UK:

> [Y]ou'd be hard pressed to see it, to show any examples of where that has happened . . . I know of no lobby groups or public lectures funded by these companies to say 'let's lock up more' or however subtly they do it. They are big companies, they have glossy PR machines, they provide lunches and all that. But I don't think you can say they behaved improperly in any respect.
>
> (Stephen Shaw, personal interview)

There was some commercial lobbying in the arena of EM, though respondents differed on how significant it was in bringing about policy change. Harry Fletcher of NAPO suggested that commercial companies had more influence in placing EM on the agenda of policy-makers than did the activities of the OTA: 'The real lobbying was from the private sector.' However, other respondents played down the importance of commercial lobbying. Hugh Marriage remembered some low-level contact from US companies, occasional invitations to lunch and so on, but that the lobbying was 'not heavy'. Dick Whitfield confirmed this impression, reporting that one US company had invited him for an expenses-paid holiday in Colorado in order to 'show him a few things' while he was there. However, he said this was in total contrast to the contractors involved in EM in the UK:

> I actually found them very well behaved. There were one or two companies who had the reputation of being very aggressive . . . but I have to say that in terms of co-sponsoring and being responsible, they've been brilliant.
>
> (Dick Whitfield, personal interview)

Clearly, then, commercial companies have played some role in helping to transfer the more concrete aspects of policy into the UK context, both through some initial lobbying for policy change, and subsequently though their involvement in commercial contracts in both running prisons and EM schemes. However, this influence is relatively minor compared with the role played by the commercial sector in many parts of the USA.

Policy transfer processes

This section explores in more detail the actual processes via which policy transfer in this arena occurred, drawing in particular upon the work of Dolowitz and Marsh (2000) and also that of Bennett (1991), discussed in Chapter 2. For example, it is helpful to consider how we might characterize policy transfer in this field in terms of Dolowitz and Marsh's notion of degrees of transfer ranging from 'copying' (complete and direct transfer of an entire programme), emulation (transfer of ideas behind a particular policy or programme) and combinations (mixtures of different policies) to inspiration (where developments in another country inspire change but the eventual policy outcome does not resemble the original in any detail). It is also important to consider the degree to which policy transfer arises as a result of Bennett's distinct paths of policy convergence, including emulation, elite networking, harmonization and penetration. An additional key objective of this section is to examine how far these processes provide evidence that knowledge about policy developments in the USA was actually used to inform and shape subsequent developments in the UK.

The emergence and growth of a commercial corrections sector in the UK involved a complex combination of processes, and it is difficult to categorize these in a straightforward way. In terms of Dolowitz and Marsh's terminology, the notions of direct copying and combinations of policies do not seem to correspond to the UK developments in commercial corrections. However, there does seem to have been a significant degree of both inspiration and emulation in the development of EM and of contracting out of prisons. The basic ideas concerning both policies clearly had their roots in the USA. But what happened went beyond mere inspiration. Those promoting the policies from outside government drew on specific US exemplars, and both politicians and policy-makers undertook visits to the USA in order to inform their thinking on this. The British Embassy in Washington DC played (and still plays) an important role in facilitating policy learning from the USA. Sir John Wheeler and Hugh Marriage recalled that the British Embassy arranged the visits of politicians and officials to commercially run prisons and EM schemes. This was confirmed in interviews with representatives of the Public Affairs Unit of the British Embassy in Washington DC. According to one official, acting as facilitators for policy transfer should be 'a core function of an Embassy in a developed country'. This official felt that policy learning from the USA had been occurring for some time in the fields of economic management and science and technology, and now this was a developing field in criminal justice. A particular focus for the Public Affairs Unit at the time of our meeting was in exchanging best practice in law enforcement, and this point is developed further in Chapter 5. For the purposes of this chapter, however, it is sufficient to note that a similar process of identifying particular policies and initiatives arranging programmes of visits for travelling UK officials and politicians was also carried out by Embassy staff in the area of privatization of corrections.

As far as Bennett's models of process are concerned, the first two are most relevant here. We have already discussed emulation (which Bennett uses in a similar way to Dolowitz and Marsh). In addition, there is strong evidence for the role of 'elite networking' and the development of transnational policy networks involving a combination of policy entrepreneurs, politicians, policy-makers and practitioners. In terms of the soft policy transfer of broad policy ideas and principles (Evans and Davies 1999), the elite networking of major neo-liberal think tanks was crucial in spreading ideas about contracting out of prisons from the USA to the UK. In the United States the key players in this regard were the Heritage Foundation and the Manhattan Institute; in the UK, the Adam Smith Institute and the Institute of Economic Affairs (IEA) (Wacquant 1999b). On both sides of the Atlantic these major think tanks have played a key role in the promotion and dissemination of neo-liberal ideas, some of which have clearly influenced developments in the field of corrections (Smith 1991; Stone 2000). In relation to crime control they have not only been important in disseminating such ideas domestically, but transatlantic ties between these bodies have arguably been centrally implicated in the process of policy transfer. As we saw above, the Adam Smith Institute was prominent in the promotion of contracting out of prisons, leaning heavily on study visits to the USA and the experience of its head of research who worked previously for the Heritage Foundation in Washington. In terms of the more substantive elements of policy (content and instruments), the role of elite networks was also important, but arguably less so. The representative from the Home Office Contract and Competitions Group reported that international conferences involving a range of commercial companies, policy-makers and correctional officials did have some influence in terms of sharing ideas across national boundaries. However, despite the existence of growing transnational networks in this arena, the details of the contracting out of prisons policy developed in a quite distinctive way in the UK (see below for a discussion of the limits of policy transfer).

In the arena of EM, the elite networking of think tanks was less important, but once again, international conferences (involving significant input from US commercial companies and correctional officials) played a role in promoting the general ideas and principles of EM. In addition, there was significant contact between policy-makers and practitioners in both countries. Elements of US experience were clearly imported, as reported by the key players. As Nellis (2000) points out, the US influence was clear:

> In developing electronic tagging in England both new and old players
> in the criminal justice policy networks learned – some blindly, some
> selectively and some critically – from what various states and counties
> in America were already doing, at least to begin with.

However, US experiences were also used as 'negative lessons' and, as with contracting out of prisons, the way that EM subsequently developed in the UK was
very distinctive. This illustrates the limits of policy transfer, and the abiding
importance of domestic influences, and this general issue is discussed in more
detail in the next section.

In Chapter 1, we outlined Nils Christie's (2000) argument that a 'penal
industrial complex' has emerged, consisting of contacts between commercial
corrections companies, politicians and policy-makers. In this way, the expansionist policies of multinational corporations are shaping the public policy
process in the interests of their own profit-making. Our study did not find any
extensive evidence to support this view of privatization in the UK. As we
have seen above, commercial corrections corporations did appear to play an
important role, to a degree, as agents of policy transfer in the commercial
corrections field. However, this was rather limited when compared to the situation in the USA, and was limited to some lobbying activity to promote EM
and contracted out prisons in the first instance, and then some more substantive input in terms of being involved in consortia that actually won contracts
in the UK. There was no evidence of any major attempt to influence the political process as has been noted in the USA. As we have discussed elsewhere, the
American Legislative Exchange Council (ALEC) has become an increasingly
important national player in the USA, promoting both harsher sentencing
policies across state legislatures and pro-privatization policies more generally
(Jones and Newburn 2005). ALEC is a conservative public policy organization
based in Washington DC and it is estimated that 40 per cent of state legislators
are members (Sarabi and Bender 2000: 3). ALEC draws up 'model legislation' to
promote conservative policies, and it has been highly effective in influencing
policy in many US states. Corporate donations form a major source of income
for ALEC, accounting for almost 70 per cent of the total budget in 1998
(Sarabi and Bender 2000). Commercial corrections corporations have been
prominent supporters of ALEC, including both CCA and Wackenhut. ALEC's
'Criminal Justice Taskforce' takes the lead in developing model legislation to
sell to state governments, and included senior representatives from commercial corrections companies. As well as promoting legislation to allow the
contracting out of prisons, the organization successfully promoted 'truth in
sentencing' and 'three strikes' legislation during the 1990s. In addition to the
work of bodies like ALEC, private corrections corporations have taken more
direct action in the form of increasing amounts of money paid to professional
lobbyists, and in terms of making direct donations to political campaigns.

Sarabi and Bender (2000) note that in 1998, contributions were made by private corrections companies or their associates to 361 candidates in 25 states. They argue that 'this total represents a significant and growing effort to ensure access to policy-makers at the state level at crucial moments' (2000: 8). It seems to us, therefore, that the operation of a penal–industrial complex is much more visible in the spread of policy ideas and innovations in the field of commercial corrections in the USA, but there is little evidence of this kind of overt behaviour in the UK. This is not to say that commercial interests do not exert influence over policy-making in more subtle ways. However, it seems clear that crude parallels should not be drawn with the US situation.

Limits to policy transfer

We would argue that there is sufficient evidence from the discussion so far to meet Smith's (2004) three criteria of an empirical test of policy transfer. First, the broad similarities between the policy ideas/principles and content/ instruments in the USA and the UK, and the time lag between developments in the two countries, are consistent with a hypothesis of policy transfer. Second, we have been able to identify a number of key 'transfer agents', and third, highlight processes within which policy actors actively used knowledge about developments in US jurisdictions to shape subsequent developments in the UK. However, there were also important differences in the ways in which policies developed subsequently in different jurisdictions. Such differences are important because they highlight the constraints and limitations to policy transfer, and the continued importance of domestic influences. This section first considers differences in the policy outcomes in the USA and the UK. It then relates these to contrasts in the particular context of policy-making as shaped by political and legal institutions. Finally, it considers the important role played by the agency of key policy actors, and the essential unpredictability of the policy process.

Policy differences

The first key difference concerns the manner in which the privatization of prisons related to broader governmental programmes in the USA and the UK. It is clear that the policy of privatization as a national governmental programme was far more significant in the UK than in the USA (Feigenbaum et al. 1999). Even though the Reagan administration did latterly promote privatization across a range of areas, including corrections (President's Commission on Privatization 1988), in the USA at that time there was much less opportunity for privatization at the federal level. However, this situation was to change from the late 1990s onwards (Jones and Newburn 2005). Since 2000, state governments have been a shrinking source of private corrections contracts; the federal government has stepped in and provided 'a source of salvation for the industry' (Sentencing Project 2002: 3). By 1997, the Federal Bureau of Prisons was the main customer for privately operated custodial facilities in terms of number of prison places (McDonald *et al.* 1998). An important factor behind the expansion in federal prison privatization has been the implementation of mandatory minimum sentencing and the 'war on drugs' (Sentencing Project 2002). Further pressure on the federal system has resulted from the 1996 Immigration Reform Act, which meant that even minor offences, when committed by non-US citizens, can be prosecuted under federal law. This has led to a further expansion in levels of incarceration in federal prisons. In 2001, the Immigration and Naturalization Service and the US Marshalls Service renewed five contracts with CCA worth over $50 million annually (Mattera and Khan 2001).

Notwithstanding these later developments, it remains the case that the UK government privatization programme was on a far greater scale than anything that occurred in the USA. This was partly because in the US there was much less to privatize, unlike the UK which had a far more significant public sector both in terms of national and local public service provision and a substantial state-owned industrial sector at the beginning of the 1980s. In terms of privatization and criminal justice in particular, the relatively limited role of privatization as a national policy in the USA also relates to the very different constitutional and institutional context (considered in more detail below) within which the federal government traditionally had limited jurisdiction in criminal justice matters. These largely remained the responsibility of state administrations. For much of the 1980s, the radical governments of Margaret Thatcher were ideologically committed to a programme of liberalization and privatization in the economic sphere, and in many areas of social policy. This enthusiasm for the market, however, did not initially extend to the penal system. An important strand within Conservative thinking advocated the strong state in the sphere of law and order, while championing the 'rolling back' of state influence elsewhere (Windlesham 1993). However, from the early 1990s onwards, Conservative governments sought to extend their programmes of market-based reforms to the heart of the criminal justice and penal systems. Thus, general policy shifts in the UK provided fertile ground for the germination and rooting of ideas about privatization in the penal system.

Taking the contracting out of prisons first, there are a number of important contrasts between the way that this has developed in the USA and the UK. Cummins (2000) demonstrates the process by which private contractors in Texas cut costs by abandoning work and rehabilitative programmes, and simply 'warehousing' inmates in their facilities. These are the kinds of developments that were highlighted in campaigns against the introduction of contracting out in this country (see, for example, Prison Reform Trust 1994).

Some of these experiences were used as what Dolowitz and Marsh (2000) call 'negative lessons'; that is, learning what *not* to do from the perceived mistakes committed in other jurisdictions. We discuss examples of this in more detail below in the section on agency.

Another distinctive feature of the US approach to commercial provision of corrections, and one which relates directly to some of the structural and institutional differences discussed below, concerns the practice of exporting prisoners between jurisdictions whereby, for instance, state prison authorities contract with commercial companies to export some prisoners to out-of-state facilities (McDonald *et al.* 1998). This tradition of a vibrant 'prisoner export' market is simply not a feature of the much smaller and more centralized system in the UK. Another contrast concerns speculative prison building by some US corrections companies (McDonald 1994), which has not been a feature of the UK experience, where companies would be constrained by relatively stringent planning regulations and the lack of available cheap land. Thus, the commercially contracted prisons sector in the UK has developed in a distinctive British way. Important contrasts with the USA include the integration of the commercial sector within the broader prison system, a more stringent approach to contract specification and the subsequent monitoring of contracts, and a considerable degree of accountability and external control over commercially run prisons. Commercially run prisons have an on-site Home Office monitor and, as for publicly run prisons, are regularly inspected by Her Majesty's Inspector of Prisons and come under the responsibility of the Prisons Ombudsman. This was a point stressed to us by the current Prisons Ombudsman, Stephen Shaw, and a previous opponent of contracting prisons out to commercial companies:

> The information about how [private prisons] run is freely available; the chief inspector goes in . . . They've not tried to stop, well, they couldn't stop, me going in, they're pretty open institutions . . . If you want to know anything about our prisons, I mean, most of it is published, or it's on the web site . . . The range of information that you've got freely as an academic or as a campaigner or as a public servant . . . is remarkable, compared to most administrations, remarkable.
>
> (Stephen Shaw, personal interview)

This general point was developed by a representative of the Home Office Contracts and Competition Group who outlined how the contracting and procurement process has become increasingly rigorous since the introduction of contracting out:

> I think it's probably fair to say that, although we followed the Americans in terms of involving the private sector in managing

prisons, since then . . . our approach and theirs have diverged somewhat. And I think that's more to do with the culture issues and our
approach to what prison is and what it's meant to do and what it's
meant to achieve compared with the Americans.

A final interesting area of contrast concerns the proportional impact of
the policy on the system as a whole. Given the massive increases in the US
incarcerated population over the past 30 years or so, despite substantial
growth in the private penal sector, it still only accounts for a rather smaller
proportion of the total number of prisoners. In the smaller (albeit growing)
and more centralized UK system, privatization has had a greater proportional
impact on the system as a whole. For example, recent estimates from the USA
indicate that about 6 per cent of the total adult imprisoned population were
held in private facilities (US Department of Justice 2001). In the UK, now that
the two most recent commercially run prisons have opened, it is estimated
that about 10 per cent of the total adult imprisoned population are held in
private facilities. Although these differences are not huge, in the smaller –
though rapidly expanding – UK system, the impact of the existence of a
significant private sector in terms of being a lever of reform in public sector
prisons has been more influential.

The emergence of EM as outlined above has already demonstrated how
negative lessons from the USA helped to shape what became a distinctively
British tagging system. This was true in a number of ways including the ways
in which tags were deployed and the actual equipment used (one company
simply imported the US software and was unsuccessful, whereas another company designed a system specially for use in the UK). Hugh Marriage deliberately emphasized the distinctive nature of the UK model of EM when
attempting to defuse resistance from prison governors to the development of
HDC using EM. Governors repeatedly called upon evidence from the USA to
suggest that HDC would not work, but Marriage persuaded them that, in his
words, 'we have a completely different system here'.

Institutional and legal structures

We have outlined elsewhere the huge geographical, institutional and political
differences between the USA and the UK that have had a major impact on
the subsequent development of policy (Jones and Newburn 2005). A highly
important contrast concerns significant differences in the political institutions
of the two nations, most particularly the decentralized and relatively open
nature of the US system (at least compared to that in the UK), with more
points of influence for interest groups to target key decision-makers at federal, state and local level (Chandler 2000). This helps to explain the greater
significance of commercial lobbying in the USA than was the case in the UK

(Sarabi 2000). British penal policy-making has traditionally been a far more closed world, with relatively few opportunities for outside influence. Professional groups and practitioners have traditionally exerted considerable power within the British criminal justice policy-making network, with trade unions and professional associations operating in some senses as a buffer against radical change. The relatively closed British system arguably provided such interest groups with the space and resources to resist radical reform. As we see below, with regard to both the contracting out of prisons and the development of EM, it seems that there was considerable resistance to the commercialization of corrections from a number of groups, including Home Office officials, professional associations and trade unions, penal reform groups, and even some senior Conservative ministers.

The wider political and institutional differences between the USA and the UK manifested themselves in particular ways within the correctional systems. In particular, many of the differences relate to the sheer size of the country, and the division of responsibilities between the federal government, the 50 states and local government below this. This means that the market for prison places is far larger, considerably more open, and more complex in the USA. Although the UK prison population has been growing, this is massively outstripped by what has happened in the USA over the past 30 years. The possibilities for commercial involvement are much greater in a huge continental country where responsibility for corrections is shared among the federal government, 50 states (plus Washington DC), over 3000 counties, plus a large number of big cities (Lilly and Knepper 1992).

Political agency and happenstance

Of course, differences in political and constitutional structural contexts do not in themselves determine policy outcomes. This requires the agency of key actors to take advantage of the opportunities, and overcome the constraints, that such structures provide. The importance of political agency shaping the trajectory of commercial involvement in the corrections system has been apparent at every stage. At key 'policy windows' (Kingdon 1995) in the trajectory of policy change, political agents took crucial decisions that could have been very different. The particular actions of key transfer agents outlined above, and in particular the Conservative members of the HAC, were crucial in placing the idea of contracting out of prisons on the edges of the political agenda. Then there was the intervention of the No 10 Policy Unit – because it is suggested that the Prime Minister changed her mind on the issue – to ensure that the principle of contracting out of prisons was included in the 1991 Criminal Justice Act. Various backbench Conservative MPs worked hard during the Committee stages of the Bill to ensure the final legislation would relatively easily allow the remit of privatization to be extended. Senior POA officials decided against taking industrial action in protest against prison privatization, a decision that they later regretted. Labour Party politicians executed their own U-turn on private prisons once in power, and became enthusiastic supporters of the policy of contracting out. At each of these stages, it is quite conceivable that some key players could have chosen to act differently – indeed, in precisely the opposite way.

A number of other bodies resisted the growing commercial involvement in corrections. These included trade unions and staff associations (in this area, the POA and NAPO), and penal reform groups such as the Howard League, the Prison Reform Trust and NACRO (who have adopted a consistent line against privatization). Ultimately, these constraints to policy transfer were unsuccessful in so far as the commercial involvement in corrections was introduced and did expand in the UK. However, the fact that these opposing forces existed, along with the broader contextual differences outlined above, have, in our view, provided important limitations to the extent of policy transfer and helped to shape particular policies in distinctive ways. In addition, the continued interpretation and reshaping of the initial ideas regarding contracting out helped to remould the policy into a different form than existed in many parts of the USA. One example of active resistance of US approaches to prison management came from the Home Office Contracts and Competition Unit. An official from this unit told us about a competitive tendering exercise during the late 1990s in which a consortium involving a US company was unsuccessful mainly because their bid was deemed to be 'too American':

> And one of the reasons . . . they weren't successful is that their operating proposals and methods of work may well have been fine for the American culture but they weren't fine for the British Prison Service and culture. It was a far too Americanized regimented approach, concentrating far too much on incarceration, to use an American term, rather than rehabilitation.

The Director of a commercially-run UK prison also highlighted what could be taken as an example of 'negative lesson drawing' from the USA. He summarized US influence over the UK policy of contracting out in the following way:

> I would have said if . . . other than the fact of demonstrating that it can happen, if there was any influence at all in terms of how it has happened in the UK, it's been to say we mustn't make the same mistakes as America has made, and actually are still making . . . The only way that [some commercial companies] are going to make a profit is to treat people badly, which is what they do. And I don't have to quote to you numerous examples of where it's happened and people have been treated extraordinarily badly in pursuit of a profit motive.

We have already discussed the ways in which US experience was used to inform the policy of electronic monitoring in the UK. Initially, US research evidence was deployed by Home Office officials to advise ministers against the adoption of EM in the UK. When it became clear that there was a political imperative to introduce EM despite this advice, the implementation team in the Home Office actively drew upon the best practice elements of a range of US schemes to develop a distinctive model that was deemed more appropriate for the UK. Thus, in both areas of commercialized corrections that are considered in this chapter, following the initial transfer of basic policy ideas and principles from the USA, domestic influences intervened (in the form of direct opposition to policy developments, the learning of negative lessons from US experience, and the wishes of UK policy-makers to design policies that fit with the UK contexts, as well as unintended consequences and happenstance), so that the policies that eventually emerged in the UK had a distinctive British flavour, and were distinct from their US forebears in a number of significant ways.

Commercial corrections and policy transfer

In this chapter we have explored in more detail the development of one apparent area of penal policy transfer from the USA to the UK. As noted in Chapter 2, there is an occasional tendency to make exaggerated claims about policy transfer, which should not simply be inferred from similarities between two jurisdictions in policy outcomes (Evans and Davies 1999). However, it is clear that in the case of privatized corrections there is strong evidence that in terms of basic policy ideas and principles, and (to a degree) in terms of policy content and instruments, there has been a degree of policy convergence between the USA and the UK. In addition, there is also evidence to support the contention that, at least in part, this convergence reflects a degree of deliberate policy transfer from the USA. This is suggested by the policy similarities in the UK and the USA, consistent timescales, the existence of a number of key 'transfer agents', and the active use of knowledge about US developments to inform the introduction and implementation of policy in the UK. Of the three areas considered in this book, the privatization of corrections provides the strongest evidence of policy transfer, visible in the way that policy ideas emerge, travel, and are implemented in different jurisdictions when the political conditions are right (Jones and Newburn 2005).

However, it would be misleading to present the story of privatized corrections as a straightforward policy export from the USA to the UK. These policy developments must be viewed as part of a more general shift towards the commodification of crime control in Western societies (Christie 2000). Most developed economies have been, to a greater or lesser extent, transformed by governmental programmes of neo-liberal reform promoting privatization, new audit-based forms of management, contracting out of public services, and the development of rigorous frameworks of performance management in the public sector. The UK was at the forefront of such developments globally, and was undoubtedly fertile ground for the germination and flourishing of ideas concerning the marketization of corrections. Involvement of the commercial sector in the delivery of punishment had – and has – a kind of consonance with what is going on in many other areas of social policy. This should by no means suggest that the adoption of such ideas as policy was inevitable. However, it did mean that when faced with pressing problems of growing prison populations, the need for effective alternatives to custody, a growing perception that community punishments were viewed by the public as too lenient, a belief that trade union power was a barrier to reform of prisons and probation, and the ever present politician's problem of needing to appear radical and innovative, it is not surprising that these ideas took root. As a number of our key informants suggested, US exemplars were used to promote already-held ideas about the alleged benefits of commercial involvement in the penal system, rather than simply imported into 'virgin territory'. In this sense, ideas from the USA were important, but so too were home-grown influences.

Our study supports the findings of other authors about the difficulty of isolating specific processes of transfer from the broader policy development process (Evans and Davies 1999; Dolowitz and Marsh 2000). It is clear that this is not a straightforward case of 'copying' in which US policies were used as a blueprint for change in the UK. Rather, we characterized the process as one of 'emulation' (Bennett 1991; Dolowitz and Marsh 2000). To the degree that experiences from the USA gained some purchase within the policy process, we suggest that the role of elite networks has been crucial, and in particular the role played by such networks involving free market think tanks, other 'policy entrepreneurs', policy-makers and practitioners. Although the initial US impetus within these networks is clear, it is also true that there were significant processes of resistance, reworking and fine-tuning. Combined with the inevitable messiness and unpredictability of the policy-making process, these resulted in policy outcomes that significantly diverged from US experience. Thus, unpicking the different levels of policy and analysis of the process of policy formulation on both sides of the Atlantic underlines a number of significant distinctions between the experiences of the two nations. These differences apply to the substance of policy, in terms of the specific ways in which it was implemented, but also apply to the processes that led to the adoption and subsequent development of particular policy ideas. Many of these differences arise from specific structural differences between political structures and cultures of the various jurisdictions of the USA and the UK. In addition, the study of policy transfer in this arena again underlines the importance of happenstance, and the essentially haphazard nature of public policy-making.

In Chapters 1 and 2, we identified two contrasting approaches to the analysis of penal policy developments – one that highlights broad global tendencies, and the other that focuses upon the local and the particular. Each approach has much to offer. The first identifies important commonalities between societies and explains them with reference to global cultural, political and social changes taking place in advanced democracies or late modern societies. The latter reminds us of the abiding importance of national and sub national cultural and historical traditions in mediating and reworking global trends, and preserving significant degrees of difference. We can begin to make links between these two approaches by exploring more closely the details of particular policy developments. The story of the emergence of privatized corrections in the UK supports Garland's (1990) observation that penal policy is the outcome of 'swarming circumstances'. On the surface, the privatization of corrections in the UK initially appears as a straightforward example of Americanizing tendencies in penal policy, and policy importation from the USA. However, it is clear that the story is more complicated than this, one in which complex relationships between political actors at the local, national and global level shape domestic penal policy in distinctive ways.

4 'Three strikes' and mandatory sentencing

This chapter turns to the arena of sentencing policy and considers the hypothesis that UK sentencing reforms during the late 1990s involved a degree of policy transfer from the USA. As with some other areas of criminal justice and penal policy, it has been suggested that sentencing policy has been subject to a degree of globalization leading to a perceived convergence of approaches across many Western industrialized democracies (Frase 2001). It has been reported that a number of commonalities are now observable, including 'not only broadly similar sentencing purposes, procedures, and alternatives but also similar recent trends (e.g. toward increased severity, particularly for violent, sex and drug offenders)' (Frase 2001: 259).[1] The key questions considered in this chapter are: to what extent was there convergence between particular sentencing policies in the UK and the USA, and how far (and in what ways) can such convergence be explained by a process of policy transfer? Our specific focus is upon the sentencing reforms introduced during the 1990s, following the appointment of Michael Howard as Home Secretary. As part of a broader 'populist punitive' agenda, Howard promoted the ideas of increased 'honesty' in sentencing (that is, removing the automatic right to early release), and mandatory minimum sentences for certain categories of repeat offence. The 1997 Crime (Sentences) Act, initially developed under Howard and later implemented by the post–1997 Labour government, emerged from this period. This included a number of provisions for mandatory minimum sentences that are broadly comparable to the 'two' and 'three strikes' legislation that spread through the USA during the early to mid-1990s, which raises the possibility that the UK policy was, in some sense, influenced by developments across the Atlantic. This chapter begins with an account of the emergence of mandatory minimum sentences in the UK. The following section compares the timescales and similarities in policy between the USA and the UK, while the next section explores the role of 'transfer agents' in this area. The fourth section examines the policy process and the nature and extent of transfer within this, and the fifth discusses constraints on policy transfer and the impact of domestic influence on policy development. The final section draws some broad conclusions about the nature of sentencing reform and the role of policy transfer within this.

Mandatory minimum sentencing in the UK

The early 1990s saw a marked move away from the just deserts-influenced sentencing approaches in England and Wales, as promoted by the Criminal Justice Act 1991, and towards increasingly populist punitive policies (Bottoms 1995). This period saw increasing criticism of the alleged leniency of judges and magistrates. Michael Howard had become Home Secretary in 1993, and at the Conservative Party conference in the autumn of that year, he had signalled a major change from the dominant approaches to penal policy in recent years (broadly aimed – with limited success – at reducing the use of imprisonment) by famously announcing that 'prison works'. However, it was not until two years later that Howard signalled his 'unexpected conversion' (Windlesham 2001) to mandatory minimum sentences, when once again the Conservative Party conference was the arena for the announcement of a key policy change. During his conference speech, he promoted two sets of changes in particular. First, he called for more honesty in sentencing ('no more half-time sentences for full-time crimes') and thus proposed to abolish automatic early release and increase the actual amount of time served in prison. Second, he argued for the introduction of a variant on the 'two' and 'three strikes' sentencing policies that had become widespread in the USA (although importantly he did not use the slogan). The two strikes bracket was appropriate, according to Howard, for serious violent and sexual offenders: 'Anyone convicted for the second time of a serious violent or sexual offence should receive an automatic sentence of life imprisonment' (cited in Dunbar and Langdon 1998). Howard also stated his support for mandatory minimum sentences for burglars and drug dealers, though he neither specified a minimum sentence length nor the number of previous convictions that would be required to trigger such a sentence.

Howard's speech led to an immediate critical response from penal reform groups and also senior judiciary, who began to use the media extremely effectively to put the case against the proposed reforms (Ashworth 2001). The Lord Chief Justice, Lord Taylor of Gosforth, issued a press statement, on the same day as Howard's proposals were announced, in which he attacked the reasoning behind mandatory minimum sentences: 'I do not believe that the threat of longer and longer periods of imprisonment across the board will deter habitual criminals' (cited in Dunbar and Langdon 1998). He further attacked the principles behind such reforms, arguing that mandatory minimum sentences 'are inconsistent with doing justice according to the circumstances' (cited in Dunbar and Langdon 1998). This set the scene for an unprecedented public battle between government ministers and senior members of the judiciary over the following months (Windlesham 2001). In December 1995, Lord Donaldson described the proposals as 'an attack by politicians on the judiciary as a whole' (*Guardian*, 2 December 1995).

The White Paper arising from Howard's conference speech, *Protecting the Public*, was published in March 1996, and proposed (among other things) an automatic life sentence for those convicted of a second serious violent or sexual offence, a minimum seven-year sentence for those convicted of a second class A drug dealing offence, and a minimum three-year sentence for a third conviction for domestic burglary (Home Office 1996). Automatic early release and parole for prisoners were to be abolished, with provisions introduced whereby prisoners would have to earn time off their sentences. This, it was argued, would 'introduce greater honesty and clarity into the sentencing process, so that the sentence actually served will relate much more closely to the sentence passed by the court' (Home Office 1996: 45). Regarding the proposed mandatory minimum sentences, the White Paper already included what was to become an increasingly important phrase in the subsequent development of legislation. In the section on automatic life sentences, the White Paper stated: 'The court should be required to impose an automatic life sentence on offenders convicted for the second time of a serious violent or sexual offence, *unless there are genuinely exceptional circumstances*' (Home Office 1996, emphasis added). With identical wording, the proposed mandatory sentences for drug dealers and burglars were also qualified in the White Paper.[2] For violent and sexual offences, and for the drug dealing provisions, it was proposed that convictions before the commencement of the proposed legislation were to be included. By contrast, and primarily because this provision was likely to have the greatest effect on the prison population, the burglary provision was only to apply to convictions following the introduction of the law.

The White Paper listed a number of specific offences that would come under the definition of serious violent or sexual crimes. It also included a discussion of implications for the prison population of the proposed changes. This stated that there would be little immediate impact on the prison population arising from the sexual/violent crime and drug dealing provisions, since such offenders would be likely in any case to receive long jail sentences. However, the burglary provision clearly had bigger resource implications, given the greater volume of such offences, and the White Paper stated that the implementation of such a provision would have to wait until a significant prison building programme had been implemented in order to provide the necessary prison spaces. The White Paper also claimed that the proposals would have some effects in the opposite direction. First, in terms of the restriction of parole and the abolition of automatic release, it suggested that trial judges would take this into account in their sentencing (and thus average sentence lengths would be reduced). Second, it suggested that there would be a deterrent effect of the new minimum sentences that would lead to a 20 per cent reduction in offences.

The Penal Affairs Consortium (PAC), an umbrella group representing a range of organizations including all the main penal reform groups and representative bodies for criminal justice professionals (probation officers, prison officers and prison governors), strongly condemned Howard's proposals (Penal Affairs Consortium 1996) and was very active in lobbying parliamentarians against the Bill. In a detailed discussion document published in response to the White Paper, it argued that automatic life sentences were unjust and unnecessary. In serious cases, judges already had the power to give a discretionary life sentence but this required an individual assessment of the gravity of the case, the risk posed by the offender, and the just deserts required. The proposals on mandatory minimum sentences for drug dealing and burglary were described as 'highly objectionable', and the PAC argued that judges be allowed to set sentences to be proportionate to the seriousness of the offence. In practical terms, the drug-dealing proposal would have the greatest impact upon small-time addicts sharing drugs among themselves. The discussion document also provided a detailed critique of the White Paper's projections regarding the resource implications of the sentencing reforms. The document concluded that the proposals 'would sacrifice justice and effectiveness to a desire to appear tough at all costs' (PAC 1996: 12).

The Crime (Sentences) Bill received its First Reading in the House of Commons in October 1996, and then followed a difficult passage through Parliament. These difficulties were not, however, related to any activities of the Official Opposition. The Labour Party adopted an equivocal stance towards the proposals, determined to avoid accusations of being soft on crime with a general election looming. As Windlesham (2001: 24) noted: 'In the last months before that long awaited moment, it was inconceivable that the Labour Party leadership would allow a tactical parliamentary decision to jeopardize its overall objective of obtaining power after so long.' In effect, this resulted in Commons opposition to the Bill being left to smaller parties. For example, Liberal Democrat and Plaid Cymru MPs made crucial interventions at the Committee stages, along with some dissenting Tory backbenchers such as Peter Lloyd. The Bill came up against considerable opposition in the House of Lords, not least from senior Law Lords and several former Conservative Home Secretaries. The House of Lords delivered the only defeat to the Bill, and introduced amendments that extended the 'exceptional circumstances' clause. The amendments would allow judges to have regard to 'specific circumstances' relating either to the offence or to the offender, when considering whether it was appropriate not to apply the mandatory life sentence and the minimum custodial sentences. A further condition was added to the minimum custodial sentences; that the court should have regard to any specific circumstances that would render the prescribed sentence 'unjust in all the circumstances'. This, according to Windlesham, was intended to widen the range of factors that judges could take into account when considering 'exceptional circumstances', and would allow them to interpret the clause more broadly than had been the intention of the framers of the Bill.

The timing of the Crime (Sentences) Bill was also crucial to subsequent developments. When the general election was announced on 18 March 1997, all unfinished legislation either had to be completed or abandoned by the end of that week. This meant that there was little time for the Bill to return to the Commons, where it was strongly suspected the Lords' amendments would be voted down (with the acquiescence of the Labour Party). This gave opponents of the Bill, who already had significant impetus due to the strength of opposition inside and outside Parliament, considerable leverage. Under the threat from Liberal Democrat peers to keep the Report stage going (and thus prevent the Bill returning to the Commons in time), Michael Howard negotiated an agreement that if the Bill was returned to the Commons in its amended state, the government would not seek to overturn the amendments to the exceptional circumstances clauses. The significance of the changes cannot be underestimated. For example, Ashworth (2001) argued that the addition of the 'unjust in all the circumstances' clause to the drug-dealing minimum sentence effectively 'emasculated' the Bill. Michael Howard himself acknowledged the significance of these amendments when he made the following comments in the House of Commons: 'The Lords' amendments drive a coach and horses through the provisions of the Bill that deal with burglars and drug dealers . . . [They] would allow the present pattern of sentencing broadly to continue' (Parliamentary Debates, House of Commons, Column 982, 19 March 1997).

The Crime (Sentences) Act 1997 became law before the general election, and it introduced three sets of mandatory sentences.[3] First, it provided for an automatic life sentence for a second serious sexual or violent offence, unless there were 'exceptional circumstances' relating to the offender or the offence that justified the court in not giving such a sentence. Second, the Act prescribed a minimum seven-year prison sentence for third-time 'trafficking' in class A drugs; and third, a minimum three-year sentence for third-time domestic burglary. Both these latter sentences were subject to the wider judicial 'escape clause' (Ashworth 1998: 234) that allowed the court not to impose the required sentence if it considered that to do so would be 'unjust in all the circumstances'. The proposals for 'honesty in sentencing' were enacted in Chapter 1 of Part II of the Act, which abolished early release, and laid down a change in sentencing practice to take this into account. However, this part of the Act was never implemented (Faulkner 2001). The mandatory sentences for sexual and violent crimes and for drug trafficking were implemented fairly soon after the 1997 election, though the mandatory sentence for third-time burglars was initially left dormant on the statute book (Dunbar and Langdon 1998). Eventually, the measure proved irresistible and in early 1999 Jack Straw announced plans to implement the final 'three strikes' provision in the Act in December 1999.[4] Given the proportion of all criminal offences accounted for by burglary (23 per cent in 1997) compared with the other offences subject to 'three strikes' penalties, the impact on the prison population was likely to be much more significant.

Developments subsequent to the Act demonstrate how important the exceptional circumstances amendments have been, particularly in the case of the drug dealing and burglary provisions. A number of newspaper articles over the subsequent years highlighted the limited practical impact of the two and three strikes laws, with judges using the exceptional circumstances clauses to preserve their discretion in individual cases. By December 2000, a year after its implementation, not a single three strikes sentence had been passed on a convicted burglar (Cavadino and Dignan 2002). However, perhaps this is not surprising given the requirement for relevant previous convictions to have occurred after the implementation of the Act. Nevertheless, the symbolism of this news story was important, and attracted both praise and criticism. Harry Fletcher of the National Association of Probation Officers made a press statement in which he expressed his delight that the courts were exercising their discretion (Travis 2000). On the other hand, Julian Lewis, the Conservative MP for New Forest East, urged the government to amend the legislation in order to curb judicial discretion on this matter, because in his view judges were 'out of touch' with public opinion (*Independent*, 31 January 2001).

As noted above, the exceptional circumstances clause in the case of the second violent or sexual crime was more narrowly defined, and clearly did circumscribe judicial discretion in important ways. On the whole, judges appeared to interpret exceptional circumstances in these cases more narrowly, and this is reflected in the greater number of people sentenced to life imprisonment under this provision (although as we point out later, we cannot know how many of these offenders would have received a discretionary life sentence in any case). The years following implementation of the Crime (Sentences) Act saw Court of Appeal guidance clarify the extent of the 'exceptional circumstances' clause in particular cases. Of particular importance were the cases of *Kelly* (1999) and *Offen No. 1* (2001), which confirmed the interpretation of the 'exceptional circumstances' clause to include circumstances that were unusual, special and uncommon (and thus not things that are regularly encountered before the courts) (Easton and Piper 2005). For example, Offen's first appeal was based on the argument that the offender's history of childhood mental illness, along with the fact that the robbery was considered 'amateurish' (having been committed while the offender was wearing slippers) and that the money was recovered shortly after the offence, could be construed as 'exceptional circumstances' by the court. This appeal was rejected. After the Human Rights Act 1998 became operational in October 2000, the Court of Appeal under the (then) Lord Chief Justice (Lord Woolf) reinterpreted and further widened the meaning of the 'exceptional circumstances' clause in the two strikes penalty for serious and/or violent offences. Following Offen's further appeal (*Offen No. 2*) in 2001, the Court ruled that if an offender was not felt to present a significant risk to the public, then this would be an 'exceptional circumstance' that would allow the court not to pass a life sentence. Thus, so long as this rule was applied in a way that was consistent with Parliament's aim of protecting the public, Articles 3 and 5 of the European Convention on Human Rights would not be contravened. This, according to Cavadino and Dignan, would 'presumably allow sentencers to avoid passing life sentences in many – possibly most – of these "two strike" cases' (2002: 106). It is generally held that this further narrowing of the exceptional circumstances clause significantly curtailed the use of the automatic life sentence introduced by the Crime (Sentences) Act 1997 (Easton and Piper 2005).

The 'two strike' clause for automatic life imprisonment was eventually repealed by the Criminal Justice Act 2003, which established a new sentencing framework for dangerous offenders. Sections 225–8 of this Act provide sentences of life imprisonment and imprisonment for public protection, plus a new extended sentence, that can be imposed in relation to a list of specified offences, within which a separate list of 'serious' offences are laid down as being punishable by life imprisonment or by a determinate sentence of a minimum of 10 years (Easton and Piper 2005). It is generally accepted that these amount to mandatory sentences, although again the conditions in which the courts must impose a particular sentence leave some room for interpretation. The crucial factor is the court's assessment of the level of risk to the public posed by the offender. Among other indicators of dangerousness, whether an offender has committed a similar offence before is an important consideration, thus preserving some element of the 'two strikes' principle. If a convicted offender has a previous conviction for a relevant offence (that is, an offence specified in the Act), then the court must assume there is a significant risk to the public, unless it considers it 'unreasonable' to so conclude (s.299(3)). Easton and Piper observe that these provisions are still open to challenge under the Human Rights Act, on the grounds that 'the presumptions of risk inherent in the provisions militate against the full consideration required, especially as the Act does not make it mandatory for the court to receive medical reports in relation to all these decisions' (2005: 146).

Timing and policy similarity

Timing

The timing of policy changes in the USA and the UK is consistent with a picture of policy transfer from the former to the latter. We discuss mandatory minimum sentencing first, before briefly turning to 'truth in sentencing' approaches. The emergence of 'three strikes' in the USA was built on a long history of 'habitual offender' legislation that allowed for enhanced sentences for repeat offenders (Jones and Newburn 2006). Since the 1970s, there has been a significant number of mandatory minimum sentence provisions operating within state and federal jurisdictions, particularly in the area of drug enforcement. In 1973, the state of New York passed laws requiring draconian mandatory minimum penalties for drug offences (known as 'the Rockefeller Drug Laws'). Five years later, the state of Michigan enacted the infamous '650 Lifer Law' (mandating life imprisonment without parole for offenders convicted of intent to deliver 650 grams or more of heroin or cocaine). Mandatory minimum sentences for drug offenders have also been applied within the federal system. In 1986, Congress passed the Anti-Drug Abuse Act, which prescribed mandatory minimum imprisonment terms for drug offenders (most commonly of five or ten years, depending on the weight of drug and presence of a firearm). These mandatory minimums were strictly defined, and prevented sentencers from considering other relevant factors to the case. The more recent history of 'two' and 'three strikes' sentencing is most associated with developments in the early 1990s in the states of Washington and California. In each state, horrific crimes committed by repeat offenders led to major campaigns in which relatives of the high-profile victims promoted tougher sentencing laws and attracted nationwide media coverage (Gest 2001; Jones and Newburn 2006).

The actual term 'three strikes' – a baseball metaphor – was first employed in Washington State in connection with a campaign for a repeat offender law mandating long sentences for third-time offenders, in certain circumstances (Jones and Newburn 2006). In November 1993, the 'three strikes' law in Washington State was passed by voter ballot. In California, the slogan 'three strikes' rapidly gained currency, and though the campaign for its introduction overlapped to some extent with that in Washington, it was not until November 1994 that a more extreme version (see below) of mandatory minimum sentencing was passed by voter initiative. Between 1993 and 1995, 24 states added three strikes legislation to already existing laws that enhanced sentencing for repeat offenders. Similar sentencing reforms emerged at this time in the federal system. Although mandatory minimum sentences were far from uncommon in the federal system prior to this, the form that the new sentencing provisions took in the mid-1990s closely mirrored what was happening in many states across the USA. The idea was endorsed by President Clinton in his 1994 State of the Union Address (Surette 1996) and was eventually incorporated into federal legislation in the Violent Crime Control and Law Enforcement Act 1994 (Windlesham 1998).

The emergence of 'truth in sentencing' (TIS) provisions in the USA is associated with the above mentioned 1994 Crime Act, federal legislation that authorized the US Department of Justice to provide incentive grants to eligible states to build or expand prison capacity.[5] However, many such states had TIS laws prior to federal legislation, the term first appearing in the USA in 1984 when Washington State enacted the first TIS law (Ditton and Wilson 1999). The definition of TIS varied between states, in terms both of the kinds of offenders to whom it applied and the proportion of sentence that has to be served in prison. In the year following the 1994 federal legislation, 11 states added TIS laws that met with the requirement to receive federal funds for prison building. These grants were awarded to states with laws that require offenders convicted of a violent crime to serve at least 85 per cent of the sentence imposed. The following four years saw the spread of these sentencing provisions across the USA, and by 1998 there were 27 states with TIS laws that met the federal requirement for prison grants (United States General Accounting Office 1998). A further 13 states had adopted TIS laws requiring that some offenders serve a specific proportion of their original sentence. In addition, by 1998, 14 states had abolished parole board release for all offenders, and a further six states abolished such release provisions for particular crimes (usually involving violence) (Ditton and Wilson 1999).

These developments, particularly those concerning 'two/three strikes' received widespread media attention in the UK but, as outlined above, it was not until the autumn of 1995 that Michael Howard suggested a version of mandatory minimum sentences in the UK and the introduction of what he termed 'honesty in sentencing'. It took a further two years for legislation to be introduced in the form of the Crime (Sentences) Act 1997. Thus, in the case of mandatory minimum sentencing, the timescales of the sentencing reforms in both countries are clearly consistent with the possibility of policy transfer, with developments in the USA predating the initial UK proposals by at least two years (longer if we broaden the comparison from specific 'three strikes' proposals to habitual offender sentencing provisions more generally).[6] Although the timing of 'truth in sentencing' reforms in the USA and 'honesty in sentencing' proposals in the UK appears closer, when the focus is upon the 1994 federal legislation, as the above discussion shows, TIS has a far longer history dating back to 1984. Thus, again, the timing is consistent with the possibility of some form of policy transfer from the USA to the UK.

Policy similarities

A further condition for policy transfer is, of course, sufficient degrees of similarity between policies in two jurisdictions. It is certainly possible to detect similarities in the broader contexts within which these sentencing reforms were introduced. For example, the key problems facing policy-makers in the USA and the UK prior to the introduction of these reforms were similar in several important regards. In both countries, there was growing public and media concern about crime, an increasing perception in media and political circles that judicial discretion was being exercised to deliver overly lenient sentences and a growing tendency for the media to focus upon particularly horrific crime stories involving ideal type victims and 'monstrous offenders' (Kennedy 2000) to exacerbate popular pressures on policy-makers. Within both countries, sentencing reforms took place within a broader context wherein policy-makers had faced the problem of trying to structure the sentencing decisions taken by powerful judicial elites (Ashworth 2001; Reitz 2001).

In drawing comparisons with the USA, however, there is the inevitable danger of over-simplification. As Reitz (2001: 223) observes, 'there really is no such thing as "US sentencing practice" . . . primary responsibility for criminal justice resides at the state level – and the states have varied greatly in their individual experiences of crime and their governmental responses to it'. We discuss in more detail below some of the important differences that emerged between 'two' and 'three strikes' laws in different jurisdictions. However, for current purposes, we feel that there is an initial case for the existence of policy transfer in the arena of sentencing, because there are sufficient similarities in elements of the policies between those that emerged in parts of the USA and the UK. In particular, on both sides of the Atlantic there was a significant emphasis on the expressive aspects of policy over and above the instrumental impacts (Jones and Newburn 2006). In particular, it seems the strongest case for policy transfer from the USA can be made regarding the political symbols and rhetoric associated with three strikes and other punitive sentencing provisions such as 'truth in sentencing'. However, even in terms of the more substantive manifestations of policy, there is sufficient broad similarity to support the possibility of policy transfer.

A US Department of Justice review of 'three strikes' legislation observed that, 'from a national perspective the "three strikes and you're out" movement was largely symbolic . . . it was not designed to have a significant impact on the criminal justice system' (Austin et al. 2000). In the US federal system, and states other than California, the reforms had a rather limited practical impact (Clark et al. 1997; King and Mauer 2001). This reflects the fact that many penal laws are deliberately designed to have a 'bark' that is worse than their 'bite' (Zimring et al. 2001: ix), so that they sound sufficiently tough to attract votes but have rather limited resource implications in practice. It seems that much of the 'three strikes' reform in the USA came under this category, being focused primarily on a small number of violent or dangerous offenders who would have received long prison sentences in any case. Similarly, in Britain, the symbolic elements of the policy changes clearly overshadowed their substantive impact. These elements were key to Labour's decision not to oppose the original Bill (because of fears of the possible electoral consequences), and they were widely seen as central to the subsequent decision of Jack Straw to implement all provisions of the Act. Some observers who were close to developments at the time clearly felt that the Labour front bench spokespeople,

Paul Boateng and Alun Michael, had strong sympathies with arguments against the Bill, but simply had to stay silent because of the position of the Party leadership. For example, Elfyn Llwyd MP said:

> I had the odd nod from Alun Michael and I could see that his natural instincts lay with what I was saying but that he was constrained in what he could say. And whereas in some instances he might have got up and, as a matter of form, said, 'Well, we're not in favour of this amendment because . . .' – sometimes he would just sit on his hands. So I perceived that that was really saying, 'Well, you know I can understand the force of your argument but I can't get involved.' And Paul [Boateng] was the same.
>
> (Elfyn Llwyd MP, personal interview)

The former Liberal Democrat MP Alex (now Lord) Carlile had a similar recollection:

> My take on it was that Jack [Straw] himself was very uncomfortable about all this stuff, and was quite happy for the rest of us to make some running. Because it didn't sit well with the kind of social liberalism that Jack himself has always espoused. At the same time they were on a major roll . . . and they weren't running any risks of being seen to be feeble on law and order. But I think Jack Straw as a lawyer Shadow Home Secretary knew perfectly well that there was potential for perfectly ludicrous results from 'three and out'.
>
> (Lord [Alex] Carlile, personal interview)

Leading commentators on sentencing policy saw Labour's position on this as primarily about symbolic politics. For example, Thomas (1998: 83) predicted that the practical effects of the legislation would be negligible, and that its 'importance is in what it symbolises'. In a similar vein, Ashworth (2001) emphasized the symbolic aspects of the British version of 'three strikes'. He argued that the Crime (Sentences) Act was an example of a more general decline in the importance of values in decisions about sentencing policy, and the continued elevation of political expediency: '[P]olitical symbolism was more important than mere evidence and argument . . . What mattered was how the new laws would look to the public, media and other politicians, not whether they would actually "work" as claimed' (Ashworth 2001: 85). These circumstances left some Labour politicians in a difficult position, not least the Labour Leader in the House of Lords, Lord McKintosh:

> [Lord McKintosh] took the Bill for them through this house [the Lords], and I taunted him once or twice, you know, 'Are you going to

support us in this business?' and his powers were very limited by what he was being allowed to do on the other end of the corridor by a very conscious Shadow Home Secretary concerned in the run-up to the election that if they spoke out they would be seen as being weak on crime.

(Lord [Mark] Carlisle, personal interview)

The importance of symbolism in crime policy to New Labour in general, and of particular relevance to this case, was underlined by the leaking of a memo written by Tony Blair to his advisers in July 2000. Blair was concerned about growing public criticism of the government in general and his leadership in particular. The leaked memo reportedly referred to the mandatory minimum sentences introduced by the Crime (Sentences) Act as a tough measure that needed to be highlighted to the public (*Guardian*, 17 July 2000). The symbolic importance of mandatory minimum sentences to New Labour is perhaps underlined by the fact that one of the few people to actually use the phrase 'three strikes' in Parliament was none other than Tony Blair, in contrast to Michael Howard (there is no public record of his ever using the term in Parliament or public speeches). In interview, Michael Howard could not recall using the US terminology:

No, I don't think I did [use the term] because 'three strikes and you're out' really, as I recall it, was to do with life imprisonment, wasn't it, and that wasn't at all what we were about. In my mind it's associated in America with life imprisonment, and that's a completely different thing.

(Michael Howard, personal interview)

In addition to similarities in terms of the symbolic dimensions of policy, there are also similarities in terms of broader sentencing principles, and in terms of policy content and instruments. In both countries these reforms were part of a move away from a 'just deserts' sentencing rationale that allowed judges discretion according to the particular circumstances of the offence, and towards an incapacitation approach that was based on mandatory enhanced sentences for repeat offenders. In terms of the more concrete manifestations of policy, there is sufficient similarity between the policy content and instruments of the sentencing reforms (both in terms of 'three strikes' and 'truth in sentencing') in each country to be consistent with a broad picture of policy transfer. Both countries saw jurisdictions introduce legislation with the aim of ensuring that certain categories of repeat offender would be incarcerated for longer periods than had previously been the case. In the case of mandatory minimum sentencing, this would be done via the instrument of a statutory curtailment of judicial discretion to set shorter sentences via a mandatory minimum. Regarding 'honesty in sentencing' (UK) and 'truth in sentencing' (USA), this would be done by removing the automatic right to early release and requiring that offenders serve a higher percentage of their original sentence in prison. As with mandatory minimum sentencing, the variation between TIS laws in different US states makes a straightforward USA–UK comparison impossible. In some important ways, the UK proposals differed from what was in operation in many parts of the USA. First, they applied (in different forms) to all offenders, rather than just offenders convicted of violent offences (as in many US states, and as in the focus of the federal legislation). Second, prisoners could still earn early release of up to a maximum of 20 per cent of the original sentence by cooperative behaviour and compliance with prison pro-grammes. Third, the UK proposals suggested that judges would allow for the changes in parole and early release policy when setting the original sentence, and thus the average time served in prison would not increase (Home Office 1996: 43–5). By contrast, it appeared that the intention of TIS in many US states was actually to increase time served. Although in the USA it appears that sentencers took TIS into account (and thus in many states, initial sentences were reduced), average time served for violent offenders increased significantly following the implementation of TIS laws (Ditton and Wilson 1999). Thus, unsurprisingly, it is possible to identify differences in the specifics of policy content between the UK proposals and many of the TIS laws in the USA. However, we would argue again that there existed sufficient similarity (in the initial idea, the terminology employed, and the specific policy content and instruments) to be consistent with a case of *attempted* policy transfer (since, as we have seen, this was a policy that did become law, but was never implemented due to a change of government).

Policy transfer agents

Although the timing and nature of the reforms to UK sentencing policy in the mid-1990s suggest the possibility of transfer from the USA, there is actually only very limited evidence within the sphere of sentencing regarding actual policy transfer from the USA. To recap, the second element of our empirical test of policy transfer requires the identification of policy actors who deployed knowledge about developments in the USA to inform policy formulation in the UK. In terms of the specific UK developments, the US links are tenuous, to say the least.

Unlike the arena of privatized corrections, there is no evidence of signifi-cant influence by policy entrepreneurs, such as free market think tanks or campaigning organizations, in actively promoting 'US-style' sentencing pol-icies in the UK.[7] There is little evidence of concerted activity by backbench MPs in lobbying to promote 'US-style' changes in sentencing, although, unsurprisingly, *Hansard* accounts of Commons debates throughout the 1990s are peppered with calls for a more punitive approach towards law and order from various MPs. But this could not be said to amount to a campaign in the way that certain backbenchers, for example, promoted contracting out of prisons. Nor can we find evidence of any contact between British Home Office civil servants and policy-makers/practitioners in the USA in the manner that was clearly apparent in the stories of privatized corrections and Zero Tolerance Policing (ZTP). There is no evidence of lobbying by commercial organizations to promote changes in sentencing policy (as has occurred in the USA). Nevertheless, despite all this, there remains a sense that these sentencing reforms, or at least the broader ideas that inspired them, had their roots in previous developments in the USA. The key 'transfer agent' to consider within this process was Michael Howard, the Conservative Home Secretary. This is therefore an area within which senior politicians, and one politician in particular, appear to have been the vital influence in driving policy change.

Politicians

The central importance of Michael Howard in promoting change in this area of policy during his time as Home Secretary was underlined to us by a number of informed commentators, including a range of people who had argued against him at the time. For instance, the former Conservative minister Lord [Mark] Carlisle saw Mr Howard's role as absolutely key:

> I think it was a clear decision by Michael Howard that he wanted to do something totally different. He believed his approach was right, and he turned the Home Office around, didn't he, on these issues? The Home Office has always been dead against mandatory sentencing . . . they didn't believe that necessarily 'prison works'.
>
> (Lord Carlisle)

Ann Widdecombe MP, who served as a Home Office minister when Michael Howard was Home Secretary, also placed primary emphasis upon Mr Howard's personal beliefs and agenda when she expressed strong support for his original plans for mandatory minimum sentences. In interview, Miss Widdecombe also stated that she believed the initial idea came 'from abroad', although she arrived at the Home Office after the Bill had been introduced. Even though she did not mention the USA specifically, without prompting, she used the 'two' and 'three strikes' terminology. Interestingly, Ann Widdecombe's comments also suggested a significant link between two of our chosen policy case studies. She explicitly said that without the Private Finance Initiative (PFI) and commercial contracting out of prisons, the proposals of the Crime (Sentences) Bill would have been out of the question. She reported that most of the concern from Home Office officials was regarding the likely impact on the prison population. However, the advent of PFI and private contracting offered an opportunity to provide new prison places quickly:

> Now if we hadn't had the PFI and the private sector initiative, then you could have forgotten it, you know, we wouldn't have been able to do it. As it was, they were putting prisons up in, you know, eighteen months.
>
> (Ann Widdecombe, personal interview)

In interview, Michael Howard himself also supported this general view-point, although, interestingly, he significantly played down the role of lesson-drawing from the USA within the specific realm of sentencing policy. The main US influence, as he pointed out, was over his broader 'prison works' agenda:

> . . . One of my beliefs, which owed something to the American experience, was that if you were able to incapacitate by imprisonment serious and persistent offenders, that would have an impact on crime . . . Charles Murray is one of the people whose writings influenced me and I think he demonstrated pretty conclusively that falling crime in the United States had been accompanied by increased use of imprisonment. And that's why I said 'prison works' and that sort of thing.
>
> (Michael Howard, personal interview)

Mr Howard went on to say that this broader belief – in the deterrent and incapacitating functions of imprisonment as key levers of crime reduction rather than particular examples of US sentencing reform – is what initially informed his proposals for mandatory minimum sentences and honesty in sentencing. He reported that his discussions with senior police officers had led him to believe that incapacitation would be a particularly effective policy with regard to persistent burglars. Mr Howard said that he was 'astonished' by the typical sentences for burglary at the time, which he felt were very low in the first place, even before one considered the fact that in most cases only half the sentences were served, which he found 'completely unacceptable'. According to his account, it was this that led him to develop his proposals for sentencing reforms. To the extent that there was any influence of particular sentencing developments in the USA, this applied only some time after his initial interest in mandatory sentencing:

> And the possibility of mandatory minimum sentences arose and so I asked the question 'Do they exist anywhere?' And the answer came,

'Yes, they exist in the United States.' So it wasn't saying 'Let's go to the United States, see what they do, and import everything willy-nilly.' It was, we've got a problem here, persistent burglars are not sufficiently incapacitated. The risk–reward ratio is all wrong . . . What can we do about that? Mandatory minimum sentences is one answer. Has it been tried anywhere? Yes, it's been tried in the States.

(Michael Howard, personal interview)

The interview with Mr Howard also supported the perception that there had been very little direct lesson-drawing in terms of visits to the USA by Home Office officials, or even analysis of published research on US experience of mandatory minimum sentencing. When asked if he could recall visits by officials to the USA to explore US sentencing practices, he responded: 'I don't think they [advisers and officials] went there; you didn't need to go there to find that out.' Although there may have been a number of parallels between Mr Howard's sentencing reform proposals and developments in certain parts of the USA, Mr Howard was clearly keen to present them as primarily a home-grown response to the particular problems, as he perceived them, with criminal justice in Britain. This is clear from his following comments on his support for 'honesty in sentencing':

I believed there was a serious loss of public confidence in the criminal justice system . . . And I thought, and I still think, that one of the things that contributes to the lack of public confidence in the criminal justice system is when a victim hears her assailant being sentenced to what seems quite a long time in prison, say four years, that actually means to the person that knows, two years. Furthermore, because of the parole and because of the time you spend in the community before you're released on parole in order to acclimatize yourself to life in the community – which is a perfectly sensible thing of course – very often the victim of crime will see their assailant walking up the high street of the local community possibly nine months after sentence. I'm plucking these figures out of the air to illustrate the point. They had been ostensibly sentenced to four years. And that led to fury which I thought was entirely understandable, on the part of these people; it's a kind of conspiracy to make people think the sentence was tough when in fact it isn't and I thought it would be much better if we had an honest system. It didn't really owe very much to what was happening in America.

(Michael Howard, personal interview)

The question arises as to what motivated Mr Howard in his embracing of such a different approach to sentencing, and one that was likely to lead to significant and entrenched opposition. It is certainly clear that his original conversion to mandatory minimum sentences surprised his ministerial colleagues (Windlesham 2001). There is no doubt that a degree of political opportunism played an important part in these developments. Mr Howard was Home Secretary in what was widely perceived as a government under pressure on the crime issue from the Opposition, who had reinvented themselves as a party of law and order, with the famous 'tough on crime, tough on the causes of crime' mantra. As Ashworth (2001: 85) observed: 'It may not be pure chance that the period of greatest penal repression in England (1992–97) coincided with the term of a weak government with a slender majority, anxious to exploit any means of political survival.' Similarly, it has been suggested that the 'punitive turn' in Conservative policy at this time reflected, rather than some kind of unilateral shift, an urgent need to respond to the pressure from a reinvigorated Labour Party that had drawn its inspiration from the successful electoral strategies of the New Democrats in the USA, within which a tough law and order approach was central (Newburn and Jones 2005). This point has also been made by Downes and Morgan, who have argued that the Tory Party and Michael Howard at that time should be viewed as 'prisoners of Blair and Straw's agenda rather than – as generally assumed – the reverse' (2002: 297). However, it would be an over-simplification to argue that electoral opportunism was the key factor here. There is also evidence of genuine commitment and belief on Michael Howard's part. For example, his familiarity with and broad agreement with the writings of neo-conservative US intellectuals such as J.Q. Wilson and Charles Murray have already been remarked upon by a number of informed observers. In interview, as we have seen, Mr Howard himself reported the influence that neo-conservative US writing and research on crime and punishment had had upon his position. Key opponents of Mr Howard's proposed reforms who were involved in negotiations with ministers over the Crime (Sentences) Bill also told us that, in their view, these proposals were about more than symbolic politics:

> There was a sort of convention that Tory Home Secretaries went to the Party Conference, made vicious speeches on law and order and then allowed legislation that was determined on its merits . . . That convention of the tough speech, and then legislation quietly getting on with it, continued until Michael Howard became Home Secretary. Then suddenly we discovered there was a Home Secretary who not only said it, he believed it! And this was a shock to us all. We weren't ready for this kind of stuff. And he did mean it, and he did believe it . . . It was certainly not posturing.
>
> (Lord [Alex] Carlile, personal interview)

The key point with regard to the balance between substance and symbol in Mr Howard's proposals relates to his willingness to, in his words, 'put his money where his mouth was'. He was politically committed to providing the considerable extra expenditure resources required to fund the building of new prisons. As he said in interview:

> I had some tough talking with the Treasury but I got a lot of what I wanted. We did get the money to build more prisons. As a government, we put our money where our mouth was, which is something that has been notably lacking since 1997.

Thus, although we should pay due regard to Michael Howard's willingness to appeal to a populist agenda, we should not underplay the fact that he also intended these reforms to have real impact. As we have argued elsewhere:

> . . . Howard's intentions went beyond the expressive; he meant business. He was actively seeking to pass measures that would increase sentence lengths, would reduce parole opportunities and would mandate minimum terms for repeat offenders (in circumstances, unlike most American states, where such a principle was not already established). This position is consistent with Howard's stated beliefs in the effectiveness of incapacitative sentencing, his willingness to provide the resources to expand the prison estate, and his general views about the need to bring sentencing policy under greater political direction.
>
> (Jones and Newburn 2006: 792)

Notwithstanding his personal importance in the original attempt to introduce mandatory minimum sentences and honesty in sentencing to the UK, Michael Howard was not the only senior politician who might be loosely regarded as an agent of transfer. As we have seen, senior Labour Party politicians played a key role in this story. First, senior Labour Party figures made the strategic decision not to oppose the Crime (Sentences) Bill in the House of Commons. Second, the Labour Party took the decision to implement the mandatory minimum sentence provisions of the Act after returning to office in 1997. Finally, and perhaps most tellingly, in terms of directly importing US symbols and rhetoric, it was Tony Blair, and not Michael Howard, who subsequently deployed the terminology of 'three strikes and you're out'.

Policy transfer processes

The evidence about precise processes of transfer in the case of sentencing is also somewhat sparse, reflecting the rather more modest and generalized nature of US influence in the story of these particular UK policy developments. In a broad sense, the US 'prison works' movement (including the work of prominent US neo-conservatives such as Charles Murray and John DiIulio, and various econometric studies of incarceration and crime rates published during the mid-1990s) influenced the broader policy framework within which these proposed changes were designed. The Institute of Economic Affairs (IEA) had links with the American Enterprise Institute in Washington DC, and was instrumental in publicizing the work of Charles Murray in the UK via special conferences and events (see Murray 1997). The IEA also independently published work in the same vein by a British economist, making the econometric case in favour of increased incarceration (Pyle 1995). So from the early 1990s, partly drawing upon US experience (as well as making broader philosophical arguments in favour of incapacitation and deterrence), the IEA began promoting the 'prison works' agenda in the UK. Michael Howard certainly had some involvement with these developments in that he spoke at a number of these IEA events during the early 1990s. However, as David Green, formerly of the IEA, told us:

> I don't know if he ever came to the IEA and discussed crime when he was the Home Secretary. He may have, but he didn't while I was there. So we certainly can't trace a direct link from what we did to what he did.
>
> (David Green, personal interview)

Despite these developments, however, there is little evidence to suggest that 'elite networking' – in the sense of links between think tanks, policy-makers and practitioners on both sides of the Atlantic – was a significant influence over the specific policy changes in sentencing proposed by Michael Howard. Although transatlantic contacts between think tanks provided a degree of intellectual backing for politicians keen to promote the notion that prison works, there is no evidence of anything that might approximate to a transnational 'epistemic community' (Stone 1999) in the arena of sentencing policy. In any case, it seems that much of this activity occurred after Mr Howard's proposals on increased use of imprisonment and mandatory minimum sentencing appeared. As we noted above, the primary element that appears to have been transferred from the USA is the general ideas behind sentencing reform, and the political symbolism and rhetoric associated with getting tough on crime. Even in their original form, Michael Howard's proposals on minimum sentences were significantly milder and more focused than their much-discussed counterparts in California (as we will discuss further below). In this sense, Dolowitz and Marsh's (2000) term 'inspiration' appears to be more appropriate than 'emulation' to describe the nature of transfer in this particular instance. In particular, this inspiration was indirect,

relating more to general beliefs about deterrence and incapacitation as an effective tool of crime reduction than to a focused inspiration linked with particular
US sentencing practices. The less complex nature of the transfer process within
sentencing policy is related to the central importance of just one key player
in the early part of this story. Michael Howard was convinced of the need for
a more punitive approach to sentencing in this country, but used US experience
more as general inspiration than as detailed blueprints for policy.

Thus, broader ideas and symbols from the USA were more important
than the details of particular sentencing policies or the research evidence
about their effectiveness (or lack of it). In this, the story of the 1990s
sentencing reforms concurs with Nelson's (1996) observation: 'Ideas, not
evidence, are the mainstay of political decision-making in an increasingly
nationalised and media-driven political system.' Majone (1996) outlines how
the importance of ideas in policy-making has been having something of a
renaissance in political science. For a while, discussion about the role of
rationality in the policy process was obscured by the popularity of the concept of political science as being the straightforward study of power. This was
in part a reaction against the 'rationalist fallacy' that undertook studies based
on the notion that the policy process was a kind of intellectual exercise.
Increasingly, however, although authors still see the role of interests and
power as important, there is growing evidence for the independent role of
ideas, and a growth of literature on 'ideational' factors in policy-making. This
does not remove politics from the equation but simply means that particular
ideas and examples of overseas experience are increasingly used as post-hoc
justifications for policy decisions.

A process of policy learning can perhaps also be identified in later developments of sentencing policy under New Labour. As we have observed, symbolic politics were if anything more important within the Labour Party's initial
approach to mandatory minimum sentencing than they were to the Tories. As
discussed above, the Crime (Sentences) Bill was being rushed through parliament as the country approached a general election. This had a number of key
effects, including the Labour Party's reluctance to oppose the Bill outright, and
Howard's ultimate acceptance of the Lords' amendments broadening the
exceptional circumstances clauses. The decisions taken by Jack Straw and his
New Labour colleagues demonstrate once again the central importance of
symbolic politics. New Labour has continued to support the policies once in
office. Once the election was won, arguably they had the choice not to implement the provisions of the Act regarding mandatory minimum sentencing.
However, the Labour government implemented the MMS provisions of the
Act on violent/sexual crime and drug trafficking soon after taking office.
Furthermore, the burglary provision was also implemented two years later.
Thus, although the symbolic and rhetorical elements of policy-making were
clearly central in the early story of 'three strikes' in Britain, it should not

be suggested that the developments had negligible practical consequences. Indeed, developments since the Crime (Sentences) Act demonstrate that there is clearly a genuine belief among senior Labour politicians in the importance of using imprisonment as an incapacitation and deterrent tool if necessary (Morgan 2002). This is further evidenced by the very substantial rises in prison populations in Britain under successive Labour governments.

It is important, therefore, to consider, given the limited evidence of transfer, why it became so widely assumed that these sentencing reforms were imported from the USA. It appears clear that the basic ideas and terminology associated with 'three strikes' were transferred from the USA to the UK, but only after the original proposals were made. Much of the UK debate – on both sides of the argument – referred explicitly to the US experience. For example, there was considerable UK newspaper and other media discussion during 1994/95 of the development of 'three strikes' laws in the USA. Both supporters and critics of the proposed sentencing reforms called upon US experience. The Prison Reform Trust undertook primary research in a number of US states and published a series of papers on US sentencing reforms as part of its campaign against Michael Howard's reforms. In a robust defence of Howard's original intentions provided as a memorandum of evidence to the Home Affairs Select Committee Third Report in 1997 (Home Affairs Committee 1998), a retired senior probation officer repeatedly quoted US research evidence about the crime reduction effect of increased incarceration (Coad 1997, cited in Home Affairs Committee 1998). In particular, Coad referred to the work of Charles Murray undertaken at the American Enterprise Institute in Washington DC. The neo-conservative think tank, the Institute for Economic Affairs, also published a short piece by Murray that promoted US-style sentencing reforms for the UK on the basis of the argument that increased incarceration significantly reduces crime levels. Overall, Coad concluded:

> The evidence is that [crime reduction] can be achieved by increasing the use of custodial sentences for serious and persistent offenders; it has been successful in many states in America . . . The considerable evidence from America is that tough prison sentences either control or reduce crime.
>
> (Coad 1997)

In a 1999 House of Lords debate on penal policy, Lord Windlesham argued that Michael Howard had made clear the US inspiration of his mandatory minimum sentence proposals during Commons debates on the Crime (Sentences) Bill:

> So what lay behind these policies? It is well known that they were an adaptation of the American 'Three strikes and you're out' sentencing

policy; a fact that was recognised not least by Mr Howard, in the debates in the House of Commons.

(Lord Windlesham, House of Lords Debate, *Hansard*, 8 December 1999, column 1363)

Despite the general perception about the origins of the sentencing reforms in the Crime (Sentences) Act 1997, it does seem that at most a 'soft' version of policy transfer can be identified here. Michael Howard was clear that his reading of the significant body of US research suggesting that increased imprisonment reduces crime (see, for example, Levitt 1996) was the general inspiration for his support for mandatory sentencing (and restricting parole). It is difficult to make a case that government politicians transferred US rhetoric and terminology, at least during the initial development of the sentencing reform proposals in the UK. We can find no record of the actual terms 'two strikes' or 'three strikes' being used by Howard at any point. In fact, the term has been used sparingly during House of Commons speeches and debates (only on 13 occasions, according to a search of *Hansard*). The US terminology of 'three strikes' was employed extensively in media discussions of Howard's proposals, and by some of his opponents at the time. As we discussed earlier in the chapter, US terminology was also employed at a later stage by Tony Blair after the Labour government had implemented the proposals. In terms of the concrete details of policy content and instruments – the subject matter of 'hard' transfer – there is little evidence of policy transfer from the USA. As noted above, while there was similarity at a very broad level, there were very substantial differences in detail between the forms that the legislation took in the two countries. Thus, although it does appear that the broad policy ideas and – after some delay – the particular rhetoric behind three strikes were transferred from the USA to the UK, it seems equally clear that the practical policy manifestations of these ideas were very different in their original inceptions. Even these subsequently underwent considerable resistance and reworking in the context of British (and latterly, European Union) political and legal institutions.

A final comment on process concerns the influence of 'harmonization' (Bennett 1991) in the arena of sentencing policy. This had an important impact, although it was in terms of constraining the US influence rather than promoting it. The Human Rights Act 1998 saw the incorporation into UK law of the European Convention on Human Rights. The full effects of the HRA are yet to become apparent but are likely to be enormously significant in UK crime control. As noted above, in late 2000, the Court of Appeal ruled that elements of the mandatory sentences contained in the 1997 Crime (Sentences) Act ran counter to the principles enshrined in the HRA and expanded judicial discretion in relation to the sentencing of repeat offenders.

Limits to policy transfer

As outlined in the first section of this chapter, the original proposals for two and three strikes sentencing in the UK met with huge resistance from the judiciary, penal reform groups, the House of Lords and backbench MPs. This resistance resulted in significant amendments and limited the degree to which more radical sentencing reform proposals could be implemented in the UK. In turn, substantive differences in policy content between the US and the UK were reflected in a relatively limited impact of the legislation, in terms of numbers of offenders actually sentenced to prison. These limits to policy transfer can be related to two factors in particular. The first concerns the broader political, legal and cultural circumstances within which policy developments unfolded. The second focuses upon the strategies and actions of key political actors, as witnessed in the energetic campaign against the proposals and their subsequent implementation.

Policy differences

As we have seen, a distinctive British version of 'two/three strikes' was to emerge in the UK that contrasted a great deal with experiences in some parts of the USA. In fact, when we examine the details of policy content, it is clear that there are very significant differences, both within the USA and between the USA and the UK. Even within the USA, the 'two' and 'three strikes' sentencing laws that spread during the mid-1990s varied significantly (Clark *et al.* 1997). First, there were variations according to how broadly the 'strike zone' was defined, including, for example, the sale of drugs (Indiana), carjacking (New Jersey), and any class A, B or C felony (North Dakota). Second, states differed on how many strikes were required to be 'out': two (California, Montana and North Dakota), three (Florida, Nevada, New Jersey), and four (Louisiana and Maryland). Third, there were variations in what it means to be 'out': mandatory life in prison and no parole (Montana), enhanced sentence of up to 25 years (Pennsylvania), and five years to life (Utah). As Vitello (1997: 402) observes, these variations 'have an enormous impact on a state's prison population'. California has attracted the most attention from UK media, partly 'because that state stands alone in the breadth of its policy' (King and Mauer 2001: 3).[8] Mainly because of the breadth of the laws, the effects in California went far beyond those in any other state, partly because its 'three strikes' law 'was designed to operate even more broadly than its specialised title would suggest' (Zimring *et al.* 2001: ix). This relates in particular to the fact that offenders can receive significantly enhanced mandatory sentences after only two strikes, and that should the offender have two official 'strikes' on his/her record, any simple felony offence can trigger the mandatory minimum sentence. In addition, the sentences that are actually laid down (and provisions regarding the time that must be served) are significantly more severe in California than in other jurisdictions (Greenberg 2002).

Thus, in some US states the two and three strikes laws were wider in scope than those in Britain, whereas in others, the scope was much narrower. In terms of another key variable within the three strikes movement – the degree of sentence enhancement available – the USA/UK comparison appears far more straightforward. In almost all cases, the penalties required by the 'three strikes' legislation in US states (and the federal system) were substantially more punitive than those in England and Wales. This is partly because, in England and Wales, the judge retained discretion to set the recommended number of years of a life sentence that should be served in custody. This is a considerable contrast to the more draconian sentences passed under US laws. In the US states that implemented tougher versions of two and three strikes, there seems to have been less discretion for sentencers to circumvent the minimum sentences, what counts as a 'strike' has been more widely defined, and the actual sentence enhancements were more severe than was the case in England and Wales. The contrast was greatest with the legislation in California, which, as we have noted, was the most extreme form of this sentencing approach. For example, there was never any suggestion by the supporters of mandatory minimum sentencing in the UK for sentences as severe as 25 years to life with no parole. In addition, the 'exceptional circumstances' clauses allowed UK judges some discretion to circumvent the minimum sentence requirement in some cases.

These differences in policy content between jurisdictions have significant implications for the impact of the sentencing reforms in terms of actual numbers of prisoners sentenced under the legislation. In England and Wales, the figures for convictions under the 'two' and 'three strikes' provisions tend to support the general predictions that the provisions would have a rather marginal effect in terms of prison populations. Table 4.1 shows the numbers of sentences given by the courts under the provisions of the Crime (Sentences) Act 1997, later consolidated under the Powers of Criminal Courts (Sentencing) Act 2000.

Table 4.1 confirms the very small effects of the minimum sentences for drug trafficking and burglary, though it clearly shows more significant numbers of people being sentenced under the 'two strikes' provision for a second serious violent or sexual offence. However, as we have noted, it is likely that many of these cases would have attracted a discretionary life sentence in any case. The predictions that the new sentencing provisions would directly add over 5000 to the prison population were thus considerably overstated (White and Cullen 2000).

There was also considerable variation between different states within the USA in terms of the practical impact of three strikes laws with regard to

Table 4.1   Persons sentenced under the Powers of Criminal Courts (Sentencing) Act 2000 (England and Wales)

	Life for 2nd serious offence (Section 109)	Minimum 7 years for 3rd class A drug dealing offence (Section 110)	Minimum 3 years for 3rd domestic burglary (Section 111)
2000	57	2	0
2001	51	1	6
2002	44	0	2
2003	48	3	13

Source: Home Office (2005)

numbers of offenders sentenced. A recent study has shown how the number of people incarcerated under two/three strikes laws is negligible in many states (Schiraldi *et al.* 2004). This confirmed earlier findings about the enormous impact of the legislation in California (where at the time of the study over 42,000 people had been imprisoned under two/three strikes laws) compared to over half the states with such laws where the total of those imprisoned was well under 100 (King and Mauer 2001). The relatively limited practical impact of the UK legislation, when compared with the symbolic messages portrayed by the Act, should not be taken to imply that the measures were 'all talk and no action'. As Garland (2001a: 22) has argued, 'political rhetoric and official representations of crime and criminals have a symbolic significance and a practical efficacy that have real social consequences. Sometimes "talk" *is* "action".' Although the actual numbers of prisoners sentenced under the provisions of the Crime (Sentences) Act 1997 has been relatively small compared to early predictions, we should not forget that the English and Welsh prison population has been growing significantly over the recent period. This growth has accelerated under Labour administrations since 1997. The reasons behind the growth in the prison population are complex, but experts agree that a key factor has been the growing punitiveness of the courts. It does seem that sentencers respond to a growing climate of punitiveness, within which the rhetoric of politicians plays an important part. Indeed, it has been convincingly argued that, rather than simply responding to punitive popular opinion, politicians actively construct and lead populist punitiveness as part of a deliberate electoral strategy (Beckett 1997). Although it has been argued that the British legislation was primarily symbolic, it has been suggested that there may be longer-term substantive impacts of such symbolism (Thomas 1998). First, the implementation of the burglary provision promised to have much more practical impact in terms of prison population, given the larger number of offenders that would come under the remit of the 'three strikes' law as the years go by. Second, there could also be wider practical impact in terms of setting a precedent for more mandatory minimum sentences for other kinds of crime.

Political, legal and cultural contexts

A key factor to consider here is the importance of national (and sub-national) political and legal institutions and cultures as sources of constraint over policy transfer, both within the USA and from the USA to Britain. A key contrast between many parts of the USA and Britain in this regard is different legal and historical traditions concerning judicial independence. Although historically US judges have opposed restrictions on their discretion, the history of sentencing commissions and guidelines in many US jurisdictions contrasts with the relatively wide level of discretion under which sentencers in England and Wales have operated (Reitz 2001). In addition, as we noted above, the emergence of 'two' and 'three strikes' sentencing during the early 1990s was built upon a long tradition of habitual offender laws in many parts of the USA. The Californian legislation in particular was framed so as to reduce as far as possible the discretion of judges to avoid passing mandatory sentences.[9] As we have noted, the practical impact of three strikes legislation overall was vastly greater in California than in other US jurisdictions. It seems that this arose from a combination of the (deliberately) more restrictive remit of the legislation in other states, and the ways in which the laws were implemented by sentencers. Turning to the UK, the twentieth century saw a very strong tradition of judicial independence develop. As Ashworth (2001: 77) notes: 'For most of the century [Parliament] had done little more than set maximum penalties and introduce new penal measures, and the judges had come to expect a wide and unfettered sentencing discretion, with a form of self-regulation (appellate review) to guard against excesses.' The importance of this discretion was vital in that the amended legislation in Britain provided judges with opportunities to limit further the practical impact of the new laws.

As noted above, the development of three strikes sentencing reforms in many parts of the USA built on a long history of habitual offender laws, which provided for enhanced sentences for repeat offenders. Indeed, in many cases it appears that the 'three strikes' laws could simply be described as 'old wine in new bottles', in so far as they were unlikely to lead to substantial increases in prison populations. In California, as we have seen, things were different. Indeed, such was the breadth of the proposed three strikes legislation that a number of bodies concerned about the practical implications of the bill put forward detailed alternative proposals, designed to focus the provisions more narrowly on repeat violent offenders. In England and Wales, although there was some provision for enhanced sentencing of repeat offenders, Michael Howard's proposals came somewhat out of the blue. The most recent govern-ment attempts to constrain judicial discretion had been designed to have exactly the opposite effect. The 1991 Criminal Justice Act was based on the premise that the use of prison needed to be restricted (Cavadino and Dignan 2002). In interview, Michael Howard stated that he felt that in the arena of sentencing, as in a number of other areas of reform that he personally promoted, he faced the opposition of an entrenched Home Office culture:

> Oh, you know, officials weren't very comfortable with most of the things I did. It was a break with the criminological, penal establish-ment view. That was why I was subjected to such a tirade of abuse for most of the time I was there. So of course, Home Office officials . . . weren't very keen on most of the things I was trying to do.
>
> (Michael Howard, personal interview)

Thus, differences in political institutions, legal traditions and bureaucratic cultures between jurisdictions have played a key part in shaping differences in policy outcomes. We noted in the previous chapter the relatively open system of democracy in the USA in which there are more points of influence for interest groups to target key decision-makers at federal, state and local level. This was a significant part in the story of three strikes in the USA, which began as voter initiatives in Washington and California. By contrast, the pressure for change clearly came from the top in the UK (in the form of a decision by the Home Secretary). The more direct forms of US democracy and the tradition of law making via referenda and voter petition are clearly a key contrast (Freed-land 1998; Garland 2005). These distinctive features of the politics of crime and punishment in the USA have played an extremely important part in the story of three strikes. Another key structural contrast with the UK is the fact that in the majority of US states judges have to face re-election (rather than being appointed for life, as in the UK). In the majority of US states judges are elected, sometimes with the explicit endorsement of political parties (Cole and Smith 2001). Thus, it has been noted that 'judges and politicians often appeal to the public demand for more rigorous criminal justice policies in the hope of enhancing their own electoral prospects' (Roberts and Stalans 1998: 31). Though popular sentiment has been an increasingly important influence over UK penal policy in recent years, it remains the case that judicial, governmental and academic elites still provide something of a buffer between public opin-ion and penal policy-making.[10] In the UK, the stronger tradition of judicial independence was illustrated by previous successful circumvention of execu-tive attempts to structure discretion by courts, via the 'destructive interpret-ation' of judges (Cavadino and Dignan 2002). The wider judicial interpretation of the 'exceptional circumstances' clause described above is one of a range of examples of such destructive interpretation of sentencing legislation by the courts in Britain.

Another critical difference in the political histories of 'three strikes' in the USA and the UK concerns the very different politics of 'victimhood' in the two countries (Dubber 2002). Garland (2000) has argued that a key feature of the 'culture of control' that has arisen (in both the USA and the UK) is the important part played by a 'projected, politicised image of "the victim" ' (2000: 143) in penal politics. This, he suggests, is reflected in the naming of particular laws and penal measures after particular high-profile victims. Although Garland's analysis focuses on similarities between the USA and the UK in this regard, other commentators have drawn strong contrasts between the political construction of crime victims in the UK and in many parts of the USA (Rock 2004). It is striking that there were no high-profile 'figurehead' victims in the British three strikes story. The history in the USA is very much one of specific campaigns with symbolic victims at their heart. The UK story was partly about the general wish to project political toughness and partly about the ongoing battle the then Conservative government were having with the judiciary. There continued to be deep scepticism about using victims as flagships upon which to base a campaign. The other important contrast is the very differing degrees to which these policies were racialized in the two countries. In the USA, historically, much of the push to mandatory minimum sentences was related to drug control policy and, directly or indirectly therefore, about race. This was simply not the case in the UK; had street robbery been the focus of political and public concern behind the drive to three strikes, then this might have been different. Two of the three broad categories of offending that formed the target for the British version of two and three strikes (violence/sexual offences and burglary) are not predominantly the offences for which black people are convicted.

Political agency and happenstance

The different sets of political institutions and legal structures referred to above provided policy actors with both constraints and opportunities. Differences in policy content and impact reflect the highly effective campaign of resistance to the development of mandatory minimum sentencing reforms. For example, the Penal Affairs Consortium (PAC) energetically campaigned against the Bill by lobbying MPs and peers, and undertaking a large number of media interviews. Central in this was Paul Cavadino of NACRO, who described 'an intensive lobbying effort'. Elfyn Llwyd MP, who played a leading role in opposing the Bill at the Committee Stages in the House of Commons, remembered that he had a number of 'very helpful' meetings with Paul Cavadino who had provided him with a range of 'facts and figures' to draw upon in the debates over mandatory minimum sentencing. Individual penal reform groups also continued to attempt to exert influence over the debate on sentencing reform.

Some attempted to use the USA as an example of 'negative lessons'. For example, the Prison Reform Trust published a series of papers in 1996/97 entitled *Lessons from America*. These papers provided critical scrutiny of US developments such as 'truth in sentencing', 'three strikes' and other forms of mandatory minimum sentencing (see, for example, Prison Reform Trust 1996a, 1996b, 1997). These short papers were explicitly aimed at influencing the ongoing debate surrounding the Crime (Sentences) Bill, and highlighting what the PRT saw as the likely negative impacts of the Bill's key provisions. As we have seen above, the lobbying effort had a significant effect on the eventual shape of the legislation. So much so, in fact, that Paul Cavadino of NACRO argued that they amounted to presumptive sentences, rather than mandatory minimums. However, the campaign continued after the Act came into force. Soon after the change of government in 1997, NACRO met with the new Home Office ministers and argued the case against the burglary clause. When the Labour government implemented the burglary clause, NACRO issued a statement condemning this.

As noted above, although the judiciary had previously shown themselves more than willing to engage in public debate about sentencing policy, the debate about mandatory minimum sentences in the UK saw this rise to an unprecedented level (Ashworth 2001). In fact, it seems fair to argue that judicial opposition, in terms of high-profile public campaigning, the activities of Law Lords (serving and retired) in the House of Lords, and subsequent inter-pretations of the legislation by the Court of Appeal and judges in individual cases, was absolutely central to reshaping the original proposals into a highly muted form of 'two/three strikes'. It is important here to note also that the notion of an essentially US-based idea being resisted and reworked by pri-marily domestic influences is an over-simplification. We mentioned above the important role played by European Union pressures, in the form of the incorporation of the European Declaration on Human Rights into British law in the Human Rights Act 1998. This provided further levers for practical judicial opposition to 'two strikes', with Lord Woolf's utilization of the Act to expand further the 'exceptional circumstances' clause in the 'two strikes' cases of serious sexual and violent crimes.

The 'three strikes' story helps to highlight once again the haphazard and contingent nature of the policy-making process. Although the wider eco-nomic, cultural and social forces that provide the context of policy-making have clearly had an impact (Garland 2001a), the direction and substance of policy change have been shaped by the specific legal, political and cultural contexts within which it has emerged, along with the strategic agency of key policy actors. The emergence of mandatory minimum sentencing again underlines the truth in Kingdon's (1995: 206) observation that in examining the detail of public policy change 'we still encounter considerable doses of messiness, accident, fortuitous coupling and dumb luck'. In particular, the contingent nature of the timing of the Bill, in that legislation had to be rushed through Parliament in the immediate run-up to the 1997 general election, had a crucial impact on the eventual shape that it took. In particular, it forced Michael Howard to allow revisions to the Bill that he otherwise would not have accepted. In his words:

> I saw exceptional circumstances as really meaning *exceptional circum-stances* and I would have limited them, required the judge to give reasons and all that sort of stuff. Now, that was made into a bloody great loophole by what Labour did in the run-up to the 1997 election. The answer to one of your questions – would I have done it differently if the election hadn't been imminent – yes, bloody sure I would have done. But I didn't have time. When an election is imminent, you have to make a judgement. And in the end I had to choose between allowing the legislation to fall and allowing these changes.
>
> (Michael Howard, personal interview)

Sentencing reform and policy transfer

The story of two and three strikes sentencing in the UK presents some interesting similarities and contrasts with the story of privatized corrections. Overall, it is again possible to detect the important structural and cultural preconditions in both the USA and the UK that rendered the promotion of 'get tough' penal policies more probable. In particular, there was in the 1990s a general political climate in both countries that provided fertile ground in which certain ideas and approaches to sentencing policy might take root in the minds of some politicians. In this sense, these sentencing policy ideas had a certain consonance with wider socio-political developments. We can thus regard the emergence of this kind of sentencing proposal in the USA and the UK, at roughly similar times, as arising as much from a wider coincidence in domestic social and political conditions as from any deliberate process of international policy transfer. Despite a seemingly strong association (at least in media discussion and wider debate) between the reforms of the Crime (Sentences) Act in the UK and prior US developments, this appears to be an area of policy where US influence was rather limited and indirect. In terms of broad policy ideas there is evidence, from the timing and some similarity in policy (along with the specific terminology and rhetoric that were later employed by its Labour inheritors), that there was a degree – albeit 'soft' – of transfer from the USA to the UK. This picture of generalized and indirect US influence was conveyed to us by the original architect of the UK reforms, Michael Howard himself. Both the nature and degree of policy transfer therefore differ significantly from the story of privatized corrections explored in the previous chapter. First, there is an important difference in what was transferred. Although subject to considerable reformulation and resistance, the policy of contracting out of prisons and EM in the UK drew in some detail on the policy content and instruments employed in the USA. In terms of substantive policy, far more was transferred than in the case of two/three strikes. The main import in the arena of sentencing policy was a general inspiration about the use of imprisonment as a tool of crime reduction via deterrence and incapacitation, rather than major changes in the substantive details of policy content and instruments. At a later stage, there developed a willingness on the part of some Labour politicians – in telling contrast to Michael Howard – to deploy the specifically US terminology of 'three strikes'.

Second, in terms of the 'who', these sentencing reforms were directly associated with one key policy player – the then Home Secretary Michael Howard. He was known for his interest in conservative US thinking on crime and punishment. He had a genuine belief in the crime reduction potential of sentencing for deterrence and incapacitation (Windlesham 2001) and, indeed, explicitly reiterated this belief in interview. In contrast to developments in the commercialization of corrections, the role of policy entrepreneurs, civil servants and backbench politicians in promoting change was limited. Indeed, civil servants and backbench MPs were active participants in the coalition of opposition that campaigned against these sentencing reforms. There is no evidence of campaigning organizations and lobbying groups promoting changes in specific sentencing policies in the way that occurred in the USA (see Chapter 3). Not surprisingly, given the rather general and diffuse nature of the US influence in this policy area, we found little evidence relating to the processes of policy transfer, in that there seem to have been no *specific* examples in which US experience was used to promote changes in UK policy. In particular, neither our documentary research nor our interview accounts gave rise to examples of visits by UK politicians, policy-makers or sentencing practitioners to the USA to observe and discuss sentencing developments there. Indeed, the only way in which US evidence was explicitly utilized during debates about mandatory minimum sentencing was by key opponents of the proposals (see, for example, Prison Reform Trust 1996b, 1997), who deployed such experience as 'negative lessons' (Dolowitz and Marsh 2000). The final contrast with the privatized corrections story concerns the relative success with which the substantive policy changes associated with two/three strikes sentencing were opposed and reshaped by domestic influences. While the initial proposals were considerably less severe than those in the most high-profile US jurisdictions, even these were weakened by a combination of opposition from peers in the House of Lords and a cross-party coalition of backbench MPs. Following this, those tasked with the implementation of the laws, the judges, used the 'exceptional circumstances' clauses to avoid sentencing under the provisions of the Act in all but relatively few cases. Thus, although it would be an exaggeration to argue that the initial proposals were completely neutralized, it is clear the actual impact of the changes in the UK has been very limited.

Thus, mandatory minimum sentencing in the form of 'three strikes' emerged in the USA and the UK in distinctive legal, political and cultural circumstances. Although in very broad terms it seems that the idea did have roots in the USA (in terms of wider political commitment to the use of imprisonment as a crime reduction policy), in general, the role played by policy transfer was rather limited. This was, out of our three case studies of policy change, the 'softest' example of policy transfer. There was much that was home-grown about the emergence of these sentencing reforms in the UK. This raises interesting broader questions about the processes of international policy diffusion and convergence, to which we return in the final chapter. To the degree that there is convergence in this area (and, as we have seen, there remained significant differences between jurisdictions within the broad remit of 'three strikes'), this arose from a complex mixture of domestic and international influences, only a very small part of which involved policy transfer. The initial proposals of Michael Howard – already very different from sentencing practices in the USA – were then subject to the national and subnational resistance, mediation and reworking within the particular political and legal cultures and institutions of the UK. A key part of this process involved the deployment of US experience as 'negative lessons' by key opponents of the proposals. Important contrasts between the institutional context of policy-making in the UK and in many US states were also highly significant in the contrasting histories of 'three strikes'. The key contrast with US experience here concerns the greater degree to which criminal justice policy in the UK remains buffered from the direct impact of popular sentiment. Notwithstanding the noted shift towards populist punitiveness in the UK (and the important influence this has had in particular on the stance of the Labour Party), the voter-led developments in the US states of Washington and California were something of a completely different order when compared to UK political traditions.

5 Zero tolerance policing

The term 'zero tolerance' has become an established feature of the crime control landscape. Used in various settings by politicians, policy-makers, police
officers and others, the signals it sends about toughness have been enormously
seductive in these punitive times. Though to many observers it may seem to be
a relatively new term, zero tolerance has a fairly lengthy and quite complicated
history. Initial uses of the term in North America appeared in connection first
with the war on drugs and then later with specific campaigns against violence
against women (Newburn and Jones, forthcoming). In much of the world,
however, the term is currently most commonly associated with policing, and
this is the primary focus of the current chapter. 'Zero tolerance policing' (ZTP)
is associated with a vigorous enforcement-oriented policing approach that
focuses upon minor offences and disorder as much as upon more serious
crimes. During the first half of the 1990s, there was considerable attention paid
by the British media to developments in the policing of New York City where
there had been very significant drops in crime. This became associated, at least
in popular consciousness, with a zero tolerance approach to policing (Bowling
1999; Karmen 2001). Zero tolerance is rather a slippery idea. As we have outlined elsewhere, the term has been used in a number of distinct arenas,
and means different things in these different contexts (Newburn and Jones,
forthcoming). Even within one context, such as policing, it is difficult to
list a definitive set of goals, contents, or instruments that might help us
define what a zero tolerance policy is. We will argue later that zero tolerance
policing represents a set of ideas and symbols, and a distinctive policy style,
rather than a concrete set of interventions. However, a general impression of
the strategy adopted by the New York Police Department, that has become
lastingly associated with the term zero tolerance, is captured in the following
quote from Bill Bratton, Commissioner of Police under Mayor Giuliani from
1994–96:

Boom boxes, squeegee people, street prostitutes, public drunks, panhandlers, reckless bicyclists, illegal after-hours joints, graffiti – New
York was overrun . . . We could solve all the murders we liked, but if
the average citizen was running a gauntlet of panhandlers every day
on his way to and from work, he would want that issue solved . . .
Previous police administrations had been handcuffed by restrictions.
We took the handcuffs off. Department attorneys worked with precinct commanders to address the problems. We used civil law to
enforce existing regulations against harassment, assault, menacing,
disorderly conduct and damaging property. We stepped up enforcement of the laws against public drunkenness and public urination
and arrested repeat violators, including those who threw empty bottles in the street or were involved in even relatively minor damage to
property. No more D.A.T.s.[1] If you peed in the street, you were going
to jail. We were going to fix the broken windows and prevent anyone
from breaking them again.

(Bratton and Knobler 1998: 229)

From 1996 onwards, something that became labelled ZTP appeared in
parts of the UK, with policing initiatives in London and Cleveland that
shared at least some of the terminology with zero tolerance approaches. More
broadly, the rhetoric of zero tolerance became increasingly popular with politicians who applied it in a number of contexts from failing schools to under-
performing hospitals. In this chapter, we explore what this term is taken to
mean and the ways and means by which yet another seemingly American
crime control concept crossed the Atlantic to become embedded in British
consciousness. The chapter begins with an overview of the emergence of the
idea of zero tolerance; in connection with policing in the UK. The next section
compares the timing of its emergence and the nature of policies associated
with it with developments in the USA. The following two sections discuss
respectively the key agents of policy transfer, and the processes via which
transfer came about. The fifth section explores the limits to policy transfer and
the influence of intervening factors such as domestic resistance to proposed
policy changes. The final substantive section outlines the broader influence of
the ideas underpinning ZTP in more general government crime control policy,
outside of the immediate arena of policing.

Zero tolerance in the UK

Interestingly, in Britain, the initial usage of the term zero tolerance appeared,
not in connection with policing approaches, but in the context of work and
campaigning regarding violence against women. Two campaigns, the first in

Canada, the second in Scotland, used the term as the core of their strategies to heighten the profile of the problem of violence against women. As in other parts of the world, it was the women's movement that identified violence against women as a political issue, and campaigned for social and structural reform in the face of widespread public and professional ignorance. Almost simultaneously with the Canadian campaign, though clearly influenced by the Canadian model, the Zero Tolerance Campaign (ZTC) was launched in Edinburgh in November 1992 by the City Council's Women's Committee. It was one of the first major UK crime prevention campaigns to focus on the issue of male violence against women. The Edinburgh initiative developed as a public education campaign that aimed to raise awareness about male violence against women and children, send out a clear message that such crimes should not be tolerated, and campaign for a national strategy to combat such violence. ZTC used posters, billboards and cinema advertising, all carrying a stark 'Z' symbol, to raise awareness and carry the central message of the campaign that 'male abuse of power is a crime'. In 1995 the Zero Tolerance Charitable Trust was established following the success of, and interest in, the Edinburgh campaign. The campaign has been taken up by many local authorities in Scotland and has spread internationally as far as South Australia and intriguingly, given what has happened since to the term zero tolerance, New York City.

During the early 1990s New York City experienced a steep decline in its crime rates. For example, between 1990 and 1997 felony crime rates were halved and homicides fell from 2245 to 767 (Dixon 2005). It was far from alone among major American cities in doing so. However, partly because of its reputation as a high crime city, its status as America's most important urban centre and, as we will see, the visibility of some of its leading public figures, the crime drop in New York became a very significant source of news both domestically and abroad. More particularly, the message that this crime drop was associated with reformed policing practices in the city received a considerable amount of attention in the international media. As we outline later, this period saw a large number of visits to the USA (and New York in particular) by British government and opposition politicians, civil servants, and representatives of the police service. In late 1996, for example, a number of senior police officers from the UK visited New York to observe developments there and to talk directly with the Chief of Police. Richard Monk, at the time an Assistant Inspector of Constabulary, was directly commissioned by the Home Secretary 'to identify the principal means by which the New York City Police Department had achieved such dramatic reductions in crime during 1994 and 1995' (Monk 1998: 25). Zero tolerance policing continued to attract significant attention, so much that in the run-up to the 1997 general election it appeared that 'zero tolerance looked likely to become a main plank of any new government's thinking about the future of policing, irrespective of its political complexion' (Weatheritt 1998: 1).

During the 1990s, there were a number of localized experiments with so-called 'zero tolerance policing' in the UK. The Metropolitan Police in Kings Cross undertook a vigorous and, they allege, successful campaign to 'clean up' the area by focusing as much on minor infractions and incivilities as on major crimes. One of their operations, entitled Operation Zero Tolerance, ran for six weeks in late 1996 and involved 25 police officers 'who have been instructed to clamp down on all crime in the area, however apparently trivial or irrelevant' ('The petty crime way', *Guardian*, 21 November 1996). The only major explicit attempt to introduce a form of zero tolerance policing was that in Hartlepool from mid-1994 under the guidance of Detective Superintendent Ray Mallon. Mallon is one of the few British police officers of any seniority to have embraced the idea of zero tolerance. According to him, what zero tolerance meant in Hartlepool was 'that the police would "return peace to the streets" by controlling minor situations in the interest of the "decent" and "respectable" citizen' (Dennis and Mallon 1997: 65). Critics of zero tolerance have long alleged that its encouragement of intolerance of offenders and offending is likely to lead to serious misconduct by police officers. Such critics viewed the subsequent suspension of DS Mallon on charges of corruption as an indication of the veracity of their fears.

Another police operation associated with the idea of zero tolerance – Operation Spotlight in Glasgow – massively increased arrests for drunkenness and public order offences in an attempt to reduce late night disorder problems. However, as so many others have sought to do, Strathclyde Police have been keen to dissociate themselves from the idea of zero tolerance despite the keenness of others to attach the label to their activities (Orr 1997). What 'Spotlight' shared with the NYPD was an explicit attachment to the Wilson and Kelling 'broken windows' thesis (1982). Indeed, it is an element of this thesis – the notion that in order successfully to have an impact on serious crime it is important to target and prioritize action against low-level disorder – that has had the greater influence on recent crime control policy in England and Wales. As one time junior Minister in the Home Office Alun Michael (1997) put it:

> One interpretation of 'zero tolerance' is fast police action to stop crime in its tracks and to protect the public. That interpretation has its place. But another interpretation is to 'nip things in the bud' when they start to go wrong, to recognise the patterns of behaviour which, if left to grow, will go from bad to worse. If graffiti start to creep along a wall, they will soon take it over; while one broken window left unrepaired will start to feed a sense of decay as others follow.

New Labour's adoption of such a philosophy is most visible in both the title and the contents of the 1998 Crime and Disorder Act, the more recent

Anti-Social Behaviour Act 2003 and the architecture of government anti-social behaviour policy more generally (Burney 2005; Squires and Stephen 2005). Indeed, as we will later argue, it is here that the greatest influence of North American ideas is visible. What has become known as the Labour government's 'anti-social behaviour agenda' has been profoundly influenced by a very particular reading or understanding of, among other things, Wilson and Kelling's original 'broken windows' article.

The strong opposition from most chief police officers to both the general principles and concrete policing practices associated with zero tolerance makes the persistent popularity of the term even more interesting. The popularity of the term is largely political. The emergence of zero tolerance in British political life occurred during the mid-1990s. Jack Straw, then Shadow Home Secretary, visited New York in July 1995, and was the first to use the new terminology. In a speech to launch the London Borough of Lewisham's community safety strategy he was critical of the 'aggressive begging of winos and addicts' and the 'squeegee merchants who wait at large road junctions to force on reticent motorists their windscreen cleaning service . . . Even where graffiti is not comprehensible or racialist in message', he went on, 'it is often violent and uncontrolled in its violent image, and correctly gives the impression of a lack of law and order on the streets' (quoted in Newburn 1998). Echoing his Shadow Home Secretary, Tony Blair made a major, and controversial, speech in January 1997 in which he outlined his view of zero tolerance. Asked by the editor of the *Big Issue* whether he supported the policy, he replied: 'Yes, I do. It is important that you say we don't tolerate the small crimes. It says you don't tolerate the graffiti on the wall.'[2] He went on: 'Obviously, some people will interpret this in a way which is harsh and unpleasant, but I think the basic principle is here to say: yes, it is right to be intolerant of people homeless on the streets.' During the election campaign, while appearing in Hartlepool, Jack Straw sought to soften the message of intolerance by pointing out that New Labour's strategy was much broader. 'Tackling youth crime is an integral part of our strategy to reduce anti-social behaviour and create a more decent society.' This he called 'zero tolerance with a British face'.[3]

As early as December 1995, Tony Blair had signalled his willingness to use the term in a much broader manner to signify a more general style in which New Labour would operate, given the opportunity. In launching proposals for improving educational standards, he promised to 'sweep away the second rate and tackle head-on the half-baked and the ineffective', adding: 'There will be zero tolerance of failure from any government I lead.'[4] The same message eventually found its way into the Labour Party election manifesto in 1997. Under the heading, 'Zero tolerance to underperformance', the manifesto (Labour Party 1997) said:

Every school has the capacity to succeed. All LEAs must demonstrate that every school is improving. For those failing schools unable to improve, ministers will order a 'fresh start' – close the school and start afresh on the same site. Where good schools and bad schools coexist side by side we will authorize LEAs to allow one school to take over the other to set the underperforming school on a new path.

Later in the manifesto, the party reiterated its support of a crackdown approach to 'quality of life' offences:

> The Conservatives have forgotten the 'order' part of 'law and order'. We will tackle the unacceptable level of anti-social behaviour and crime on our streets. Our 'zero tolerance' approach will ensure that petty criminality among young offenders is seriously addressed.

It was at this stage that zero tolerance rhetoric from politicians really took off. Whereas there had been occasional sightings prior to this, particularly around major speeches by Blair and Straw, in the run-up to the 1997 general election and in parliamentary debates during the six months afterwards it regularly reappeared. Though both the Conservative Home Secretary and his Shadow visited New York and made positive statements about what was happening there, the term zero tolerance was appropriated primarily by New Labour. This period from mid-1995 to late 2000 was the high point for deployment of the term. In more recent times talk of zero tolerance has lessened, though it still reappears from time to time in connection with matters such as abuse against public sector workers,[5] especially within the NHS[6] and in relation to discipline in schools.[7]

Occasionally, though infrequently, the term 'zero tolerance policing' still arises. Wherever it is deployed, the 'New York miracle' is almost always invoked. Speaking in Hartlepool in August 2004, and accompanied by the City's former Chief Superintendent, now Mayor of Middlesbrough, Ray Mallon, Michael Howard summarized much of the recent story of ZTP:

> We need to police our streets – not de-police them. We need a police force which intervenes, confronts and challenges every kind of crime and disorder – from graffiti and litter to burglary and robbery. In short, we need zero tolerance policing. As Ray has shown in Middlesbrough, and Rudi Giuliani showed in New York, by challenging disorder you begin to claim ground back from the yobs and hoodlums controlling our cities. You demonstrate that there is a line people cannot cross – and as police confidence rises in challenging unacceptable behaviour, so public confidence rises in the police. By challenging so-called small crimes head-on, you push back the burglars, car thieves and drug dealers responsible for so much of the crime in Britain today.[8]

Continued sightings of the term are testimony to its enduring power and resonance. At the Conservative Party Conference in 2000, Ann Widdecombe drew explicitly upon the New York experience in 2000 in support of the introduction of zero tolerance policing approaches in the UK:

> Today I am able to announce a new policy. Earlier this year, I visited New York, where under Mayor Giuliani crime has plummeted. Although we can't replicate exactly what I saw there, we can learn the lessons. . . . And so, from the possession of the most minimal amount of soft drugs right up the chain to the large importer, there will be no hiding place. There will be zero tolerance.

Although Widdecombe's speech received a standing ovation in the conference hall, there were considerable reservations about it among her Shadow Cabinet colleagues, particularly after a number of senior police officers appeared on radio and television criticizing the idea of a zero tolerance drugs policy. Matters quickly became worse for Widdecombe when it became apparent that she had seemingly failed to clear the details of her speech with the Shadow Cabinet.[9] She was quickly ordered to backtrack and in due course the policy was quietly dropped. This point seemed to mark the point at which the term zero tolerance began to lose some of its lustre in British political life. While it could still galvanize an audience, it was far from unproblematic as a policy prescription. Although the term has appeared occasionally since this time, sometimes with regard to policing, it has undoubtedly been sighted far less frequently than during the second half of the 1990s. There are now relatively few politicians or police officers[10] who invoke the term zero tolerance in any serious way in connection with policing policies or strategies. As we have already implied, and return to below, it is in the field of anti-social behaviour that 'quality of life'-influenced ideas and strategies have had a greater effect.

Timing and policy similarity

To what extent is it realistic to talk of policy transfer in relation to zero tolerance policing? In this section we consider this question by looking at the timing and nature of policy developments in the USA and the UK in this area. First of all, the relative timescales of the appearance of zero tolerance terminology, and the wider promotion of particular policing practices associated with it, are consistent with a picture of transfer from the USA to the UK. The term emerged first in North America and then appeared some years later in the UK. Second, although the specific policing practices associated with ZTP in New York City were not transferred wholesale across the Atlantic, a number of small-scale experiments in ZTP were undertaken in the UK in the mid- to late

1990s. More importantly in terms of policy transfer, the political rhetoric and some more general policy ideas associated with 'zero tolerance policing' were similar in both the USA and the UK. Indeed, a general concern with tackling the problems of 'disorder' and 'anti-social behaviour' has been a central plank in Labour governments' anti-crime policies from the late 1990s onward.

Timing

Let us begin by looking at the emergence of zero tolerance; as a crime control concept and, more particularly, when and how it became attached to policing. The initial sighting was in President Reagan's 'war on drugs' during the 1980s. Military metaphors abound in political discourses surrounding crime and justice. The most often used is that of 'war'. The 'war on crime' was famously declared by President Nixon and was followed by a full-scale 'war on drugs' declared by Ronald Reagan in 1982, and heightened by his successor George Bush. It was with the Reagan–Bush-inspired 'war on drugs' during the 1980s that the term 'zero tolerance' first gained prominence (Newburn and Jones, forthcoming). Despite the relatively long history of the term it is, as we have implied, now most closely associated with policing and, in particular, with a particular period of policing history in New York City (NYC). A brief examination of the recent history of policing in NYC and the UK clearly demonstrates that the rhetoric and symbols of zero tolerance – as well as any more concrete manifestations of policing policy associated with the term – emerged first in the USA and subsequently appeared in the UK.

The very significant drops in crime, especially violent crime and homicide, in New York City in the early 1990s came to be associated with changed policing practices, largely as a result of some very successful image management by the Mayor, Rudy Giuliani, and the then Commissioner of Police, Bill Bratton. Influenced by James Q. Wilson and George Kelling's (1982) 'broken windows' metaphor, the NYPD under Bratton (and under his successor Howard Safir) pursued a vigorous campaign against both crime and disorder. In terms of timing, the majority of policing practices that became associated with ZTP were introduced to the NYPD[11] following the election of Giuliani in 1993, and his appointment of Bratton in early 1994 (Silverman 1999), though elements, particularly the use of civil measures, began under the previous Commissioner. As we have already noted, the emergence of the terminology and policing approaches associated with ZTP did not occur in the UK until Ray Mallon took up post in the Hartlepool division of Cleveland Police in April 1994. Thus, Mallon's appointment predates most of the major UK media coverage of the crime drop in New York and the policing reforms that became associated with it. So far as Mallon himself was concerned, what he was doing in England was largely contemporaneous with developments in New York City. In interview he suggested:

As far as zero tolerance policing is concerned, it didn't come from New York. What actually happened was that they were practising something in New York and by coincidence we were practising something similar in Hartlepool. Now a television company got hold of Bratton and, words to this effect, said to Bratton, there's been a lot of publicity about what's happening in New York, but there's also something similar happening in Hartlepool in the North East of England. Both environments are completely different. But they're both successful, which indicates there's merit in this kind of strategy. So Bratton had just ceased as the Commissioner of the NYPD. So they fly him over to Hartlepool. He's there for three days. This was July 1995 and we were getting quite a bit of publicity because we were going quite well – and suddenly there was loads and loads of press on top of us. So that's the first thing. It didn't come from New York. It was just coincidence that we were doing something similar.

(Ray Mallon, personal interview)

The subsequent spread of terminology associated with ZTP occurred in the UK later, about 1996/97, a timescale that is clearly consistent with a picture of policy transfer. However, in its initial form at least and confined to a small experiment in the north of England, the British version of ZTP developed almost simultaneously with, and independently of, the developments in New York City.

Policy similarities

The next question we must face is what, if anything, might have been transferred? This requires a close look at what is meant by zero tolerance policing, in terms of broader policy ideas and rhetoric, as well as at the more concrete manifestations of policy.

One level of broad similarity between US and UK experience comes at the level of the basic ideas that inform ZTP approaches. The strategies employed by the NYPD under Giuliani and Bratton have, in practice, rarely been referred to using the term zero tolerance. More frequently the description of choice has been 'quality of life policing'. The idea of 'quality of life' offences derives from Wilson and Kelling's (1982) 'broken windows' thesis, which emphasized the role of informal social controls in helping contain crime levels in local neighbourhoods. The original broken windows article was published in 1982 and, though it received some coverage, was by no means immediately influential, nor was it necessarily expected to be. As George Kelling noted, 'Jim Wilson and I at times chuckle about the legs of the article. Had we known it was going to have the legs that it has, we might have been a little more cautious in our writing at times!' The thesis has been interpreted in a range of ways. Kelling

(1998: 4–5) himself suggests that 'broken windows' is a metaphor: 'Just as a broken window left untended is a sign that nobody cares and leads to more damage, so disorderly behaviour left untended is a sign that nobody cares and leads to worsening disorder, serious crime and urban decay.' He goes on to argue that the first two parts of the theory – that untended broken windows lead to more serious vandalism, and that disorderly behaviour gives rise to fear of crime – are supported by evidence. The third and final part, that disorderly behaviour leads to worsening disorder, serious crime and urban decay was, he says, 'a hypothesis at the time' (1998: 5).

The question raised by the use of this metaphor, and only partly answered above, is what are the 'broken windows' (the disorderly behaviours) that need to be kept in check if crime is not to spiral out of control? According to Wilson and Kelling (1982: 34), they are 'the ill-smelling drunk, the rowdy teen-ager, or the importuning beggar . . . The unchecked panhandler is in effect the first broken window.' The central focus of the broken windows approach therefore is 'incivilities', or 'quality of life' offences. The basic ideas inspiring ZTP (and its variants) on both sides of the Atlantic, and the Labour government's anti-social behaviour agenda, have been clearly influenced by this particular element of the broken windows article – as Bill Bratton's description of policing in New York at the beginning of this chapter illustrated. Policing in Bratton's NYPD involved a renewed focus upon public begging, low-level incivilities, public drunkenness and urination, fare dodging and, most famously of all, 'squeegeeing' – and, more particularly, 'crackdowns' on these offences. It was these crackdowns, and related actions against more serious offences, that became primarily associated with the term zero tolerance. The fifth of the eight policing strategies adopted by the NYPD was called 'Reclaiming the Public Spaces of New York' (Giuliani and Bratton 1994). It was, according to Bratton, the 'lynchpin' strategy in New York City: 'We were going to fix the *broken windows* and prevent anyone from breaking them again' (Bratton and Andrews 1999: 229, emphasis added). This concerted police action against such 'quality of life' violations became associated with the term zero tolerance in the UK. Though the phrase was rarely used in New York to describe such strategies, and Bratton generally avoided using the term, towards the end of his first term as mayor, and seeking ways of securing a second term, Mayor Giuliani highlighted these quality of life strategies and it was these that he 'took to calling "zero tolerance" ' (Barrett and Fifield 2000: 345).

A clear parallel can be found in the description of what underpinned the zero tolerance policing approach in Hartlepool. Dennis and Mallon (1997) wrote that a key aim was 'retaining or recovering the control of the streets on behalf and with the consent of the law-abiding population' (1997: 66). Furthermore, this involved 'paying attention to, not ignoring, anti-social behaviour and "nuisance crime" ' (1997: 66). Although not referred to directly, again the rationale behind this was very much that outlined in the broken windows thesis. The streets would be reclaimed for the 'respectable' and 'law-abiding' citizens. 'Quality of life' offences would be targeted by the police, and partly as a result of this 'nipping of things in the bud', more serious crimes would fall. Similar ideas lay behind the particular 'zero tolerance' policing initiatives in Strathclyde and London (Griffiths 1997; Orr 1997). Overall, the practical policing initiatives in the UK that became associated with the term ZTP, although limited in their application, were quite clearly underpinned by ideas and assumptions that appear to have informed developments in New York. Indeed, as we will later argue, although these ideas have not gone on to influence British policing more generally, the broken windows thesis has been more generally influential in broader government prevention policy in the UK, with landmark legislation explicitly using the kind of language drawn upon by Wilson and Kelling (see, for example, the Crime and Disorder Act 1998, the Anti-Social Behaviour Act 2003).

When we turn to the more concrete dimensions of policy in terms of actual policing practices associated with ZTP, then the evidence for similarity between the USA and the UK is more limited. Yet there is arguably a sufficient degree of similarity to provide reasonable cause not to dismiss the possibility of policy transfer – at least in relation to the specific zero tolerance initiatives undertaken in London, Glasgow and Hartlepool. Although admittedly the links here are more tenuous, we would argue that we can identify a sufficient number of similarities between policing reforms in New York and UK experiments in ZTP (and its variants) during the 1990s to meet this condition.

What, then, are the core components of 'quality of life'/zero tolerance policing under Bratton and Giuliani? We have already noted the emphasis placed upon crackdowns on low-level incivilities and disorderliness. A second attribute would be the significantly increased use of the civil law as a mechanism for reducing crime or criminal opportunities (Kelling 1998; Greene 1999). This strategy was initially developed under Bratton's predecessors as Commissioner of the NYPD, Lee Brown and Ray Kelly. The Deputy Commissioner responsible for its development, Jeremy Travis, describes it thus:

> . . . we started finding statutes that had never been enforced, civil remedies, all these sorts of things, and my instructions to them were to be as aggressive as you can within the limits of the law, and let's see what works. And so we starting developing what became the civil enforcement initiative, which was a number of non-criminal legal options that helped to expand the repertoire of the problem-solving process in terms of their strategic and tactical interventions. Such as for street prostitution, the traditional response was either do nothing or arrest the prostitutes. And we said, well, we can arrest the patrons, and we had a legal statute that allowed us to seize their cars. So we started an operation and street prostitution went down. Drug selling,

we said, we can make lots of arrests of drug sellers, but why don't we talk about the legal liability of the owner of the building from which they're selling the drugs in terms of his supporting the criminal enterprise? So we started taking owners to court and drug selling went down. Problems with kids drunk on weekends, we can arrest the kids, or you can say, well, there's the responsibility of the bar owners and you can, without necessarily doing anything, it brings them into court and threatens them that if they continue to do something they will face legal consequences . . . And we also did some things that were sort of at the high end in terms of severity, but most of them were low level quality of life offences. And a lot of them had to do with the sort of intersect between that and broken windows, the notion of order in public spaces, so the theoretical view here would be that if you take care of these irritants, then it would help communities to rebound.

(Jeremy Travis, personal interview)

The third component of the NYPD's approach involved the development of a management information and control system for regulating and directing policing at precinct level – Compstat (Bratton 1997; Silverman 1999). Mark Moore (2003) describes Compstat in both narrow and broad perspectives. The narrower view, he says, would see Compstat as a technical system for measuring demands on police services at a local level, together with levels of police activity. More broadly, however, it is a '*combined* technical and managerial system that embeds the technical system for the collection and distribution of performance information in a broader managerial system designed to focus the organization as a whole, and a subset of managers who are relied on to exercise leadership in meeting the organization's objectives, on the task that the organization faces'. More prosaically, Bill Bratton (1997: 38) described the twice-weekly Compstat meetings as requiring precinct commanders 'to be ready to review their up-to-date computer-generated crime statistics and relate what things are going to be done to achieve crime reduction'.

Targeted crime reduction was Bratton's aim and another part of his strategy involved highly publicized target-setting for himself and his department. This involved regular use of the media as a key element of the means by which he communicated both with his department and with the citizens of New York. The final core element of the strategy involved high-visibility order maintenance involving a specialist NYPD team called the 'Street Crimes Unit'. This was a plain clothes, elite unit that worked across the city – rather than being located in particular precincts or even boroughs. The unit was tasked with aggressive action against street crime and notched up many successes. However, it also contributed to many of the less positive aspects of 'quality of life' policing, not least the shooting of Amadou Diallou, an unarmed 22-year-old black man shot 19 times by street crimes unit officers.

Thus, although it is difficult to identify the concrete elements of the 'policy' of ZTP (since this, in many senses, was a media invention), the key elements of 'quality of life' policing in New York (which came to be (mis)labelled 'zero tolerance') were:

- vigorous law-enforcement responses to minor crime and disorder;
- the use of civil remedies against those perceived to be involved in criminal activities;
- enhanced accountability, using Compstat, of local police managers for crime and disorder in their areas;
- public target-setting in relation to crime reduction;
- conspicuous use of the media as a public relations tool on behalf of the police and policing strategies; and
- aggressive action against street crimes.

Those areas in the UK that did introduce policing initiatives that became associated with zero tolerance employed at least some of the elements that formed 'quality of life' policing in NYC – most particularly the focus on enforcement strategies targeting low-level crime and disorder, and the use of media and public target-setting as a means of highlighting the new strategic approach. In this way the UK policing initiatives that became associated with ZTP to differing degrees all involved enhanced levels of uniform patrol, a more vigorous approach to enforcing the law against minor offences and disorder, a heightened use of 'stop and search', the use of high-profile 'crackdowns' against particular kinds of street offences, all packaged together in a rhetoric that promoted the 'reclaiming' of public spaces for 'decent' and 'law-abiding' people (Dennis and Mallon 1997). Certainly, those who introduced what they termed 'confident policing' in Cleveland themselves saw significant parallels with the New York experience:

> The police's failed and successful initiatives have been surprisingly similar in the two places both in content and timing, to such an extent that William J Bratton . . . thought it worthwhile to pay a visit to Hartlepool to examine police work there.
>
> (Dennis and Mallon 1997: 63)

A core part of this policing strategy involved encouraging high-profile uniform patrols and police targeting of 'anti-social behaviour'. As described by Mallon himself:

> My style of zero tolerance policing didn't stand for locking more people up or reporting more people for summons. What it stood for is intervention. The police shouldn't walk past anything. Whether it be

litter on the pavement, people parking on double yellow lines . . .
Whatever it is, there should be intervention. And intervention by the
police officer should be enough.

(Ray Mallon, personal interview)

In addition, the police actively targeted suspected burglars with a view to 'taking out of circulation' many of the most high-profile offenders locally (Dennis
and Mallon 1998: 69–70). This involved the systematic use of intelligence-led
policing methods such as the cultivation of informants, and increased intelligence feedback from community constables. A key objective was to target stop
and search upon 'known malefactors going about their business at suspicious
times or in suspicious circumstances' (Dennis and Mallon 1997: 71). In a
broader sense, Mallon's noted use of charismatic leadership approaches, and
the mass media, as a more general attempt to increase self-belief and morale
among police officers had strong parallels with Bratton's approach in New
York. Indeed, this was noted by Bratton himself:

> There was a similarity in that [Mallon] was seeking to do a number of
> things. He understood that we were using quality of life offences to
> gather information. He understood that the quality of life enforce-
> ment did bring the cops closer to the legitimate community and he
> also understood strategically that it would be an essential element in
> getting crime down. Many of those engaged in quality of life offences
> were in fact the more significant criminals in a community, and so he
> got it, he understood it, and he also understood the need to publicise
> it, to move toward a tipping point . . . you know he's got the BBC up
> there, he's got all these international TV stations paying to bring me
> over from the United States to spend three days up there with him. He
> got the media big-time, he's a good-looking guy, made major state-
> ments, it was interesting watching what happened to him. He was a
> man before his time.
>
> (Bill Bratton, personal interview)

One can also see broad similarities in the actual policing approaches
deployed in the 'Spotlight' initiative in Scotland. Although, as we have noted,
the then Chief Constable explicitly rejected the term zero tolerance, the focus
of the initiative upon heightened levels of uniformed patrol and the prioritiza-
tion of 'quality of life' offences as part of a strategy both to address fear of crime
and reduce more serious crimes drew explicitly upon the New York experience
in general and the broken windows thesis in particular (Orr 1997). The 1996
Metropolitan Police initiative in Kings Cross, although rather small-scale
and localized, displayed some broad similarity in its emphasis on increased
deployment of uniformed officers to target a range of minor crimes and

disorders (Jones and Newburn 2002b). Later, the Metropolitan Police also became more cautious about using the term zero tolerance, but in the late 1990s presented an account of their 'intelligence-led' crime reduction strategy that explicitly drew upon elements in best practice from New York (Griffiths 1997).

So far as these discrete British experiments were concerned, it certainly seems plausible to argue that a degree of direct policy transfer occurred. In Kings Cross and Strathclyde, those responsible for local policing policy drew directly on policies and practices associated with ZTP or 'quality of life policing' in New York City. Even in Hartlepool, where Mallon's 'positive policing' developed contemporaneously with the reforms in New York, there was clearly an exchange of ideas with senior players in the New York story. However, as we shall argue in greater detail below, there were also some substantial differences between these UK policing initiatives and what was implemented in New York. More importantly, arguably, mainstream British policing remained successfully inoculated against much of what became known as ZTP, and much of the enforcement orientation advocated by Ray Mallon and others was criticized by many senior police officers and rejected by most British police forces.

Policy transfer agents

As we have seen, one of the issues focused upon by political scientists interested in the area of transfer and policy convergence is who is involved in, and helps bring about, policy transfer. It is possible to identify a number of key individuals and organizations that were active in promoting the ideas and practices associated with zero tolerance within the UK. As with the case of privatization of corrections, an important role was played in promoting zero tolerance by what have been referred to as 'policy entrepreneurs' (Kingdon 1995; see Chapter 2). In addition to these individuals, the activities of a number of organizations, notably free market think tanks, were vital in facilitating the spread of ideas about ZTP and 'quality of life' policing.

Policy entrepreneurs

A number of free market think tanks on both sides of the Atlantic were centrally involved in the promotion of 'quality of life' policing, and the ideas that underpin such approaches. In the United States the key player in this regard was the Manhattan Institute; in the UK, it was the Institute of Economic Affairs (IEA) (Wacquant 1999b). On both sides of the Atlantic these major think tanks played a key role in the promotion and dissemination of neo-liberal ideas (Smith 1991; Stone 2000). In relation to crime control they have not only been important in disseminating such ideas domestically, but trans-atlantic ties between these bodies have been centrally implicated in the process of policy transfer. This should not be surprising on one level given, as Stone (2000: 47) argues, 'comparison and lesson-drawing is innate to [the] intellectual endeavours' of think tanks.

In the USA the Manhattan Institute promoted the work of Charles Murray and, subsequently, that of James Q. Wilson and George Kelling. Through its promotion of 'broken windows' and its connections with similar organiza-tions in the UK, the Manhattan Institute also played a central role in the international promulgation of the idea of zero tolerance policing. In terms of its early role, the Manhattan Institute held a series of seminars to promote the 'broken windows' philosophy – George Kelling being a Fellow at the Institute. One of those in attendance at these seminars, and who also received consider-able backing from the Manhattan Institute, was Rudy Giuliani. The Manhattan Institute was a contributor to Giuliani's mayoral campaign (Barrett and Fifield 2000) as well as providing financial support for, and promoting, George Kelling and Catherine Coles' book-length follow-up to the original *Atlantic Monthly* article, *Fixing Broken Windows* (Kelling and Coles 1996). After his period as Commissioner of Police under Giuliani, Bill Bratton became a regular lecturer at Manhattan Institute events and later an international consultant in urban policing. Through seminars at this and other similar organizations like the Heritage Foundation and articles in the Manhattan Institute's house magazine, the *City Journal* (see, for example, Bratton and Andrews 1999), Bratton became the key proselytizer on behalf of 'quality of life' policing (Wacquant 1999b). Myron Magnet, editor of the *City Journal*, described part of its activities in the following way:

> One of the things that we do at the Manhattan Institute, and this is not my department so I'm not quite sure how it's organised, but we go down to South America with Bill Bratton and some of his former lieutenants, and try to help them. And this is not national govern-ments, but this is city governments in various Latin American cities, . . . like Rio, where crime is just off the chart, and try to teach them how to police. And, you know, they're incredibly receptive to it.
>
> (Myron Magnet, personal interview)

Bratton subsequently, through his autobiography (Bratton and Knobler 1998), and widespread travels, took his message around the world, including to the UK primarily at a seminar organized by the IEA in London in 1997.[12] According to David Green, who worked at the IEA at that time, the initial invitation to Bratton did not come about through the organization's contacts with the Manhattan Institute. In fact:

> There was a lunch at the IEA and Conrad Black [the then owner of the *Daily Telegraph* newspaper] was there and he said he'd met this great guy in New York called William Bratton, who'd sorted out the policing. And actually I didn't really know about the New York policing story till that day. That must have been '96 or something. I said why don't you . . ., next time you're in New York ask Bratton if he'll come over, and he did it, funnily. There was no reason why he should have . . . None of us really knew the policing of New York at the time. So that was a coincidence. And then, he gave us his e-mail address and we got his phone number and we made direct contact. He was quite keen to come over, but he'd been doing some visits anyway.
>
> And then he came over and did – we had two or three seminars, lunchtime seminars, evening things and a big conference, which was mainly attended by police, about a hundred and odd people from all over police forces, various police forces in England and Wales, and he was a very impressive guy. He just stood up, walked away from the lectern, stood in the middle of the stage at the front . . . you know, didn't have any notes, just spoke as if he were . . . briefing his chaps before he sent them out on the street. You know there were all these constables, sergeants and inspectors. He was a very impressive person. You could see how he would be an inspirational leader. And I think that had some kind of influence. Ray Mallon also spoke that day.
>
> (David Green, personal interview)

Nevertheless, Bratton himself is very clear about the genesis of the event and the role of the two think tanks in bringing zero tolerance policing to public attention in the UK:

> A sister institution . . . the Manhattan Institute, that puts out a *City Journal* and through that group I came over [to England] with the editor . . . Myron Magnet, and the president of the Manhattan Institute . . . They're both [Manhattan Institute and IEA] conservative think tanks; the Manhattan Institute had significantly influenced a lot of Giuliani's thinking, social and crime policies, and so we were asked to come over. Steve Goldsmith, the mayor of Indianapolis, came over to talk about privatisation of city services; I was asked to speak on crime, and that's how that conference came about, and [the *Zero Tolerance*] book actually.
>
> (Bill Bratton, personal interview)

Such events, and the publications associated with them (Dennis 1997), have been vital in disseminating the idea of zero tolerance policing. Bratton's many well-publicized trips to the UK, including to the event organized by the

IEA in 1997, have all involved the term zero tolerance in some shape or form. The IEA conference, for example, the most highly publicized of all, was organized to coincide with the publication of a short book entitled *Zero Tolerance: Policing a Free Society*, though Bratton commented that he 'did not know that was going to be the title of the book', and in its second edition explicitly sought to distance himself from the term. Indeed, Bratton argues that he never consciously used the term in relation to the strategies adopted by the NYPD under his command:

> The term was used in New York and applied to the issue of police corruption which we had a major problem with, a major scandal back in '93/94, and the use of drugs by police officers. New York City has a zero tolerance policy for use of drugs – [use drugs and] you're fired. Other cities they give you a second chance. So the term zero tolerance was used, to my awareness, in those two arenas . . . I can't find any place where I used it, in terms of writings or speeches. There were seven written strategies put out when we came in – on drugs, youth crime, etc. And I think it may have been used there . . . Did Giuliani possibly use it? Possibly, but I don't have a recollection of hearing him saying it either.
>
> (Bill Bratton, personal interview)

The IEA event garnered significant publicity. According to David Green, it was attended by a number of influential journalists including John Witherow (one-time editor of *The Sunday Times*), Sir David English (editor-in-chief of Associated Newspapers) and Conrad Black (the owner of the *Telegraph* titles). With connections like these, policy entrepreneurs such as the Manhattan Institute and the IEA played a crucial role in generating publicity for the particular brand of policing associated with the crime decline in New York. Almost without exception, articles in the British press subsequent to the IEA event used the term zero tolerance as their preferred means of describing such policing strategies.

Politicians

A key figure in the US story was clearly Rudy Giuliani. It is simply not possible to understand the spreading popularity of the term zero tolerance without considering the career of Rudolph W. Giuliani, Mayor of New York City following his 1993 election. Having failed to beat David Dinkins in the 1989 mayoral election, Giuliani was looking for a way to boost his subsequent campaign. According to one of his biographers (Barrett and Fifield 2000: 289), his first year as Mayor was one of 'uncertain searching, guided by neither party nor ideology', though 'he knew he wanted to make a focused fight against crime the bedrock of his administration'. The quality of life policing strategy, particularly the demonizing of squeegee merchants, became the key element. It was also vital to his re-election four years later. According to Rosen (2000), at some stage late in Giuliani's first term 'the broken windows approach *morphed into zero tolerance*. Giuliani had found a way to promote his campaign for a second term' (emphasis added). Bratton by this stage had lost his job as a result of his own, in Giuliani's eyes, all too successful credit-claiming for the New York miracle. Giuliani played a limited, but important, role in transferring ideas about policing in New York to the UK via his contacts with senior UK politicians. According to Myron Magnet of the Manhattan Institute, Giuliani had direct contacts with Tony Blair on the issue:

> I do know that Mr Blair asked him . . . if you had to choose between increasing the size of the force or instituting Compstat, which would you pick, and unhesitatingly Rudi said Compstat, much to Mr Blair's surprise.
>
> (Myron Magnet, personal interview)

As we argued above, the appropriation and widespread deployment of the term zero tolerance were very much a New Labour strategy. In the narrower arena of crime control both Jack Straw and his one-time Minister of State, Alun Michael, were prominent promoters of zero tolerance. Indeed, this had been noted by Bill Bratton:

> Jack Straw, who when he was the Shadow Home Secretary visited New York in '95, I think it was '95 – or the spring or summer '96 before your general elections here – and I think he was the one responsible for bringing the term back [to England]. They used that rhetoric during their campaign, Labour, when they were coming back into play. It sounds great – zero tolerance – but . . . it's not a phrase I like to be associated with.
>
> (Bill Bratton, personal interview)

Tony Blair, as Leader of the Opposition and Prime Minister, was in some respects the most frequent and most promiscuous user of the term. His usage has generally been broadly focused on giving messages about his own, and his administration's, key attributes; not least the idea that they are 'tough'. We return to this below when considering the *attractiveness* of zero tolerance. For Blair, the power of zero tolerance (and therefore the incentive to use it) are almost entirely symbolic. In this he was not alone for, as we noted earlier, numerous high-profile Conservative politicians also explicitly drew upon the New York exemplar to promote similar changes to policing in Britain. Both Michael Howard and Ann Widdecombe have deployed the zero tolerance rhetoric, and made extensive references to the New York experience in public speeches. Nevertheless, in tracing the growing popularity in the UK of the term zero tolerance it was the rise to power of New Labour that was central. For a centre left party convinced that shedding its previous 'soft on crime' image was vital to electoral success, the potent political rhetoric of zero tolerance was enormously attractive.

Senior police officers

Along with ex-Mayor Giuliani, ex-Commissioner Bratton is the individual most closely associated with zero tolerance policing. As should already be clear, Bratton has been an ardent campaigner on behalf of the 'New York miracle' and how the lessons might be used elsewhere. Following his departure from the NYPD, Bratton spent some years as a consultant, speaking at seminars and addressing senior police officers in countries around the world selling the message of quality of life policing including, as we have seen, events publicized under the banner of zero tolerance. He established his own consultancy and subsequently, in 2000, joined Kroll Associates, the global security consultants, to provide 'public safety-focused administration, training and operational re-engineering and analysis consulting services' worldwide.[13]

In his own words, the New York policing experience during his tenure at the NYPD 'adds up to a textbook on how to police any big city' (Bratton and Andrews 1999: 14). Or, as he summarized it when visiting Britain in 1997: 'The good news is if you can make it in New York City, you can make it anywhere' (Bratton 1997). While many British police officers sought to keep clear blue water between themselves and the rhetoric and substance of zero tolerance policing, the major exception was Ray Mallon of Cleveland Constabulary. According to him, what zero tolerance meant in Hartlepool was 'that the police would "return peace to the streets" by controlling minor situations in the interest of the "decent" and "respectable" citizen' (Dennis and Mallon 1997: 65). Very much like Bratton, but on a much more modest scale, Mallon had both a career and an image to promote. In describing his participation in the zero tolerance seminar hosted by the Institute of Economic Affairs, at which both he and Bratton spoke, Mallon was quite clear about what he was trying to achieve:

> When I went down [to the IEA seminar] I wanted to get people's attention. I was deliberately controversial . . . What I was saying was we can reduce crime, we can save money and we can give people a better quality of life. Now that was basically changing the whole philosophy of policing. Turning it upside down . . . It was incumbent on me to get people's attention, to be controversial . . . We were trying to

sell this . . . The likes of [Tony] Blair, and particularly Michael Howard, were very keen [on the message].

(Ray Mallon, personal interview)

Mallon visited New York during 1996 in order to view policing reforms there, but did not meet with Bratton on that occasion. According to Bratton, Mallon's trip was organized and funded by a television station, the same station that later arranged for Bratton to visit the Cleveland force (after he had left the NYPD):

[That visit] came about as a result of the TV station over here, one of the big TV stations that sponsored a trip by him to the United States. He'd been aware of everything we were doing so they brought him over first-hand to look at it. He met me in New York, and then when Maple and I left the NYPD in '96 again this TV station paid for him and I to come over, spend three days up in Cleveland, then Hartlepool, and be seen with Mallon and talking about what he's doing and its relationship with what is happening in New York. But then in the '80s, particularly the late '80s, you're now starting to move into the problems we had in the '70s and early '80s and we're beginning to now wrestle with those problems and begin to find some solutions, and so I've always argued that you guys are some 10–15 years behind where we are at any given time. And so you can take a look at what we're doing and literally see the future and take what works and what doesn't work, and in the case of New York City, where they're so wary of New York-style policing because of its potential impact on the issue of race, we'll learn from that, what we do wrong, and there's a lot that we did wrong that you can examine and analyse and not do the same thing here. And so the reverse migration really began in the '90s, and then there were a lot of Brits coming over, seemed to be every time I turned around there was someone from Britain knocking on the door, or from Australia or New Zealand, and America had become the big laboratory, and also I think our technology was advancing more quickly than certainly there, and my own sense was that migration reverse was in the late '80s and '90s, and now it's become a flood so impacted by the creation of professional organisations.

(Bill Bratton, personal interview)

On both sides of the Atlantic, there were a number of police officers who played an important role in the 'export' and 'import' of zero tolerance-related ideas. Absolutely crucial to the global dissemination of a particular version of the history of policing in New York in the 1990s has been Bill Bratton.

Through public statements, international visits, and a high-profile auto-biography, *Turnaround: How America's Top Cop Reversed the Crime Epidemic* (Bratton and Knobler 1998), Bratton told and retold the tale of the crime decline in New York City and the central role played by a particular style of policing in 'reversing the crime epidemic'.

Policy transfer processes

There are a number of ways in which one can think about, and analyse, how policy travels. As discussed in Chapter 2, Bennett's (1991) work helpfully begins to examine distinct routes through which policy convergence may occur. He discusses four main routes: *emulation, elite networking, harmonization* and *penetration*. As our discussion so far has illustrated, two aspects of Bennett's framework appear to be applicable in the case of zero tolerance. These are *emulation* and *elite networking*. Emulation involves, as the word implies, direct copying of an idea, policy or programme from another jurisdiction. Elite net-working occurs in circumstances where transnational groups of actors share expertise and information about a common problem.

At the very least it appears that the basis for some form of emulation existed in the mid-1990s. Crucially in this regard, British politicians, criminal justice professionals and policy entrepreneurs made frequent visits to the USA to observe developments there, and often justified the adoption, or pro-motion, of particular policy ideas precisely on what they have observed during such visits. Thus, for example, in 1995, the then Shadow Home Secretary, Jack Straw, visited New York to see for himself the changes taking place. In interview, Bratton confirmed that he had numerous contacts with UK police officers and politicians regarding the policing reforms in New York, and remembered Straw's 1995 visit:

> Yes, he [Straw] came and saw Compstat, did some touring of the neighbourhoods. He came to see me and we spent about an hour and a half up in my office talking ... about Compstat, transferability, replicability, because he was interested in basically making this a major plank in the Labour Party platform.
>
> (Bill Bratton, personal interview)

As we have seen, Jack Straw subsequently made several speeches support-ive of the idea of zero tolerance. Indeed, the list of 'policy tourists' to New York is long and includes in addition to Straw (who went several times): the then Commissioner of the Metropolitan Police, Sir Paul Condon (in 1994); various members of Her Majesty's Inspectorate of Constabulary (in 1995/96); Michael Howard, a contingent from the Metropolitan Police (including the

Deputy Commissioner) and later Alun Michael (all during in 1996); and, more recently, Sir John Stevens and Ann Widdecombe (both in 2000) and Ken Livingstone (in early 2001). One of the Metropolitan Police officers who took part in the 1996 study visit to New York, William Griffiths, later reported that many of the members of the British study team had initially been highly scep-tical about the hype surrounding the New York experience, but the visit con-vinced them that the policing reforms had exerted a major impact on the crime drop (Griffiths 1997: 127–8):

> I was privileged to be part of a study team that visited New York in March 1996 to discover what we in the Met could learn from what can only be described as a stunning performance in crime reduction. It was a compare and contrast exercise . . . We were looking for transfer-ability. While the Met has a lot to offer the world of policing, we accept with due humility that we don't have the monopoly on good ideas . . . We were also sceptical, and spent some time in 'drilling down' and 'lifting stones' type activity to check the veracity of the figures. We were seeking the trick with smoke and mirrors. We did not find one.

Bratton supported this view:

> Shortly thereafter we got a visit from a group from the Metropolitan Police . . . I think they were coming over to do the truth test. In other words, stick the fingers in the holes, see if it was for real, and I think by and large they went back thinking that it was for real.
>   (Bill Bratton, personal interview)

The traffic has been by no means one way. Jack Maple, Bratton's deputy in New York, visited Hartlepool in September 1995, as did Bratton himself in the summer of 1996, returning to Britain for the IEA seminar in 1997. The impact of such visits is hard to doubt, for on most occasions the visitors have returned with, at the very least, some additions to their vocabulary with which to frame and discuss their approach to policy. Thus, Straw's Lewisham speech borrowed heavily from Giuliani's 1993 Mayoral campaign in New York, where the 'broken windows'-inspired approach focused particularly on so-called 'squeegee merchants'. Sir John Stevens visited New York shortly after having been appointed Commissioner of Police. On his return he announced that he was launching a 'zero tolerance' policy to 'sweep homeless people and beggars off London streets' ('Beggars to be swept away', *Observer*, 12 March 2000). Such visits were clearly designed as opportunities 'for the collection of evidence that may form the basis for "emulation": where the policy or practice in another country is employed as an exemplar or model which is then adapted' (Bennett 1991: 221).

The second element of Bennett's (1991) model that may have some relevance to this case is what he calls 'elite networking'. Such networks of policy actors may take different forms and Marsh and Rhodes (1992), looking at the ways in which state and non-state institutions can be linked by reciprocal relations and complex network relations, offer a typology which ranges from highly integrated 'policy communities' to more loosely knit 'issue networks'. In relation to zero tolerance, elite networking contributed in different ways and via different networks. Thus, for example, as well as visits by politicians and civil servants, ideas appear to have been transmitted via a series of international networks of criminal justice professionals – particularly senior police officers. We have already mentioned visits to New York by several high-ranking Metropolitan Police officers and also by HMIC. In addition, NYPD officers visited Hartlepool and Glasgow, both places where some influence could later be found. In interview, Bill Bratton argued that the growth of international policing conferences had facilitated increased policy transfer in a range of areas:

> In the 1970s there were no conferences. Where did you go to learn about anything in the police world? You didn't. You stayed where you were. Parochial. Now you can literally any day of the week find a conference some place in the world on what's going on ... the the influence of National Institute of Justice (NIJ) for example – every time you go to one of their conferences there's literally people from all over attending.
>
> (Bill Bratton, personal interview)

The clearest example of elite networking can be seen in relation to the role of the major neo-liberal think tanks in the spread of ideas about both zero tolerance and privatized corrections. We outlined above the important 'policy entrepreneurship' of think tanks such as the Manhattan Institute and the IEA in the promotion of 'quality of life' policing. The role played by such transatlantic links between think tanks has been highlighted by Wacquant (1999b) as a central factor behind the diffusion of a 'new punitive doxa' that 'originates in Washington and New York City, crosses the Atlantic to root itself in London, and from there stretches its channels and capillaries throughout the continent and beyond'. Beyond the work of these think tanks there was also important networking activity involving senior police officers. As we have seen, several groups of senior Metropolitan Police officers made visits to the NYPD to meet senior officers there, to witness Compstat in action, and to explore other aspects of the department's policing strategies. Once they had left the NYPD, both Bill Bratton and his deputy, John Timoney, made trips to the UK to promote aspects of their approach. Given the amount of contact, and the enormously positive media portrayal of the New York model in the British press, what is the most interesting aspect of the outcome of the networking and emulation activities is the relative absence of impact on British policing generally; that is to say, the relative absence of hard forms of policy transfer.

Limits to policy transfer

In exploring the limits to policy transfer in this arena there are three main points we wish to make. First, despite the evidence of some transatlantic similarity and transfer, there is also considerable evidence of significant divergences and constraints to transfer between the two countries. Second, these continuing differences are, we will argue, related to broader contextual differences between the two countries. Third, and linked to the previous point, it is important to focus on the agency of key political actors in actively resisting transfer in this sphere.

Policy differences

As we have argued above, despite the clear borrowing of elements of the New York experience in a number of high-profile policing initiatives in the UK in the late 1990s, these initiatives were usually rather isolated and localized. On the whole, in fact, there has been considerable resistance to New York-style policing reforms among senior British police officers. For example, the then Chief Constable of Thames Valley Police, Charles Pollard, authored a chapter in the 1997 IEA publication, *Zero Tolerance: Policing a Free Society*, that provided a strong critique of such policing approaches and argued that they would not be applicable in the British context. Although there has continued to be much discussion of ZTP strategies being imported from the USA, in reality there is little evidence of widespread adoption of such policing policies in the UK. The resistance to such approaches has been due in part to sound historical reasons. In the early 1980s the civil disturbances that occurred in Brixton in South London had been sparked by an aggressive policing operation, Swamp 81, which shared many characteristics with what we might think of as zero tolerance policing. The aftermath of the riots led not only to the Scarman Inquiry and Report but also to some rethinking of policing in mainland Britain. A consensus emerged within British policing that the tactics that had been employed in Brixton were in all but the most extreme cases likely to be counterproductive, leading to the alienation of the local community at best and to violent confrontation at worst. As a result, the 'dominant philosophy of the police role among chief constables [became] a broad community-oriented one' (Reiner, 1991: 114). By the time talk of zero tolerance reached British shores in the mid-1990s, most senior police officers were extremely reluctant to be seen to be advocating tactics associated with pre-Scarmanite policing

(Pollard 1997). Charles Pollard (1997: 58) offers his own particular take on this, contrasting British community policing with enforcement-oriented ZTP:

> The significance of our different policing traditions is that, in a limited sense, 'Zero Tolerance' has always been part of the English policing tradition . . . 'Zero Tolerance' in New York suggests tackling low-level disorder and incivilities, albeit through a narrow, aggressive and uncompromising law enforcement approach. Tackling 'broken windows' is something that has always happened in English policing : it is just that we use a different way of explaining it. In England it is enshrined in the concept of 'the bobby on the beat'.

In Bill Bratton's view, the reluctance in the UK was more directly linked to the politics of the policing of street crime and, more particularly, the politics of race:

> There is a big aversion to [zero tolerance policing in the UK]. I think a lot of it has to do with the belief that they just don't have enough time, and they've come to believe that, and you can't shake them in that belief, and two, the whole race issue is driving that aversion because they just feel they're going to get into trouble. They also believe that a lot of what people want addressed involve minorities as far as street activity, and you've got those compounding issues that they've not been able to make the leap that we made in the United States. I just don't know enough about all forty-three police agencies. Some have embraced it more than others . . . Ray Mallon, his chief constable was letting him move very strongly in that direction. But I think also when Mallon got jammed up that was an excuse for most of them to, aha, see, we don't want to touch that.
>
> (Bill Bratton, personal interview)

Thus, although there have been one or two minor and conspicuous exceptions, police forces in Britain have largely rejected both the terminology and the practices associated with zero tolerance. The central point is this. On the surface a plausible argument can be made that zero tolerance policing is another example of policy convergence in US and UK crime control. However, on closer inspection not only did the nature of the relationships between the various streams of influence vary on the two sides of the Atlantic but, and not surprisingly, the substantive policy outcomes were also different. More particularly, the strategies adopted by the New York Police Department, which rightly or wrongly have come to be associated with the term zero tolerance, have not been visible in other than very minor experiments in mainstream British policing. Even where there have been more apparent elements of policy transfer, in the Metropolitan Police and in Cleveland, arguably only elements of the NYC experience crossed the Atlantic. As noted earlier, the programme of policing initiatives that were introduced in New York City during the 1990s went far beyond targeting minor crimes and disorder and enhanced uniform patrol. Although the Metropolitan Police, Strathclyde and Cleveland initiatives certainly did draw upon one or two elements of the New York programmes, important points of contrast must also be noted. The first concerns the scale of what was done. There was nowhere near the same increase in police staffing resources as occurred in New York. Second, the UK initiatives did not employ civil law remedies in the same way, nor were they driven by a management-information process at the level of Compstat.[14]

To argue that the policies and programmes that developed in New York City in the 1990s were not straightforwardly imported wholesale into the UK is not, of course, meant to imply that some of the broader notions that informed the New York programmes have not been influential. On the contrary, the ideas have been enormously influential but in complex ways that go beyond the notion of policy transfer. As we have noted, the ideas associated with 'broken windows' in general, and in particular the concern with 'anti-social' behaviour, have become a cornerstone of New Labour policy. However, they have been applied in different ways in the UK. In particular, the creation of new forms of patrol provision[15] – often explicitly tasked to deal with public reassurance and relatively minor disorder in order to free up sworn police officers to deal with more serious problems – is an important point of departure from the New York approach, though clearly inspired by similar ideas. The principle of using civil law approaches as part of a broader crime and disorder control strategy has also emerged in Britain, but in a very different form from that which developed in New York. The use of anti-social behaviour orders (ASBOs) in the UK has been a central feature of anti-crime policy under New Labour, but contrasts in a number of important ways with the approaches adopted in New York during the 1990s. Similarly, although we argued above that nothing comparable to the Compstat process existed in British police forces during the 1990s, in recent years there has clearly been growing pressure from central government upon the police service to follow a rigorous, nationally shaped performance management framework. This has seen considerable investment in technology and staff in the sphere of internal management auditing, and in many forces regular performance reviews of geographical and functional divisions by senior officers, based upon regularly updated and increasingly sophisticated management information. More particularly, the emergence from within the police service of the National Intelligence Model has further increased the emphasis on information-led performance management. Within NIM the 'tasking and coordinating meeting', which operates at various levels, is a forum within which intelligence can be shared and resources allocated. Some of the principles underpinning such meetings are similar to those underpinning Compstat (Moore 2003), though the actual practices involved are far from identical.

Although points of convergence can no doubt be found, a number of long-standing points of departure continue to exist in the policing systems of the United States and the UK (Jones and Newburn 2002a). This suggests that what has been happening in policing cannot be simply presented as policy transfer. At the same time, we should take note of Dixon's (2005) argument that there remains 'considerable danger that we may complacently dismiss zero tolerance, while allowing ourselves to shuffle crab fashion into something much more significant'.

Political institutions and cultures

We have outlined in the previous two chapters how specific national, and sub-national, differences in political and legal institutions and cultures provide important constraints on policy transfer. These are also apparent in the story of zero tolerance. One key contrast here relates to the particular constitutional position of the police in Britain as compared with large American cities such as New York, and how this has traditionally provided a buffer against popular political pressures over policing policy. One of the distinctive features of the constitutional position of the police in Britain is the doctrine of 'constabulary independence' (Lustgarten 1986; Walker 2000; Jones 2003). Although this has been subject to considerable legal and political critiques, and undoubtedly has been eroded in important ways over recent years, it remains the case that senior police officers in Britain still retain a good deal of autonomy in policy-making when compared to their counterparts in many US big city forces. By contrast, in cities such as New York, the Police Commissioner is a political appointment of the Mayor, and is responsible to the Mayor (and by extension, the political process) in a way that is far more direct than has ever been the case in the UK. Thus, when Rudolph Giuliani was elected, he acted to bring William Bratton in as Police Commissioner. The change in political regime also resulted in a total change in the senior management of the NYPD, as Bratton largely brought in his own management team (with the agreement of Giuliani) (Bratton and Andrews 1999). Equally, when differences between Bratton and Giuliani arose, the latter was able to remove the former from post in a way that would be impossible in the UK. This is a key contextual difference that has allowed senior British police officers to resist some of the policy changes that national and local politicians have promoted. This difference was underlined in an interview with former Home Secretary Michael Howard, one of the high-level 'policy tourists' who visited New York City and subsequently stated strong support for similar developments in the UK. Mr Howard high-lighted the fact that, although he was impressed by Compstat, he did not feel he could direct police forces in the UK to adopt it because this would be interfering in the operational independence of police forces. When asked if he had considered promoting the use of Compstat in the UK, he replied:

> I thought about it. But it was quite difficult territory, because first of all I was fighting a lot of battles at the time. I was wary about adding more to my list of battles and of course that was something which was arguably operational policing. So, there were limits on the extent to which I could really get involved.
>
> (Michael Howard, personal interview)

There are further important contrasts between the USA and the UK in terms of the broader context of policing concerning in particular the place of law in regulating policing, and the nature of the crime problems being faced by the police. In this regard, Dixon's (2005) contrast between policing in many parts of Australia and that in New York also applies to comparisons with Britain. First, as Dixon points out, police in New York were traditionally relatively constrained by the 'legalistic, rights-oriented' culture (Dixon 2005: 488), and street policing was subject to significant constitutional limits. In Australia, by contrast, widely defined street offences provide an extensive resource for much everyday policing, to such an extent that they have been the 'bread and butter of Australian policing' (Dixon 2005: 488). We would argue that this US/Australian contrast applies in a similar way to that between the USA and the UK. The second point of contrast highlighted by Dixon also applies to the UK: that is, the very different levels and patterns of criminal offending faced by the police in New York compared to their counterparts in Sydney also apply in some respects to London. In particular, the contrasts in levels of gun ownership and gun crime and to particular features of the drugs markets, arguably heightened the initial pay-off for highly intensive saturation policing operations in a way that would not apply in Britain (Hayes 1998).

Political agency

Of course, it is not sufficient for wider contextual structures and cultures to provide constraints on policy transfer. A necessary condition for successful resistance or reworking of ideas is the political agency of key actors within the policy network. In this sense, the resistance of senior police officers has been important. It is certainly the case that some high-profile supporters of 'quality of life' policing approaches perceived strong elements of antagonism towards them among the senior British police establishment. In interview, Bill Bratton referred to what he called 'a big aversion' to this form of policing in Britain, mainly because of concerns about antagonising ethnic minorities and broader worries about devoting police time to minor offences and disorder. In Bratton's view, a combination of professional jealousy and disagreement with the methods advocated by Ray Mallon eventually led to Mallon's fall from grace:

> I think it was a combination of being resentful of him but also fearful of what he was advocating. It runs counter to anything I think the Chief Constables, Superintendents or the union that represents the cops actually want the cops to do. That it's almost beneath them . . .
> (Bill Bratton, personal interview)

We should here take note of the considerable influence that has tradition-ally been exerted, and arguably continues to be, by the police service in Britain within criminal justice policy networks. In particular, the past twenty years have seen senior police officers increasingly operating as a highly effective lobbying body (Jones *et al.* 1994; Savage *et al.* 2000), significantly enhancing the ability of this particular stakeholder group to exercise leverage with government. In the past decade or so, government ministers of both major parties have increasingly viewed this level of influence as a block to effective reform. Several of the senior officers who participated in the original IEA con-ference that first promoted zero tolerance in Britain were generally reticent to embrace both the terminology and the implications for policing practice implied by the term. The title of the presentation that day by Charles Pollard, the then Chief Constable of Thames Valley – 'Zero tolerance: short-term fix, long-term liability?' – indicates the degree of his scepticism. Pollard (1997: 61) contrasted the New York approach with 'problem-oriented policing' – his preferred model for his force – and argued that:

> [T]hat part of the 'zero tolerance' principle characterised by aggressive policing, confrontational management, opportunistic short-termism and undue emphasis on the numbers game poses an enormous threat to the future. If this culture is not tackled, then – on the basis of the British experience – the risk of serious corruption and inner-city disorder in the future is real.

Similarly, William Griffiths, then a Commander in the Metropolitan Police, concluded his examination of the New York experience and its implications for the policing of London by contrasting it, like Pollard, with another policing model – this time, 'intelligence-led policing'. His resounding conclu-sion (Griffiths 1997: 136):

> We should all be proud of the enduring magnificence of a policing system that was laid down in the late 1820s and which sees its renais-sance in the late 1990s as intelligence-led crime reduction in partner-ship with the community. 'Zero tolerance' does not do it justice!

These views, we would argue, were broadly typical of the reactions of senior officers more generally in the UK. More recently, while Deputy Commissioner of the Metropolitan Police, Ian Blair (Blair 2002: 22) argued that, 'normally liberal New Yorkers and their media were prepared [in the 1990s] for policing tactics that would not be acceptable in London or anywhere else in the UK. Zero tolerance is a misnomer: it actually means targeted intolerance, and New York's finest did not always tread lightly.'

'Broken windows' and the anti-social behaviour agenda

Although we have argued that there is relatively little evidence of direct *policy transfer* in relation to so-called zero tolerance policing, it does seem to us that one of the sets of ideas associated with, and arguably underpinning, the policing practices adopted in New York in the mid-1990s did have a more profound effect on British penal landscape: 'broken windows'. The Wilson and Kelling article, originally published in *Atlantic Monthly* in 1982, was a significant influence on Bratton when he was Commissioner of the Boston Police Department and George Kelling remained a key adviser during his subsequent stints heading up the Transit Police initially and later the NYPD. For Bratton, 'Kelling articulated and put into beautiful words what I had found from experience. I supported what he wrote because I had already lived it . . . We began to apply [the ideas] to crime in the subways. Fare evasion was the biggest broken window in the transit system. We were going to fix that window and see to it that it didn't get broken again' (Bratton and Knobler 1998: 138–9, 152).

Though British politicians of all hues visited New York to examine the causes and consequences of the crime decline, not least in the policing context, rarely did they return with the message that British policing needed to be reformed along New York lines. Rather, as we have argued, they returned with the new terminology of zero tolerance and, in the case of New Labour in particular, began to deploy such language with regularity in a variety of forums. The other element of lesson-drawing that occurred was in relation to the relatively straightforward message of 'broken windows' – along the lines outlined by Bratton above. In this context, the following exchange in 1998 (*Hansard*, 21 July 1998) in the House of Commons between the Home Secretary, Jack Straw, and a senior Conservative MP, Sir Norman Fowler, is instructive:

> **Mr Straw:** Zero tolerance is a matter for individual police forces. Interestingly, 'Reducing Offending' [a Home Office research study], a copy of which is in the Vote Office, discusses the issue, and what the research suggests. It says that there is 'moderately strong evidence that it can reduce serious crime in the short term', but that there are 'large question marks over the ability of the police to distinguish

between firm and harsh policing styles'. It adds that 'zero-tolerance may offer an attractive short-term reduction in crime, but . . . it must also be evaluated against its long-term effects on those arrested, and the communities from which they come'. 'Zero tolerance' is a phrase which is used differently in different contexts–

Sir Norman Fowler: Including by the Home Secretary.

Mr Straw: Of course. It is not a particularly scientific term, and I am not sure whether 'Reducing Offending' uses it in the context in which I would use it. What I am clear about – and the evidence supports this – is that effective police action against small crimes can stop large-scale crime developing. The research evidence for that is striking. It shows – I am happy to concede that the research was carried out under the last Administration – that there is a four times greater chance of people becoming victims of serious crimes of violence in areas of incivility where small crimes are ignored, than in areas of civility.

This relatively simple message – that tackling low-level crime, or even behaviour that is offensive even if not criminal, is important in reducing crime – has shaped a very considerable element of New Labour's criminal justice and social policy. That this was likely to be so was visible in some of the earliest discussion documents issued by New Labour prior to coming to power. The 1996 discussion document, *Tackling the Causes of Crime* (Labour Party 1996), begins:

> The rising tide of disorder is blighting our streets, neighbourhoods, parks, town and city centres. Incivility and harassment, public drunkenness, graffiti and vandalism all affect our ability to use open spaces and enjoy a quiet life in our own homes. Moreover, crime and disorder are linked. Disorder can lead to a vicious circle of community decline in which those who are able to move away do so, whilst those who remain learn to avoid certain streets and parks. This leads to a breakdown in community ties and a reduction in natural social controls tipping an area further into decline, economic dislocation and crime.

It was this, eventually, that morphed into New Labour's 'anti-social behaviour agenda'. Though anti-social behaviour was discussed in the very early Labour documents in the lead-up to the 1997 general election, the focus at that stage was still primarily on the criminal justice system, and criminal sanctions, as a means of tackling crime. Thus, the 1998 Crime and Disorder Act not only overhauled the youth justice system but introduced a raft of new criminal measures including parenting orders, child safety orders and curfew orders. Most controversially, the Act also introduced Anti-Social Behaviour Orders

(ASBOs). At the consultation stage these had been referred to as 'community safety orders' (Newburn 1998) and were designed to tackle 'anti-social behaviour [which] causes distress and misery to innocent, law-abiding people – and undermines the communities in which they live'. Though controversial even at this early stage – largely because they are civil orders that, when breached, result in criminal proceedings (Gardner *et al.* 1998) – ASBOs were less obviously at the forefront of Labour's programme than has subsequently become the case. Since this moment, however, disorderliness, incivilities and anti-social behaviour have emerged to occupy a place at the forefront of the government's policing and crime agendas. New legislation and new initiatives, most notably the Anti-Social Behaviour Act 2003, have extended governmental reach over youthful conduct and, more recently, the idea of 'baby ASBOs' – extending such order to the under-10s – has even been mooted by the Prime Minister.

Indeed, once again, it is Tony Blair who was most closely associated with developments in this area. Just as the use of Americanized rhetoric such as zero tolerance; and 'three strikes and you're out' was used by Blair more often than any other British politician, so the influence of conservative American criminology has arguably been more obvious in Blair's pronouncements than in those of any other politician – with the possible exception of Michael Howard in the early 1990s. A particular reading of the 'broken windows' thesis infuses much of Blair's vision of crime and disorder. In an interview in the *Daily Express* in December 2000, Prime Minister Blair outlined his version of these ideas:

> If you are tolerant of small crimes, and I mean vandalism and the graffiti at the end of the street, you create an environment in which pretty soon the drug dealers move in, and then after that the violent people with their knives and their guns and all the rest of it, and the community is wrecked.
>
> (Quoted in Young 2003: 41)

Jock Young, in commenting on the excerpt from Blair's article, goes on to say that he is not suggesting that either Jack Straw or Tony Blair had any direct acquaintance with commentators like James Q. Wilson, George Kelling, Charles Murray or others, merely 'that it is the ideas of such thinkers filtered through the lenses of policy advisers and speech-writers that greatly influenced New Labour's policy on law and order' (2003: 41). In large part he is undoubtedly correct in this observation. However, via the Manhattan Institute, and through contacts with Bratton, Giuliani and the NYPD, ideas associated with broken windows were also diffused in a fairly direct manner. George Kelling's contacts with British politicians and policy-makers were themselves fairly extensive:

I didn't meet the Majors, but I was at 10 Downing Street to meet with [John Major's] staff on one occasion. I know that the current Home Secretary [David Blunkett] has visited; he was scheduled to come to the Manhattan Institute right after 9/11. He had to cancel and then one day about a month ago I got a call from the BBC saying that the Home Secretary had announced that he was going to come over and visit me. It came as a surprise and last week I met with the Shadow Home Secretary [David Davis] and I'm going over for the Association of Centre City Town, Centre Town Managers (sic) in early May. Also . . . the National Institute of Justice funded a project to bring members of the Royal Ulster Constabulary here. I lectured to them and the word got back about that and a group of Northern Ireland politicians came over about two or three months ago and I spent two days with them and I'm going back to Northern Ireland in early May, again to meet with those local politicians in terms of the implementation of the Patten report . . . at the same time I had the Ray Mallon debate, I was involved with a session that included the number two man from Scotland Yard [Ian Blair].

(George Kelling, personal interview)

In whatever way it occurred, it is clear that Wilson and Kelling's broken windows article, or at least some ideas drawn from it, has been one of the most important sources of influence in shaping British criminal justice policy in the past decade. Though there has been considerable talk of zero tolerance, day-to-day British policing has been little affected by the policies and practices of the NYPD under Giuliani and Bratton. By and large senior British police officers have been reluctant to adopt what at least are perceived to be the fairly heavy-handed crackdown tactics used by the NYPD at certain stages during the 1990s or, indeed, to embrace Compstat-style managerial systems, at least in its more extreme early form – associated with Jack Maple (Maple 1999). Indeed, with a few exceptions, senior British police officers have also tended to eschew the language of zero tolerance. Rather, it has been politicians, particularly senior New Labour politicians, who appear to have found the zero tolerance rhetoric most attractive. The tactics, policies and practices associated with New York policing have not, by and large, been pursued by British politicians in their attempts at reform of domestic policing. The greatest American influence in this area, as we have suggested, is to be found in the ideas drawn from 'broken windows' – most particularly the sense that relatively minor forms of misbehaviour and misconduct will, if untended, lead to other, more serious consequences. This relatively straightforward notion underpinned the introduction of a range of measures – curfews, ASBOs, parenting orders, changes to tenancy rules and eviction regulations – all aimed at tackling what is now collectively described as 'anti-social behaviour'. The rationale for such activity was most clearly summed up in the introduction to the 2003 White Paper, *Respect and Responsibility: Taking a Stand Against Anti-Social Behaviour:*

> The anti-social behaviour of a few damages the lives of many. We should never underestimate its impact. We have seen the way communities spiral downwards once windows get broken and are not fixed, graffiti spreads and stays there, cars are left abandoned, streets get grimier and dirtier, youths hang around street corners intimidating the elderly. The result: crime increases, fear goes up and people feel trapped.
>
> (Home Office 2003b)

Zero tolerance and policy transfer

One of the most interesting aspects of the recent history of so-called zero tolerance policing is that this is arguably the area of criminal justice (at least of those we have been studying) where the greatest amount of activity associated with the potential for policy transfer has occurred but where, at least in the policing arena, there is actually only limited evidence of direct transfer of concrete policies or practices. Thus, for example, in the second half of the 1990s there was an almost incessant flow of politicians and policy-makers making their way to New York to observe aspects of policing in the city and to meet with the major figures publicly associated with the crime drop. The list includes Tony Blair, Jack Straw, Michael Howard, Ann Widdecombe, Ken Livingstone, Sir John Stevens, Ian Blair and other senior members of the Metropolitan Police, as well as representatives of other political parties and other police forces. Similarly, the key figures in New York – Rudy Giuliani, Bill Bratton, John Timoney, Jack Maple and George Kelling – also made visits to the UK, to speak about, and in some cases proselytize on behalf of, the New York success story. Moreover, they were aided and abetted in this task by pressure groups and think tanks, not least the Manhattan Institute and its associate, the Institute for Economic Affairs, in publicizing their message. And yet British policing has remained largely resistant to much of the New York message. Senior police officers, the majority of whom embraced a post-Scarman report, community policing-oriented consensus (Reiner 1991), found the more abrasive elements of zero tolerance not to their liking. Though there have been one or two minor and conspicuous exceptions, police forces in Britain have rejected both the terminology and the practices associated with zero tolerance. Even in the most conspicuous exception to this pattern, the policing initiative conducted under Detective Chief Inspector Ray Mallon in Hartlepool that embraced the idea of zero tolerance, there is relatively little evidence of 'hard' policy transfer. Mallon argued that what he was doing was happening at much the same time as the New York experiment under Giuliani and Bratton, and the timing largely supports this. He undoubtedly garnered considerably more publicity for his activities because of the New York story, but there is little evidence of direct emulation.

By contrast with the general reluctance to embrace policies and practices associated with zero tolerance policing, the terminology of zero tolerance became widespread and, indeed, eventually found its way beyond the sphere of crime control and policing. Thus, to the extent that anything directly crossed the Atlantic it was terminology and ideas (if we incorporate 'broken windows' into the broader sphere of influence) rather than policies and practices. The phrase 'zero tolerance' proved to be particularly popular with politicians and, though less so today, is still occasionally wheeled out when particular figures are seeking to emphasize their 'toughness' in the law and order arena. There is something of an irony in this, for not only was the term zero tolerance not generally used in the USA but it was perceived by many to be problematic. According to Bill Bratton (1997: 42): 'While the phrase [zero tolerance] is used more widely in Britain than in the United States, it has gained some currency there as well. The phrase is troublesome' (Bratton 1997: 42). Similarly, George Kelling (1998: 10) has argued that zero tolerance is significantly different from 'broken windows'. First, 'it denies the complexity of police work and that officers use discretion . . . [Second] zero tolerance implies zealotry'. It is not, he suggests, that the ideas in 'broken windows' imply that certain forms of crime and anti-social behaviour can be eradicated. Rather, 'all that we can really achieve is to ensure that such activities are conducted in ways that do not disrupt communities or lead to serious crime'. Indeed, it is what the term symbolizes, he argues, that helps explain its power and its continuation with NYC:

> I never used it, Bratton used it once when he referred to corruption. Giuliani used it sparingly and finally focused on . . . the term 'quality of life' . . . But I think zero tolerance gained currency because it was liked by both the Left and the Right. I think the Left liked it because it portrayed zealotry . . . and I think the Right liked it because it portrayed getting tough.
>
> (George Kelling, personal interview)

It is this attractiveness to both Left and Right on the political spectrum, or its usefulness in political circumstances where the old differences between Left and Right have very considerably diminished, if not disappeared, that lies behind the popularity of the term zero tolerance in the UK (and elsewhere), though its usage is far from unproblematic:

> I mean, I think the problem with zero tolerance is it means different

things to different people. And, you know, to some people zero tolerance means you have zero crime which is patent nonsense. You know,
I mean, we have zero tolerance of murder in this country but we still
have murders. So, I mean, other people thought zero tolerance was,
you know, sort of fining people who dropped a sweet wrapper or
something. Other people saw it through the sort of social side, the
mending broken windows side of the New York experiment, and saw
zero tolerance as wiping off the graffiti as soon as it appeared. And
everybody had different ideas of what zero tolerance meant. And so in
retrospect I rather regret using the term.

(Ann Widdecombe, personal interview)

Although the bulk of the policy transfer literature examines the extent to
which practices and policies are copied, more or less faithfully, from one jurisdiction to another, this particular example illustrates the possibility that it is
actually rhetoric and terminology that travels most easily and, below this surface similarity, local cultural and political differences may work against any
simple or lasting transfer of substantive practices. Thus, although there were a
few small-scale policing experiments that borrowed the terminology of zero
tolerance, in practice, the more extreme 'crackdown' form of policing strategy
was generally eschewed by British police forces. Indeed, given what has been
described as the post-Scarman consensus in British policing (Reiner 1991), it is
entirely predictable that senior officers should have been reticent to embrace
the styles and strategies associated with zero tolerance policing. However, a
more general look at criminal justice policy during the past decade suggests
that although British policing has not been significantly affected by political
interest in the New York experience, the rise of New Labour's 'anti-social
behaviour agenda' does owe something to North American ideas and practices, most particularly to Wilson and Kelling's 'broken windows' thesis.
Indeed, part of the popularity of the 'broken windows' thesis in Britain lies not
simply in the arguments it presents, and the degree of fit it enjoys with current political ideas, but in its association with the crime drop in New York and
therefore with so-called zero tolerance policing.

6 Policy transfer in crime control

In this final chapter we draw general conclusions about the nature and impact of policy transfer between the USA and the UK in the field of criminal justice and penal policy during the 1990s. In particular, we return to the issues outlined in the first chapter concerning how this empirical exploration of policy transfer speaks to wider debates about convergence and divergence in criminal justice and penal policy. The chapter is divided into four main sections. We begin by reviewing our three case studies of policy change, examining and assessing the evidence of policy transfer from the USA and, to the extent that such processes appear to have occurred, considering what was transferred, in what ways and by whom. There is evidence of policy transfer from the USA, in some form, in each of the areas under consideration (although this was of a very indirect form in one of the policy areas). In general, transfer occurred primarily at the level of policy ideas, symbols and labels, although this varied between policy areas. There was less evidence of substantive transfers in terms of concrete manifestations of policy such as policy content, instruments and institutions. In the second section we move on to consider the limits to policy transfer and we focus in particular upon two features of the policy process highlighted in this study. The first is the key influence exerted by domestic political and legal institutional contexts upon policy outcomes, and the second concerns the agency of political actors working within these contexts. In the third section we return to the discussion of the broader issues of convergence and divergence in criminal justice, and locate our discussion of policy transfer within broader accounts of structural and cultural change. The final section considers priorities for future research in the study of policy transfer and lesson drawing in particular, and comparative criminal justice policy making more generally.

Learning from Uncle Sam: policy transfer from the USA

Establishing policy transfer

As we outlined at the start of this book, we have explored the notion of policy transfer from the USA by undertaking detailed case histories of policy change in some key areas that have been widely associated with US developments. These included the emergence of a significant commercial corrections sector in the UK, the development of mandatory minimum sentencing and, finally, the appearance of policing initiatives associated with 'zero tolerance' during the 1990s. We chose these areas precisely because they have been widely presented – in academic, media and political discourse – as key examples of US exports in criminal justice and penal policy, and as examples of a broader process of 'Americanization' of British crime control. In each of these cases, we examined the degree of policy convergence between the USA and the UK and, as far as there was convergence, explored the extent to which this was explained by policy transfer and analysed the nature of such processes. In all three cases under consideration, the timescale of policy development on both sides of the Atlantic was consistent with a hypothesis of transfer from the USA, with the policies under consideration emerging first in the USA and then subsequently in the UK. In each of the areas we found that there was sufficient broad similarity in terms of policy ideas, content and instruments to support the contention that cross-national transfer was involved in some way. However, on closer examination only two of these areas provided clear evidence of policy transfer from the USA, at least in terms of more concrete policies and practices that could clearly be linked with developments in the USA. In the cases of ZTP and commercialized corrections, to differing degrees we found that the key policy actors who promoted developments in UK policy in each of these specific areas drew upon US exemplars, and US evidence of some kind was used to inform subsequent policy formulation in the UK. To varying extents, we identified processes and mechanisms through which this cross-national lesson-drawing occurred. In the case of mandatory minimum sentencing, however, we found no direct evidence of US experiences being drawn upon in the UK policy process and, in its initial form at least, no direct importation of US terminology and rhetoric surrounding 'three strikes'. The only evidence of conscious policy transfer in this area was in the general and 'soft' sense of the policy being linked in a broad way to US-inspired ideas about the use of imprisonment as a crime reduction tool.

The strongest example of policy transfer in our study occurred in the arena of the commercialization of corrections. Initial UK advocates of increased commercial involvement in the penal system explicitly highlighted US developments as exemplars, and in terms of the more substantive dimensions of policy (content and instruments), the USA provided the bedrock of experience upon which UK developments were built. This is not to say that US systems of contracting-out of prisons or electronic monitoring of offenders were simply imported wholesale from the USA – they clearly were not. However, there was evidence of a relatively concerted attempt at policy learning from specific developments in the USA by politicians and officials, who visited the USA to find out more about commercially run prisons and electronic monitoring systems, and subsequently used this information in the formulation of policy in the UK. Furthermore, given the lack of similar developments anywhere else in the world, it is perhaps unsurprising that US corrections corporations were directly involved in the consortia that bid for initial contracts in the penal sector, suggesting again a relatively direct form of influence. As such, privatization of corrections provides a contrast with the experiences in the sentencing and policing fields that we also examined.

Unlike other areas of public policy, where the Conservative administrations enthusiastically and explicitly championed their free market reforms, the promotion of privatization in the penal system by senior politicians was rather conspicuous by its absence. It was introduced, not as a central plank of a new government reform programme, but almost as an afterthought. According to the accounts of some senior government ministers at that time, this may have been related to concerns about likely opposition to the suggested reforms and the possibility of industrial action by the Prison Officers' Association. However, although there was initial parliamentary opposition, and strong campaigning by penal reform groups against the principles of commercial involvement in this sphere, this opposition proved rather temporary and ineffective – so much so that by the late 1990s, commercial involvement had become an accepted feature of the penal landscape in the UK. Even penal reform group representatives conceded that, in many ways, commercial involvement had improved the prison system in the UK. In terms of immediate practical impacts, it seems that privatization of corrections was a policy that both had considerable substance (in terms of the content and instruments that were transferred) and went on to have a very significant impact on the penal system in the UK. We discuss below the subsequent divergences in policy from the USA, but it appears clear that there was some evidence of both 'soft' transfer (in terms of the initial ideas and principles) and 'hard' transfer (in terms of the actual nuts and bolts of policy) from the USA in the field of commercial corrections.

The second case in which there was some evidence of policy transfer concerned 'zero tolerance policing'. It is clear that there was extensive transatlantic contact connected with these policy developments. This included visits to New York City by civil servants, politicians and police officers from the UK with the explicit aim of observing and drawing lessons from policing approaches in the NYPD. In addition, there were trips to the UK by key US players such as Bill Bratton who spoke with senior police officers and politicians about his experiences as Commissioner of Police in New York, and Rudy

Giuliani around whom British ideas of zero tolerance and crime in New York appear in many ways to have coalesced. Out of the three areas we considered in this study, it is the arena of ZTP where there appears to have been the most extensive and explicit effort to draw upon US experiences in order to inform policy development in the UK. Furthermore, it is the area in which US-based 'policy entrepreneurs' – primarily Bratton and Giuliani – were most energetic in trying to export their policy ideas and innovations from the USA to the UK (and elsewhere). Despite this, however, in terms of the more practical manifestations of policy there has been little substantive impact on British policing, other than in a few isolated examples of initiatives in particular forces. In particular, the most high-profile British policing development associated with ZTP developed in Cleveland almost simultaneously with the emergence of quality of life policing in New York City. Overall then, this is an area where, at least in relation to particular *policing* policy developments, there was more symbol than substance in what made its way across the Atlantic. However, what was imported from the USA was the tough-sounding terminology and rhetoric that proved highly attractive to politicians and, much less frequently, senior police officers. Furthermore, there was clear evidence of 'soft transfer' in the basic ideas and principles associated with the 'broken windows' approach that went on to be enormously influential in UK crime control beyond the domain of policing.

The third area under consideration, mandatory minimum sentencing (and the proposals on 'honesty in sentencing') provides us with something of a conundrum. As Chapter 4 demonstrated, although widely perceived as a US-inspired development, there is much less evidence of US influence in this area than in the other two cases. Although the timing of policy change in the USA and the UK was consistent with the possibility of policy transfer, we found no evidence that officials or politicians drew upon particular US exemplars of sentencing policy to inform developments in the UK. Unlike both commercialized corrections and ZTP, there were no study visits to the USA by policy-makers and practitioners to observe and learn from developments there. The main architect of these sentencing reforms in the UK, Michael Howard, reported that he came to support these ideas largely independently of developments in the USA. The fact of the existence of mandatory minimums was helpful to him in putting his own ideas into practice, but such a degree of influence falls a long way short of direct transfer or emulation. The connection with the USA in this area is therefore a much more tenuous one than exists in the other policy areas. Michael Howard was certainly influenced in a broader sense by the writings of US neo-conservatives such as Charles Murray, and this strengthened his beliefs about the use of increased imprisonment as a crime reduction tool. However, within the particular arena of mandatory minimum sentencing and restricted parole, there appeared to be very limited evidence even of 'soft transfer' from the USA during the initial stages of policy development. This is reflected in the fact that Michael Howard himself never actually used the particular US terminology of 'three strikes and you're out'. This was in stark contrast to Tony Blair, who did make use of such rhetoric, once Labour was in office. In effect, the story of these sentencing reforms is a rather unusual picture of a delayed 'soft' transfer in which the key actor importing symbols and rhetoric from the USA was not the initial architect of the associated policy change in the UK, but the Labour Prime Minister of the succeeding administration.

In this area of policy change, it seems that domestic and European influences – not least political and legal institutions – were particularly important. Despite clear intentions to introduce significant reforms to the sentencing system in England and Wales, Michael Howard was forced – by a combination of the constraints of UK political and legal institutions, the timing of the proposed changes and a well-organized coalition of opposition – to accept a much watered-down version of his original proposals on mandatory sentencing. Furthermore, Howard's 'honesty in sentencing' policies were immediately repealed by the Labour government after its election victory in 1997. Wide judicial interpretation of the 'exceptional circumstances' clauses subsequently rendered the mandatory minimums in the Crime (Sentences) Act 1997 largely symbolic.

In summary, the history of UK policy development in these three fields suggests that hard forms of policy transfer (Evans and Davies 1999) – in terms of large-scale importation of policy goals, content and instruments – are rather rare. In each area, although it is relatively easy to identify US roots for the ideas that were subsequently developed in the UK, in the cases of ZTP and sentencing at least, it appears that it was primarily policy ideas, symbols and rhetoric that were the objects of transfer. Subsequent developments in terms of policy content and instruments were considerably revised and reshaped in the UK context, with the result that the policies that actually developed were very different from their US forebears. This was less true in the sphere of the privatization of corrections, where, as well as the initial idea of contracting out of prisons (and that of electronic monitoring) having clear roots in the USA, there was also a more significant practical input in terms of concrete manifest-ations of the policy. However, even here the specific forms of contracting out of prisons and electronic monitoring that emerged in the UK took on a very different shape from their US precursors.

As we argued in earlier chapters, to suggest that evidence of 'hard' policy transfer is rather limited, and that there has been more symbolism than sub-stance to reforms, does not mean that these reforms did not matter. As noted earlier, talk has consequences. The importation of 'three strikes' and 'zero tol-erance' symbolism is part of a broader punitive turn that has seen a continued media obsession with crime, public anxieties about violence and disorder (dur-ing a period of sustained falls in crime), and a continued political discourse in which leading politicians play the 'crime card'. The addition of mandatory sentencing and zero tolerance rhetoric to the mix has clearly had some wider practical consequences. The rapid growth of the prison population is the most obvious of these, a development that has been largely down to more punitive sentencing by magistrates and judges. This must be related to the broader climate of public debate, in which politicians' statements have played an important part. Thus, although it is almost certainly the case that the specific policies and programmes associated with, say, 'three strikes and you're out' and 'zero tolerance' do not appear to have made their way across the Atlantic, many aspects of the broader language of punitiveness have done so, as have some more general lessons regarding crime control politics (Newburn and Jones 2005). The deployment of the political symbols and rhetoric that have been borrowed from the USA has had substantive effects on the penal systems of the UK.

Transfer agents

Looking at the three areas of policy change, in various ways policy entre-preneurs of different kinds were key agents of change in each, and to a degree acted as transfer agents. In privatized corrections, the key policy entre-preneurs were backbench Conservative MPs and members of the House of Commons Home Affairs Committee. They were motivated by a combination of ideological commitment to extending privatization to the penal sphere and a more pragmatic desire to reform the prison service. More cynical obser-vers might point to the connections between some of these MPs and the private security industry and suggest more instrumental personal motivations, although we found no evidence to support this. Another aspect of US influ-ence concerns the lobbying by US-based corporations prior to legislation on the contracting out of prisons, and then in the actual implementation stages of the policy in the UK (in terms of involvement in consortia that bid and won contracts to run prisons). In this sense, commercial corporations can also be regarded as transfer agents.

In the story of two and three strikes sentencing, the key policy entre-preneur was a politician, this time a more senior one. Home Secretary Michael Howard was determined to bring about a paradigm shift away from what he saw as entrenched approaches to sentencing and imprisonment that were prevalent among Home Office bureaucrats and many professionals and practi-tioners in the penal system. Part of this related to the changed Labour Party position on law and order, and the need symbolically to reassert Conservative appeal on crime control to what was perceived as a punitive voting public. However, as we have argued, there is significant evidence that, for Howard, this went beyond symbolic politics and party competition, and was something in which he strongly believed. Although he did not succeed in his immediate aims (in that two and three strikes sentencing was resisted and emerged in a more modest form than he intended), his broader wishes appear to have been at least partly fulfilled in so far as there has been a continued shift towards more punitive sentencing and greater use of incarceration. Although widely linked to similar developments in the USA, mandatory minimum sentencing was the area that showed least evidence of policy transfer, even at the symbolic level. Howard himself reported that he developed his ideas on mandatory minimum sentencing without knowledge of US developments, and there was no evidence of any specific visits by officials or politicians to the USA to study mandatory minimums or, indeed, other examples of drawing upon US experience (other than as 'negative lessons' by campaigners against the proposed reforms).

In the arena of ZTP, there were arguably a greater number of policy entrepreneurs who played a key role in transfer from the USA, who undertook attempts to export these ideas with a particular vigour. In contrast to the other two areas of study, this was an area in which some of the key players in attempting to initiate policy transfer were senior practitioners. The role of senior police officers Bill Bratton and Ray Mallon was central to the story of the spread of ideas (and some of the practices) associated with ZTP to parts of the UK. However, a further set of policy entrepreneurs in the form of leading politicians can be identified in this area. Jack Straw and Tony Blair stand out as two senior politicians who played a vital role in applying the rhetoric behind zero tolerance to the British criminal justice system (as well as other areas of public policy). In addition, they have played an important part in facilitating the influence of the 'broken windows' thesis in broader public policy. This has become the focus of key government legislation in a way that goes well beyond the sphere of policing.

Transfer processes

One of the very clear findings from this study concerns the growth of transnational policy networks as conduits for the transfer of ideas and policies within the sphere of criminal justice. In particular, the process categorized by Bennett (1991) as 'elite networking' has been central to the transatlantic exchange of policy ideas and initiatives. This reflects a broader trend towards growing international contact and exchange between practitioners and professionals. The fields of corrections and policing in the past two decades, at least, have seen an explosion in the numbers of international conferences and seminars, exchange programmes, and study visits involving politicians, policy-makers, practitioners and academics. A number of organizations have acted as facilitators in these networks. Particularly important in this regard has been the role of think tanks on both sides of the Atlantic. Although there is little evidence of direct and straightforward influence on particular policy decisions, think tanks have played an important role in facilitating the spread of a neo-liberal mindset via more general ideas and principles. More practical facilitation has occurred via the British Embassy. We found that Embassy officials in the Public Affairs Unit in Washington DC felt that they had a key role to play in policy transfer across the Atlantic – in both directions. These officials extensively employed the language of lesson-drawing, by identifying areas of perceived good practice and facilitating visits by policy-makers, politicians and practitioners.

This kind of elite networking was most visible in the arenas of zero tolerance policing (and related ideas) and the privatization of corrections. In both these areas, networking facilitated by major neo-liberal think tanks was crucial in the spread of the initial ideas associated with policy change. In the United States the key players in this regard have been the Heritage Foundation and the Manhattan Institute; in the UK, the Adam Smith Institute and the Institute of Economic Affairs (IEA). On both sides of the Atlantic these major think tanks played a central role in the promotion and dissemination of neo-liberal ideas. In relation to crime control they have not only been important in disseminating such ideas domestically, but transatlantic ties between these bodies were centrally implicated in the process of policy transfer. Thus, for example, the Manhattan Institute not only was heavily involved in the promotion of the 'broken windows' thesis and therefore of the idea of zero tolerance but, through its close links with the IEA, also helped to facilitate the importation of the idea to the UK. In relation to prisons, the Adam Smith Institute was prominent in the promotion of private involvement, leaning heavily on study visits to the USA and the experience of its head of research, Peter Young, who had previously worked for, and retained close contacts with, the Heritage Foundation in Washington DC.

Central to an understanding of the process of lesson-drawing in the crime control arena over the past decade has been the emergence of a transnational political elite comprising leading members of, and advisers to, social democratic administrations in modern societies. The heart of this network, particularly as far as this study was concerned, was the very close links between the New Democrats in the USA and the emergent 'New Labour' Party in the UK and, briefly at least, to 'third way' politicians across the globe. The ties between the two parties led to a sharing of electoral tactics and of political ideas across the public policy spectrum. In relation to crime control, early on, as two leading advisers put it, this was as much about style as substance (Hewitt and Gould 1993). Since the early 1990s, the sharing of ideas has included both broad policy initiatives and more specific, practical projects. In terms of direct emulation of policy ideas, there are a number of recent examples in the criminal justice field including the British government's introduction of a pilot community court in Liverpool directly modelled on the Red Hook Community Court in New York City, the gradual emergence and spread of drug courts and the establishment in 2003 of the Sentencing Guidelines Council. As an example of the attempt to import more general and strategic initiatives, we have recently argued that the most significant example is to be found in the sea change that occurred in British penal politics in the early 1990s – crudely, a decisive shift away from 'penal welfarism' toward a bipartisan populist punitiveness (Newburn and Jones 2005). Though it would be easy and convenient to reduce this sea change to the impact of Michael Howard's appointment as Home Secretary in May 1993, in our view it would be misleading. Howard's 'Prison Works' speech at the Conservative Party conference in October 1993 had signalled something of a departure from his predecessors in the Home Office – both in substance and style. Importantly, however, when he arrived in office he was faced with a challenge that no Tory Home Secretary had faced before – a Labour Shadow that sought to occupy the very law and order territory that the Conservative Party had monopolized for the previous decade and a half. Blair's 'tough on crime, tough on the causes of crime' mantra had first been aired four months before Howard became Home Secretary. Faced with rising crime, dipping popularity in the opinion polls and the prospect of being outflanked by New Labour on crime, Howard reacted quickly and consistently. From his 'Prison Works' speech and his '27-point plan to crack down on crime', through the punitive trespass and public order provisions of the 1994 Criminal Justice and Public Order Act, to mandatory minimum sentences in his Crime (Sentences) Bill, there was nothing Howard could do to shake off Labour's newfound embrace of tough penal policies. It is this conjoining of the parties in the new bipartisan consensus that is one of the key distinguishing features of the period we find ourselves in now. Though not, strictly speaking, policy transfer, the lesson-drawing between the UK Labour Party and the Democratic Party in the USA has had a profound impact on this side of the Atlantic.

Although elite networks clearly played an important role, both in the spread of particular policy ideas and in broader approaches to political style and strategy, this should not be taken to imply a straightforward 'rational' approach to policy-making. In fact, this has provided further support for the findings of Kingdon (1995) and others about the complexity and unpredictability of the policy process. This can be seen by the limited and varying ways in which 'evidence' informed policy change. In each of the policy areas we studied, evidence of some kind was deployed. In the privatization of corrections, there was some systematic evidence gathering by politicians and policy-makers who visited the USA to view contracted out prisons. The development of EM in the UK provided perhaps the clearest example of a concerted attempt by UK officials to gather systematic evidence about EM in the USA to inform UK developments. Under severe time pressure, officials from the Home Office implementation team visited the USA and developed a hybrid version of what they saw as the best elements of US systems. In ZTP, there was a very substantial amount of contact with US developments, with visits to New York from politicians (of both parties), officials and senior police officers from the UK. There were also return visits to the UK from some of the senior players in NYC, with the explicit aim of promoting similar policing reforms in the UK. However, considerable doubts remain about the degree to which evidence was systematically gathered and objectively analysed to inform the policy process. On the contrary, even where the evidence was arguably most systematically gathered and analysed (EM), arguably the key decision had already been made – Michael Howard wanted monitoring, and he wanted it to be implemented by the private sector (regardless of the other evidence about problems in the USA). In the other arenas, the use of evidence was even less systematic, and in some cases also appeared to be used to justify positions already established (Sir John Wheeler argued that he and Edward Gardner were already committed to the idea of private corrections, the US visit simply confirmed an already-held opinion). The use of US exemplars by Peter Young and the ASI was clearly a post-hoc action to justify the ideological position that they already held.

Other processes of policy convergence highlighted by Bennett (1991) have been of little consequence in the particular areas that we have studied. His notion of 'harmonization' has not really been applicable to any of our three areas other than that of sentencing reform. As we saw in Chapter 4, the effect of harmonization (in the form of the UK's incorporation of the European Declaration of Human Rights into domestic law in the Human Rights Act 1998) actually provided a barrier to the development in the UK of harsher forms of mandatory sentencing that had become established in certain parts of the USA. The Court of Appeal drew upon the Human Rights Act to extend further the interpretation of 'exceptional circumstances' in the case of the 'two strikes' life sentences for serious or violent crimes, which allowed judges to undermine Michael Howard's original intentions even more. It is important here to take note of some of the limitations of the current study. As we pointed out in Chapter 2, our use of case studies restricts our ability to generalize about processes of policy transfer beyond the areas that we have considered. Because our focus was specifically on bilateral transfers between the USA and the UK, this inevitably restricted our ability to explore interesting processes of policy convergence arising from the activities of transnational institutions. Had we explored different areas of policy change, then we might well have found very different degrees, directions and processes of transfer. In contrast with the cases we examined, other areas of policy development would be likely to high-light the growing importance of supranational organizations such as the European Union in promoting, at least to a degree, the harmonization of policies of EU member states under the 'Third Pillar' of Justice and Home Affairs (den Boer 1998).

Furthermore, our study did not explore in any detail the activities of other transnational organizations beyond Europe. It is the activities of these institutions – the United Nations, the International Monetary Fund (IMF), the World Bank, and so on that may lead to kinds of coerced policy transfer most aptly captured by Bennett's (1991) notion of 'policy penetration'. This is where transfer is coerced by international organizations (such as the World Bank requiring a country to adopt particular monetary policy approaches as a condition of making a loan) or by multinational corporations (who may make similar demands as a condition of major inward investment). We found little evidence of this in the criminal justice field in the current research, although this again reflects the nature of the two countries studied and the particular areas of policy development under consideration. In particular, had our choice of countries been different, we might well have found more evidence about other processes of policy transfer. One might expect to find more evidence of coerced forms of policy transfer in a study that included countries with considerable dependence on international aid, or post-conflict societies in transition where international organizations are more active, than in a study of two stable and relatively wealthy democracies.

Another point relevant to the processes of transfer concerns the key countries involved in policy transfer, and the directions in which transfer occurs. Undoubtedly, our focus upon our three particular areas obscured the nature and degree of policy transfer occurring in the opposite direction (from the UK to the USA and elsewhere), and also policy transfers with roots in other parts of the world. Had we explored other spheres of criminal justice and penal policy – for example, the development of community service as a sentence of the court, criminal injuries compensation, or the development of victim support – then we would have found examples of policies which appear to have had their origins in the UK and been exported abroad, not least to the USA. Similarly, the focus on a limited number of case studies also risks overlooking important international influences on UK criminal justice and penal policy that arise from countries other than the USA. One policy area where this is clearly visible is the development of restorative justice where UK developments have been widely linked to approaches that previously emerged in Australia and New Zealand (Johnstone 2003).

Thus, we should beware of generalizing too much from our small number of case studies. Empirical exploration of the wider range of policy transfer processes and directions of travel, and a focus on a larger number of exporter/importer jurisdictions is a matter for future research. The aims of the current study were to focus explicitly on particular examples of supposed bilateral US/UK policy transfer during the 1990s. Our findings bring into question assumptions that a crude form of 'Americanization' has been developing in UK criminal justice. In fact, our study demonstrates that even in these areas where such a process is widely perceived to have been active, things are much more complicated than they initially seem. If policy transfers even in these particular areas seem to have been rather partial and constrained, then we need to be very careful not to present recent policy changes in terms of a simplified notion of Americanization of British crime control. This supports the findings of other recent work that highlights how the complex changes that are emerging within criminal justice systems cannot be explained by straightforward reference to the global march of neo-liberal reform, nor to simple notions of emulation and transfer (see, for example, Crawford and Lewis forthcoming). It is to the limitations of policy transfer that we turn next.

Limits to policy transfer

We have argued that policy transfer occurred most markedly at the level of rhetoric and symbolism rather than at the level of more concrete manifestations of policy. Politicians of both major UK parties have found US-style symbols and rhetoric extremely attractive. Thus, terms such as 'three strikes' and 'zero tolerance' entered the British political lexicon more readily than did the substantive practices and policies associated with them. In addition, it is clear that even where US-inspired ideas were promoted with some success in the UK, they underwent a significant process of resistance, reworking and transformation in the British context. In particular, this reflects two particular sets of constraints on the process of policy transfer: first, the particular political institutions and structures within which policies are formulated, and second, the influence of the actions of key political actors working within these contexts.

The institutional context

In each of the areas that we have considered, irrespective of the degree of initial US influence, policies appear to have developed with a distinctively British flavour. In part, this reflects the abiding importance of particular political and legal institutional contexts which continue to structure and shape policy choices. In Britain, unlike most US states, these institutional contexts provide the space and resources for UK criminal justice elites to exert a strong influence over policy. An influential body of work in political science has shifted the gaze of scholars beyond the formal institutions of the state, and has stressed the degree to which contemporary governance is characterized by the interplay of a range of groups, both inside and outside the state, competing to organize and represent different interests (see Rhodes 1997). However, some authors have argued that some of the 'new governance' literature has taken this approach too far, in the process all but 'defining out' formal political institutions from consideration. However, detailed comparative policy histories demonstrate the importance of institutional political analysis, and an appreciation of the abiding ability of state institutions and structures to shape policy outcomes. Atkinson and Coleman (1992), for example, have underlined the importance of 'bringing the state back in' to political analyses. In particular, comparisons between the USA and the UK, such as those undertaken in this study, demonstrate the continued capacity of political and legal institutional structures to define various interests as legitimate (or otherwise), to shape the nature of political organization, and to incorporate some societal actors and not others into the policy-making process. The continued influence of particular criminal justice elites within UK policy networks is also vital to understanding policy outcomes in particular cases.

When compared with the relatively centralized and closed criminal justice policy-making structures of the UK, the federalized system of the USA provides a greater degree of freedom within which populist legislative campaigns can gather political support.[1] The decentralized and relatively open nature of the US system (at least when compared to that in the UK) allows for more ;points of influence for interest groups to target key decision-makers at federal, state and local level (Chandler 2000). This helps to explain the greater significance of corporate lobbying in relation to sentencing and correctional policy in the USA than in the UK (Jones and Newburn 2005). An additional distinctive feature of the USA is the tradition of direct popular election of many criminal justice officials – including judges, prosecutors and some police chiefs – in many parts of the country (Flanagan 1996). This system of policy-making – one that is more open to direct popular influence – is reflected in the established tradition of populist mechanisms of policy-making including voter ballot initiatives, referenda and recall provisions (Garland 2005). This clearly renders policy-making far more open to direct popular pressures in a way that does not exist in the UK, where such criminal justice officials are appointed rather than elected and consequently retain a degree of insulation from populist pressures. Within each of the policy areas under consideration, the very different political and legal traditions in the UK have shaped policies in distinctive ways.

Within the more centralized system of policy-making in the UK, criminal justice elites were able to exert a degree of influence that would be unthinkable in most parts of the USA. Even in the area where there was most evidence of 'hard' policy transfer, the commercialization of corrections, we found that within the British context the policies of contracting out of prisons and electronic monitoring developed in a very different way from the ways in which they had generally unfolded in the USA. As we discussed in detail in Chapter 3, there was significant institutional opposition to the idea of commercial involvement in corrections, both among the naturally cautious Home Office officials and also among senior Conservative politicians. According to some interviewees, this reflected some ideological discomfort about introducing privatization into institutions of law and order, but also pragmatic concerns about sparking industrial confrontation with trade unions and professional elites. While the opposition of criminal justice professionals, Home Office officials and many politicians was eventually overcome, the policy still developed in a pragmatic and rather controlled way, with the commercial corrections sector effectively being incorporated into the wider public prison system. For example, the commercial sector came under the same structures of accountability as publicly managed prisons. With regard to both the contracting out of prisons and the development of EM, it seems that there was considerable resistance to change among senior civil servants. In particular, Home Office officials drew upon US evidence about EM as negative lessons to advise ministers against introducing this in the UK. In addition, a number of other bodies offered resistance to policy transfer in these areas. These included trade unions and staff associations (in this area, the POA and NAPO), and penal reform groups such as the Howard League, the Prison Reform Trust and NACRO (who adopted a consistent line against privatization).

As a further example, the generally successful resistance of UK police officers to the adoption of 'New York-style' policing (or variants of it) was very much a product of the distinctive constitutional and institutional framework within which the police operate in Britain. One of the distinctive features of the constitutional position of the police in Britain is the doctrine of 'constabulary independence' (Lustgarten 1986; Walker 2000; Jones 2003). Although this has been subject to considerable legal and political criticism, and undoubtedly has been eroded in important ways over recent years, it remains the case that senior police officers in Britain still retain a good deal of autonomy in policy-making when compared to their counterparts in many US big city forces. By contrast, in cities such as New York, the Police Commissioner is a political appointment of the Mayor, and is responsible to the Mayor (and by extension, the political process) in a way that is far more direct than has ever been the case in the UK. Thus, when Rudolph Giuliani was elected in 1993, the change in political regime also resulted in a total change in the senior management of the NYPD. Equally, when differences between Bratton and Giuliani came to a head, the Mayor was able to remove *his* Commissioner of Police from post in a way that would be impossible in the UK, where it still remains extremely difficult for politicians to sack a chief constable. This key contextual difference has enabled senior British police officers to resist some of the policy changes that national and local politicians have promoted.

Finally, although we have argued that there was little evidence of direct US influence in the arena of sentencing policy during the 1990s, the ways in which Michael Howard's original proposals were resisted and amended are testimony to the institutional constraints that still remain in the UK on the implementation of populist criminal justice policies. As Chapter 4 showed, there was significant resistance within Parliament (and in the judiciary) to the introduction of Californian-style mandatory minimum sentences (a clause being inserted in the draft legislation to maintain judicial discretion which has had the effect of restricting the use of the mandatory minimum). This parliamentary resistance was tied in with a much broader campaign against the proposals on the part of judicial elites. Judges were able to deploy the 'exceptional circumstances' clauses to avoid giving the 'mandatory' minimum in some cases. Eventually, the Court of Appeal deliberately widened the interpretation of the exceptional circumstances clauses in the 'two strikes' cases in order to render the legislation largely symbolic.

In sum, the policy histories that we considered here demonstrate in some detail that even in an increasingly globalized world, national and local political institutions and cultures still exert a crucially important effect on policy outcomes, and provide significant limitations on the possibilities for 'hard' policy transfer into different socio-political contexts. Of course, they do not do so independently, but through the actions of key political actors who operate within the constraints and opportunities that they provide. It is to this often neglected area of agency that we turn next.

Actors and contingency

The finding that, in practice, transnational policy transfer appears to be highly difficult is related to the essentially complex and unpredictable nature of criminal justice policy-making. Contingency, happenstance and unintended effects are central to the stories of policy development in all the areas we looked at. In the privatization of corrections, for example, Prime Minister Thatcher made a vital intervention during the late 1980s to establish the legal principle of contracting out of prisons (having initially been cautious about the involvement of commercial bodies in the penal system). Several Conservative MPs worked behind the scenes to amend the legislation in order to enable the remit of privatization to be extended. National prison officer union officials decided against taking industrial action against privatization, a decision for which they later expressed regret. Following their election in May 1997, the Labour Party abandoned their previous opposition and embraced the policy of contracting out of prisons. Similar examples can be found in the other policy areas under consideration. The two and three strikes story provides examples of resistance that was relatively successful within the context of particular times and places. Arguably, whenever such a set of proposals would have been put forward, they would have met with strong opposition from the judiciary and from penal reform groups. The timing of Michael Howard's proposals in 1996/97, however, paradoxically both constrained and advantaged the coalition of opposition. The fact that the general election was approaching meant that the Labour Party took an equivocal stance on the proposals. This left the real opposition to the Bill to be undertaken by a combination of backbench MPs and peers in the House of Lords. Howard's eventual acceptance of the Lords' amendments owed everything to timing.

Labour's subsequent stance on the Crime (Sentences) Act 1997, in which it implemented the minimum sentence provisions, surprised some and demonstrated that the Party's position during the debate over the Bill was not simply a matter of symbolic politics. As we have pointed out, the Labour government has subsequently overseen the expansion of the prison population to record levels. Though these accounts of the unpredictable and serendipitous nature of the policy process may seem self-evident, it is surprising how some accounts of the penal policy change present an image of seamless, linear development that verge on the deterministic.

The fact that hard policy transfer in the field of criminal justice actually seems rather limited should not surprise us. This was also the picture presented by most of the studies in the ESRC Future Governance Programme that covered a range of policy areas as well as criminal justice (Page 2003). While it seems clear that policy ideas and innovations travel both within and between polities, they undergo a range of reshaping processes once they disembark. Although we found little evidence of the wholesale import of concrete policy content and instruments, this is not to say that what was imported was of no consequence. As already noted above, the simplistic picture of attempted 'Americanization' of criminal justice policy being largely neutralized by heroic British resistance is not supported by our research. Indeed, as we have pointed out, many of these policy changes have been part of some very significant wider developments. Thus, although the form of privatized corrections that emerged in Britain was very different from that which appeared in the southern states of the USA, we have subsequently come to a situation in which the UK commercial corrections sector is proportionally more significant than that in the USA (relative to the prison sector as a whole). Key policy actors on both sides of the original debate in the UK now generally accept that contracting out had provided a lever for positive reform of the prison system. In the USA, however, there is still active and on occasion successful opposition to the commercialization of corrections in some states. It is clear that in its specific form, the impact of mandatory minimum sentencing in Britain was largely neutralized by a combination of powerful coalitions of opposition and timing. Labour's embracing of the punitive rhetoric associated with such changes and, ultimately, its willingness to implement the sentences, was indicative of a deeper sea change in the Party's approach to imprisonment. As we write this, the prison service in England and Wales is creaking at the seams due to overcrowding, and is considering emergency measures such as expanding the early release programme in order to accommodate new prisoners. Finally, although the specific package of policing practices that emerged in New York did not appear in the UK, the broader concerns with tackling anti-social behaviour have substantially shaped government crime policy more generally. In addition, elements of the New York approach, including a more vigorous and centrally designed performance management model, are increasingly visible in British police forces.

Convergence and divergence in criminal justice

As we outlined at the outset, arguments about convergence and divergence in crime control policy across liberal democracies have become a staple of contemporary criminology. Stimulated most obviously by David Garland's hugely influential *The Culture of Control* (2001a), numerous authors have explored and compared the crime control systems of different jurisdictions in order to assess the extent of similarity and difference and to question what this might tell us about processes of globalization and diffusion (Whitman 2003; Tonry 2004a, 2004b; Newburn and Sparks 2004a; Wacquant 1999a). This book, though it has a somewhat different approach from these studies, is nevertheless a part of the same general inquiry. In matters of potential convergence and divergence in American and British criminal justice policy our particular concern has been to explore the extent to which processes of policy transfer have played any part. In fact, the particular UK policy developments we have examined provide interesting examples of simultaneous convergence and divergence in crime control policy. Of course, this is not a surprising finding at all. As we noted in Chapter 1, none of the extensive writing in this field have suggested a simplistic picture of 'total' convergence or divergence between nations. Indeed, it is clear that the closer one looks at developments in penal policy, the more complicated the picture becomes. As Levi-Faur and Jordana (2005: 194) note, 'the process of policy diffusion may involve convergence and divergence at the same time'. Their notion of 'convergent divergence' is one potential way of capturing the complex nature of what is going on here. One clear finding is that, despite widespread perceptions of strong US influence on criminal justice developments, we found no evidence of the straightforward importation of US policies by British politicians and policy-makers. This suggests that as far as convergence is visible within the arena of crime control, this relates more to underlying shifts and trends than to straightforward processes of copying and emulation. As in other areas of crime control and penal policy, parallel developments – in terms of broader structural/cultural shifts and in the politics of crime control – are clearly visible on both sides of the Atlantic. These include wider changes in social and cultural configurations conducive to increasing insecurity and the growing politicization of crime control that give rise to similar policy dilemmas and make certain policy choices more politically attractive. Similarities in policy trajectories can also be identified, in terms of the general shift towards the simultaneous adoption of primarily expressive and punitive criminal justice policies, and the promotion of more pragmatic instrumental approaches that emphasize the management of risk and the reduction of costs (Garland 2001a).

It is certainly the case that broad similarities in the structural and cultural preconditions of policy-making can be identified between the USA and the UK, and that these played an important part of the story in each of our areas of study. Both are Anglophone common law countries with 'first past the post' electoral systems, dominated by two main parties, and both have seen crime becoming an increasingly politicized issue in recent decades. In both the USA and Britain, the general political climate has been one that is apparently conducive to populist legislation. In the UK in the early 1990s, after many years out of office and facing a bleak political future, the Labour Party undertook a radical programme of 'modernization'. In many respects, this paralleled changes in tactics and presentation undertaken by the Democrats in the USA in the years leading up to the election of the first Clinton administration (Newburn and Jones 2005). For both parties a central part of this process was repositioning themselves on core public policy issues such as welfare and crime. In part, this involved the development of a much greater willingness to embrace and promote populist measures. In Britain, this involved much tougher sentencing, and consequently a rapidly rising prison population, together with a raft of measures to crack down on 'anti-social behaviour', all designed to allow the government to appear 'tough on crime' (Downes and Morgan 2002). At the same time, we have highlighted the important divergences that have existed within this broader picture of similarity. In particular, the actual manifestations of particular policies were very different from their US precursors, because of the activities of key policy actors within a distinctive set of political and legal institutions.

Understanding policy transfer

As we signalled earlier, one of the questions that has continually troubled us during the course of this work is whether any of it really matters. What is the importance or relevance of the origins of particular policy ideas and practices? Why should it matter if inspiration was drawn – or not drawn for that matter – from another jurisdiction? More concretely, given that one of our clearest conclusions is that despite apparently similar nomenclature and rhetoric in British and American crime control during the 1990s, there is actually very little evidence of the substantive transfer of 'policies', is this simply a field of research that had a brief moment of popularity only to disappear once everyone realized that there was little concrete to examine? These are, and will undoubtedly remain, important questions for those interested in the diffusion of policy ideas and practices. There are a number of things to be said in response.

First, just because despite initial appearances there seems to have been relatively little direct lesson-drawing in criminal justice and penal policy in the UK from America in the period we have been studying does not mean that the ideas of lesson-drawing and policy transfer are without merit. The entire history of 'modern' criminal justice is littered with examples of the trade in ideas. From John Howard's survey of the prisons in Britain and Europe, through Beaumont and de Toqueville's study of the American penitentiary system, to the global spread of notions of community policing and restorative justice, we are surrounded with examples which attest to the virtual impossibility of autarky in public policy-making.

Second, there is a danger in these globalized times in assuming that the speed and efficiency of the new forms of communication that link, structure and create the 'network society' (Castells 2000) mean that policy learning will also become increasingly easy and efficient. As the research reported here should indicate, this is far from something that we should take for granted. The literatures on policy transfer and lesson-drawing are replete with examples of failure. There are numerous reasons for such failure. Dolowitz and Marsh (1996), for example, examine various forms of implementation failure in seeking to explain the problems of transferring American welfare-to-work policies to the UK in the 1980s and early 1990s. In other work, focusing on the development of the Child Support Agency in the UK (Dolowitz and Marsh 2000), they identify three groups of problems with policy transfer which they term *uninformed transfer, incomplete transfer* and *inappropriate transfer.*

Finally, in this regard, it seems to us that one of the most important findings that our research points to concerns another aspect of the difficulty of policy transfer – that it is significantly easier for symbols to be exported and imported than it is for matters of substance to be transferred. As we have illustrated in some detail, for all the talk of cross-national lesson-drawing, the diffusion of ideas and so forth, policy transfer in any direct sense hardly ever occurs in its pure or 'hard' form. On reflection, despite the large and growing literature on the possibility of policy transfer, it does not seem to us at all surprising that examples of its occurrence are fairly difficult to find. As we argued above, there are many reasons why attempted policy transfer has failed and many reasons therefore why we should consider such activity to be inherently problematic. Much of the policy transfer literature, we think, has tended to skate over such difficulties and has assumed all too readily that the borrowing of practices and policies from abroad is relatively straightforward.

Now, there are undoubtedly many reasons why such assumptions have been made. One of the most important, we feel, is that such work often proceeds with an unrealistically or overly rational model of policy-making. Even if not so crude, or so explicit, much policy transfer literature assumes that policy-makers/politicians begin by identifying a problem and then travelling in search of its solution (or, alternatively, as John Kingdon might argue, identifying a solution and then looking for the problem). Having identified a likely suspect, the crude policy transfer model suggests that they then import it and set it in place. However, as those authors that have studied policy-making first-hand have demonstrated, the policy process rarely proceeds in such a textbook-like, rational choice form. Rather, as Lindblom (1959) characterized it, much policy-making activity is better conceived of as the 'science of muddling through'. Paul Rock (1990, 2004) has shown in great detail that in practice policy-making is messy, serendipitous and unpredictable. As he says, policy-making 'would be an otherwise smooth metamorphosis were it not for the sudden lurches and opportunities imposed by uncontrolled problems of timing and context' (Rock 1995: 16). Similarly, John Kingdon (1995) has argued that solutions and answers, and problems and questions, tend to circulate together in what he calls the 'political stream', and they often do so remarkably independently of each other. Now, none of this is to argue that the job of the policy analyst or criminologist is not to attempt to impose some analytical order on such processes. However, we must be constantly vigilant of the danger of imposing too much order on processes that are inherently disorderly.

If we apply this assumption to the field of policy transfer, then it is hardly surprising that while there is considerable international travel to see what others are doing, and there is much activity that looks a little like an import–export trade, in fact *policies* are not traded like *goods* (or rarely so anyway). They cannot easily be packaged, put in a container, transported to a new location, and then simply become embedded and established in the new setting. Although politicians and others are constantly on the look-out for new ideas, policies and practices, by and large they operate quite unlike the rational shopper. The circumstances under which they operate – not least the generally short timescales and the ever-shifting political terrain – mean that the difficult goal of transplanting policy initiatives lock, stock and barrel is rarely successfully achieved, or even attempted. Even where some form of 'hard' or full transfer is attempted, particular socio-economic, cultural and political contexts also inevitably shape and mould the new imports. Indeed, Melossi (2004: 144) has gone so far as to argue that translation is impossible as 'generally speaking any term, even the simplest, is embedded within a cultural context, or milieu, that gives it its meaning'. His point is that we must look beneath the surface of apparent similarities to investigate the potential for dissimilarity and divergence beneath.

What we see in the field of policy transfer, therefore, are clear differences between 'hard' and 'soft' policy transfer. Put differently, the study of policy transfer in criminal justice indicates that rhetoric, labels, and nomenclature travel much more easily than the nuts and bolts of policy (though, as Melossi counsels, we should be careful of assuming that similar labels *mean* similar things). Thus, in recent times in Britain we have had the zero tolerance label but, in practice, relatively little zero tolerance policing. We have mandatory minimum sentences, and the use of 'three strikes' labels, but not policies directly modelled on, say, the Californian experience.[2] We have sex offender registers, and campaigns for a 'Sarah's Law' based directly on US 'Megan's Laws', but we do not as yet have any concrete form of community notification. Even in the field of private prisons – the one field we have been studying where there is the clearest evidence of emulation – there is still something very distinctly *British* about the way the policy has been enacted. Crucially, though private involvement in corrections in the UK is at least as substantial, proportionately, as it is in the USA, both public and private elements of the penal estate remain subject to the same governance regime. The political and cultural circumstances into which private prisons were introduced, and the reasons they were introduced, differed quite significantly from those operating in the USA (Jones and Newburn 2005). If we shed our overly rational models of policy-making and, by implication, our overly rational model of policy transfer, then the picture of partial and piecemeal policy transfer in the crime control arena over the past decade or so appears more realistic and predictable. As Levi-Faur and Jordana have observed, 'most cases of diffusion are based not upon learning but on a myriad of mechanisms in which the rational component, if any, remains small' (2005: 192).

At this point we should reiterate a point made earlier, but one that bears repetition. Just because the bulk of what has been transferred has been *symbols* rather than *substance* does not mean that it is unimportant. As numerous authors have pointed out, symbols have important political uses (Edelman 1971) and potentially significant social and political consequences (Rock 1990; Page 2003). Much of what appears to have occurred in the crime control arena comes closer to what Page (2003) describes as 'gaining inspiration' rather than 'lesson-drawing'. Labels have been borrowed and a general steer in certain areas has occurred, rather than anything that comes close to the ideal-typical model of policy transfer. Thus, New Labour evidently gained inspiration from the New Democrats, and borrowed both language and tactics. The result has been a rightward shift in crime control policy. Even if the detail of policy owes little directly to the American experience, the consequences, not least in terms of the continuing rise in the prison population, have been dramatic.

Future research

It remains the case that detailed studies of policy-making in the crime control arena are rather rare. On a broad level, therefore, it seems to us that future research priorities should incorporate further work focusing on the detail of policy-making, especially in this highly controversial and contentious area. Within the more particular field of lesson-drawing or policy transfer there are two important areas for future work. First, we would suggest the application of similar methods of study to a wider range of specific policy areas. This will provide a broader perspective on how and why criminal justice policy change comes about. Second, it is important that future work seeks to extend comparative study beyond the 'two countries' focus of this research. For example, it is important to undertake further work that explores the impact of European harmonization in the sphere of criminal justice and penal policy or the influence of policy developments from further away such as Australia and New Zealand. Finally, this study once again highlights the need for more work in the field of comparative policy-making studies generally. There remains a relative dearth of empirically grounded comparative research, especially in the criminal justice and penal policy arena (Lacey 2003), and addressing this gap remains a priority.

Notes

1 Convergence and divergence in crime control

1 'DPP's hit at "grotesque" sentencing proposals', *Guardian* 1 September 2003; 'Lock em up: if only we'd nick America's solution', *The Times*, 2 September 2003

3 Privatizing punishment

1 There have also been important developments in private sector provision in the youth justice system in England and Wales. For reasons of space, however, this chapter focuses primarily upon developments in the adult corrections sector.

2 These amendments allowed the Home Secretary to make an order by statutory instrument giving effect to the power to contract out (with none of the previous limitations).

3 This company was jointly owned by the US corporation Wackenhut Corrections Corporation and a UK firm, Serco Ltd.

4 Group 4 lost its contract after re-tendering in 1999. Since June 2000, Buckley Hall has been run by the Prison Service.

5 KPS is a joint venture company owned 50 per cent by Serco Investments Limited, a wholly owned subsidiary of Serco Group plc, and 50 per cent by Wackenhut Corrections (UK). Premier Prison Services Limited, which has the same share ownership as KPS, was contracted to manage the day-to-day operations of the prison.

6 This followed a federal court ruling that the entire state prison system was in violation of the Constitution because of overcrowded conditions of confinement.

7 For example, two Wackenhut facilities in Arkansas were transferred to public sector control in 2001.

8 As outlined in Chapter 2, by 'policy content' we mean the formal manifestations of policy including statutes, administrative rules, court rulings, etc. The term 'policy instruments' refers to the regulatory, administrative or judicial tools used to implement and administer policy.

9 And, possibly, by Stacey and the OTA. Stacey and Douglas Hurd had attended the same school.

4 'Three strikes' and mandatory sentencing

1   Frase also highlights a number of persistent divergences between the sentencing systems of Western nations.

2   According to Windlesham (2001), the 'exceptional circumstances' clauses had not been part of Michael Howard's original plans, but the wording had been included at the insistence of Lord McKay.

3   Later re-enacted in sections 109–11 of the Powers of the Criminal Courts (Sentencing) Act 2000.

4   The announcement was made on 12 January 1999, and the provision came into force on 1 December 1999. The provisions for mandatory sentences for repeat violent offenders and drug traffickers came into force on 1 October 1997. Dunbar and Langdon (1998: 155) argue that the Home Secretary's reluctance to implement the three strikes burglary provision was not based on any principled objection to the power but 'was founded simply and solely on the likelihood (or, rather, unlikelihood) of adequate resources being available'. Similarly, its implementation in 1999 was more a matter of image management than principled policy implementation.

5   The term 'truth in sentencing' was also used extensively in Australia before this. For example, the 1989 Sentencing Act in New South Wales, Australia, was known as the 'Truth in Sentencing' Act (Clarkson and Morgan 1995).

6   Although specific measures to deal with the sentencing of 'dangerous' offenders have been an established feature of sentencing policy in the UK, there was no historical precedent of 'mandatory' sentences comparable to habitual offender legislation in the USA (Ashworth 2001).

7   This is not to say that think tanks were not active in promoting broader ideas associated with tougher sentencing policy and the use of imprisonment as a crime reduction tool. For example, the free market think tank the Institute for Economic Affairs (IEA) did undertake a lot of work promoting the idea of crime control through increased incarceration which drew extensively upon US experience (Murray 1997). However, all this work postdated Michael Howard's 1993 'Prison Works' speech and his later proposals for mandatory minimum sentences and honesty in sentencing.

8   Other factors that may lie behind the global attention paid to developments in this state concern its position as one of the richest and most powerful states in the USA, and the fact that it is much visited by many European tourists (and academics) each year.

9   Even in California some degree of discretion remained within the system. The effect of the mandatory sentencing policy was to shift discretion to the prosecutors (who could decide in some cases whether to charge offences as felonies or misdemeanours). It is clear that the application of the laws varied

between different Californian counties depending upon the approach of the particular county prosecutor (Jones and Newburn 2006).

10   Although arguably this is less the case in the UK than in some continental European countries (Whitman 2003).

5 Zero tolerance policing

1   'Desk Appearance Tickets' – where people accused of minor offences were given a court date and released.
2   'Clear beggars from streets', says Blair, *The Times*, 7 January 1997.
3   'Blair champions "zero tolerance" despite warning', *Daily Telegraph*, 11 April 1997.
4   'Teachers savage Blair school plan', *Guardian*, 6 December 1995.
5   'Blair pledges new powers to protect frontline workers', *Independent*, 31 May 2001.
6   'Assaults rise despite crackdown', *Guardian*, 27 March 2003.
7   'New moves to beat the bullies', *Guardian*, 15 July 2004; 'Task force to tackle discipline in schools', *Guardian*, 21 May 2005.
8   http://politics.guardian.co.uk/conservatives/story/0,,1280083,00.html.
9   'Widdecombe causes law and disorder', *Daily Telegraph*, 5 November 2000.
10   An exception is the current chief constable of Essex, Roger Baker, who has introduced a policy of 'zero tolerance' to local town centres (PCCG Meeting, July 2005), http://www.essex.police.uk/cms/global/meetings/cl060705.pdf) and recently declared 'Criminals are the enemy . . . We know who our core customers are' (*Mail on Sunday*, 24 October 2005).
11   In fact, Bratton had introduced a version of 'quality of life policing' to the New York City Transit when he served as head of the Transit Police prior to his appointment to the NYPD (Bratton 1997).
12   Though as Young (2003: 124), one of the attendees at the seminar, reports, Bratton 'started by totally distancing himself from the concept of zero tolerance . . . and warned of the problem of transposing too easily techniques which work in one context to another'.
13   http://www.prnewswire.co.uk/cgi/news/release?id=12346.
14   Although this was clearly a period of increased emphasis on quantitative performance management in UK policing, it would be inaccurate to equate the situation in British police forces in this regard with New York. There is no real evidence that any of the UK experiments with ZTP involved a strategic management process at the level of Compstat (with its emphasis on rapidly produced analysis of crime trends in particular neighbourhoods, elements of public theatre in the calling of local police managers to account for such trends, and its apparent sanctions in being prepared to remove from office managers whose performance was perceived as inadequate).

15 In the form of 'community support officers' or 'neighbourhood wardens'.

6 Policy transfer in crime control

1   Of course we realize that this broad comparison risks over-simplifying the important contrasts in political and legal institutions and cultures between different states within the USA. However, it does seem that notwithstanding such differences, in general the US/UK comparison does stand up to scrutiny, though clearly this contrast is greater for some states than others (see Freedland 1998).

2   One should note at this point that it is also the case that the vast majority of American states also have three strikes laws that bear little resemblance to the extreme Californian model.

References

Adam Smith Institute (1984) *The Omega File*. London: Adam Smith Institute.

Ashworth, A. (1998) *The Criminal Process*, 2nd edn. Oxford: Oxford University Press.

Ashworth, A. (2001) The decline of English sentencing and other stories, in M. Tonry and R. Frase (eds) *Sentencing and Sanctions in Western Countries*. Oxford: Oxford University Press.

Atkinson, M. and Coleman, W. (1992) Policy networks, policy communities and problems of governance, *Governance*, 5(2): 154–80.

Austin, J., Clark, J., Hardyman, P. and Henry, D.A. (2000) *Three Strikes and You're Out: Implementation and Impact of Strike Laws*. Washington, DC: US Department of Justice.

Baer, K.S. (2000) *Reinventing Democrats: The Politics of Liberalism from Reagan to Clinton*. Lawrence, KS: University Press of Kansas.

Barrett, W. and Fifield, A. (2000) *Rudy: An Investigative Biography of Rudolph Giuliani*. New York: Basic Books.

Beckett, K. (1997) *Making Crime Pay: Law and Order in Contemporary American Politics*. New York: Oxford University Press.

Bennett, C. (1991) What is policy convergence and what causes it?, *British Journal of Political Science*, 21: 215–33.

Bennett, C. (1997) Understanding ripple effects: a cross-national adoption of policy instruments for bureaucratic accountability, *Governance*, 10(3): 213–33.

Bernstein, S. and Cashore, B. (2000) Globalization, four paths of internationalization and domestic policy change: the case of ecoforestry in British Columbia, Canada, *Canadian Journal of Political Science*, 33(1): 67–99.

Bertram, E., Blachman, M., Sharpe, K. and Andreas, P. (1996) *Drug War Politics: The Price of Denial*. Berkeley, CA: University of California Press.

Blair, I. (2002) The policing revolution: back to the beat, *New Statesman*, 23 September: 21–3.

Bottoms, A.E. (1995) The philosophy and politics of punishment and sentencing: the politics of sentencing reform, in C.M.V. Clarkson and R. Morgan (eds) *The Politics of Sentencing Reform*. Oxford: Oxford University Press.

Bourdieu, P. (1999) *Acts of Resistance: Against the Tyranny of the Market*. New York: New Press.

Bowling, B. (1999) The rise and fall of New York murder: zero tolerance or crack's decline?, *British Journal of Criminology*, 39(4): 531–54.

Bratton, W. (1997) Crime is down in New York City: blame the police, in N. Dennis (ed.) *Zero Tolerance: Policing a Free Society*. London: Institute for Economic Affairs.

Bratton, W. and Andrews, W. (1999) What we've learned about policing, *City Journal* (Spring), at http://www.city-journal.org/html/cj_archives.html

Bratton, W. and Knobler, P. (1998) *Turnaround: How America's Top Cop Reversed The Crime Epidemic*. New York: Random House.

Brunsson, N. (1989) *The Organisation of Hypocrisy: Talk, Decisions and Actions in Organisations*. Chichester: John Wiley.

Bryman, A. (2002) *Social Research Methods*. Oxford: Oxford University Press.

Burney, E. (2005) *Making People Behave: Anti-Social Behaviour, Politics and Policy*. Cullompton: Willan.

Butler, D. and Kavanagh, D. (1997) *The British General Election of 1997*. Basingstoke: Macmillan.

Carter, P. (2003) *Managing Offenders, Reducing Crime: A New Approach*. London: Home Office.

Castells, M. (2000) *The Rise of the Network Society*. Oxford: Blackwell.

Castles, F. and McKinlay, R. (1979) Public welfare provision, Scandinavia and the sheer futility of the sociological approach to politics, *British Journal of Political Science*, 9(2): 157–71.

Cavadino, M. and Dignan, J. (eds) (2002) *The Penal System: An Introduction*, 3rd edn. London/Thousand Oaks, CA: Sage Publications.

Chambliss, W.J. (1999) *Power, Politics, and Crime*. Boulder, CO/Oxford: Westview Press.

Chandler, J.A. (ed.) (2000) *Comparative Public Administration*. London: Routledge.

Christie, N. (2000) *Crime Control as Industry*, 3rd edn. London: Routledge.

Clark, J., Austin, J. and Henry, D.A. (1997) *'Three Strikes and You're Out': A Review of State Legislation*. Washington, DC: National Institute for Justice.

Clarkson, C. and Morgan, R. (eds) (1995) *The Politics of Sentencing Reform*. Oxford: Oxford University Press.

Cole, G. and Smith, C. (2001) *The American System of Criminal Justice*, 9th edn. Belmont, CA: Wadsworth/Thomson Learning.

Coleman, W. and Skogstad, G. (1990) Policy communities and policy networks: a structural approach, in W. Coleman and G. Skogstad (eds) *Policy Communities and Public Policy in Canada*. Toronto: Copp Clark Pitman.

Crawford, A. and Lewis, S. (forthcoming) Évolutions mondiales, orientations nationales et justice locale: Les effets du neo-libéralisme sur la justice des mineurs en Angleterre et au Pays de Galles, in F. Bailleau and Y. Cartyvels (eds) *Les Évolutions de la Justice Pénale des Mineurs en Europe: Du Modèle Welfare au Modèle Néo-libéral?* Paris: L'Harmattan.

Cummins, C.E. (2000) Private prisons in Texas, 1987–2000: the legal, economic and political influences on policy implementation. Unpublished PhD thesis. The American University, Washington, DC.

Currie, E. (1998) *Crime and Punishment in America*. New York: Henry Holt.

Deacon, A. (1999) Learning from the US? The influence of American ideas on New Labour welfare reform, *Policy and Politics*, 28(1): 5–18.

De Maillard, J. and Roche, S. (2004) Crime and justice in France: time trends, policies and political debate, *European Journal of Criminology*, 1(1): 111–51.

Den Boer, M. (1998) *Taming the Third Pillar: Improving the Management of Justice and Home Affairs in the European Union.* Maastricht: European Institute of Public Administration.

Denham, A. and Garnett, M. (1997) *British Think-Tanks and the Climate of Opinion.* London: UCL Press.

Denham, A. and Garnett, M. (1999) Influence without responsibility? Think tanks in Britain, *Parliamentary Affairs*, 52(1): 46–57.

Dennis, N. (ed.) (1997) *Zero Tolerance: Policing a Free Society.* London: Institute for Economic Affairs.

Dennis, N. and Mallon, R. (1997) Confident policing in Hartlepool, in N. Dennis (ed.) *Zero Tolerance: Policing a Free Society.* London: Institute for Economic Affairs.

DiMaggio, P. and Powell, W. (1983) The iron cage revisited: institutional isomorphism and collective rationality in organizational fields, *American Sociological Review*, 48(2): 147–60.

Ditton, P. and Wilson, D. (1999) *Truth in Sentencing in State Prisons.* Washington, DC: United States Department of Justice.

Dixon, D. (2005) Beyond zero tolerance, in T. Newburn (ed.) *Policing: Key Readings.* Cullompton: Willan.

Dixon, D. and Maher, L. (2005) Policing, crime and public health: lessons for Australia from the 'New York miracle', *Criminal Justice*, 5(2): 115–43.

Dolowitz, D. (1997) British employment policy in the 1980s: learning from the American experience, *Governance*, 10(1): 23–42.

Dolowitz, D. (2000a) Introduction, in D. Dolowitz *et al.* (eds) *Policy Transfer and British Social Policy: Learning from the USA?* Buckingham: Open University Press.

Dolowitz, D. (2000b) Policy transfer: a new framework of policy analysis, in D. Dolowitz *et al.* (eds) *Policy Transfer and British Social Policy: Learning from the USA?* Buckingham: Open University Press.

Dolowitz, D. (2000c) Welfare: the Child Support Agency, in D. Dolowitz *et al.* (eds) *Policy Transfer and British Social Policy: Learning from the USA?* Buckingham: Open University Press.

Dolowitz, D., Greenwold, S. and Marsh, D. (1999) Policy transfer: something old, something new, something borrowed, but why red, white and blue?, *Parliamentary Affairs*, 52: 719–30.

Dolowitz, D. with Hulme, R., Nellis, M. and O'Neill, F. (eds) (2000) *Policy Transfer and British Social Policy: Learning from the USA?* Buckingham: Open University Press.

Dolowitz, D. and Marsh, D. (1996) Who learns what from whom: a review of the policy transfer literature, *Political Studies*, 44: 343–57.

Dolowitz, D. and Marsh, D. (2000) Learning from abroad: the role of policy transfer in contemporary policy-making, *Governance*, 13(1): 5–24.

Doob, A. and Cesaroni, C. (2004) *Responding to Youth Crime in Canada*. Toronto: University of Toronto Press.

Downes, D. (2001) The macho penal economy. Mass incarceration in the US: a European perspective, *Punishment and Society*, 3(1): 61–80.

Downes, D. and Morgan, R. (2002) The skeletons in the cupboard: the politics of law and order at the turn of the millennium, in M. Maguire, R. Morgan and R. Reiner (eds) *The Oxford Handbook of Criminology*, 3rd edn. Oxford: Oxford University Press.

Dubber, M.D. (2002) *Victims in the War on Crime: The Use and Abuse of Victims' Rights*. New York: New York University Press.

Dunbar, I. and Langdon, A.J. (1998) *Tough Justice: Sentencing and Penal Policies in the 1990s*. London: Blackstone Press.

Easton, D. (1965) *A Systems Analysis of Political Life*. New York: Wiley.

Easton, S. and Piper, C. (2005) *Sentencing and Punishment: The Quest for Justice*. Oxford: Oxford University Press

Edelman, M. (1971) *Politics as Symbolic Action: Mass Arousal and Acquiescence*. Chicago, IL: Markham.

Edwards, A. and Hughes, G. (2005) Editorial, *Theoretical Criminology*, 9(3): 259–63.

Epitropoulos, M-F. and Roudometof, V. (eds) (1998) *American Culture in Europe: Interdisciplinary Perspectives*. Westport, CT: Praeger.

Evans, M. and Davies, J. (1999) Understanding policy transfer: a multi-level, multi-disciplinary perspective, *Public Administration*, 77: 361–85.

Eyestone, R. (1977) Confusion, diffusion and innovation, *American Political Science Review*, 71: 441–53.

Fairclough, N. (2000) *New Labour, New Language?* New York: Routledge.

Faulkner, D. (2001) *Crime, State and Citizen: A Field Full of Folk*. Winchester: Waterside Press.

Fehrenbach, H. and Poiger, U. (2000) Introduction: Americanization reconsidered, in H. Fehrenbach, and U. Poiger (eds) *Transactions, Transgressions, Transformations: American Culture in Western Europe and Japan*. New York: Berghahn Books.

Feigenbaum, H., Henig, J. and Hamnett, C. (1999) *Shrinking the State: The Political Underpinnings of Privatization*. Cambridge: Cambridge University Press.

Flanagan, T.J. (1996) Public opinion and public policy in criminal justice, in T.J. Flanagan and D.R. Longmire (eds) *Americans View Crime and Justice: A National Public Opinion Survey*. Thousand Oaks, CA: Sage Publications.

Foley, M. (2000) *The British Presidency: Tony Blair and the Politics of Public Leadership*. Manchester: Manchester University Press.

Frase, R. (2001) Comparative perspectives on sentencing policy and research, in M. Tonry and R. Frase (eds) *Sentencing and Sanctions in Western Countries*. Oxford: Oxford University Press.

Freedland, J. (1998) *Bring Home the Revolution: How Britain Can Live the American Dream*. London: Fourth Estate.

Gardner, J., Von Hirsch, A., Smith, A.T.H., Morgan, R., Ashworth, A. and Wasik, M. (1998) Clause 1 – The hybrid law from hell?, *Criminal Justice Matters*, 31 (Spring): 25–7.

Garland, D. (1990) *Punishment and Modern Society: A Study in Social Theory*. Oxford: Oxford University Press.

Garland, D. (2000) The culture of high crime societies: some preconditions of recent 'law and order' policies, *British Journal of Criminology*, 40(3): 347–75.

Garland, D. (2001a) *The Culture of Control: Crime and Social Order in Contemporary Society*. Oxford: Clarendon.

Garland, D. (2001b) Epilogue: the new iron cage, *Punishment and Society*, 3(1): 197–9.

Garland, D. (2005) Capital punishment and American culture, *Punishment and Society*, 7(4): 347–76.

Gest, T. (2001) *Crime and Politics: Big Government's Erratic Campaign for Law and Order*. Oxford: Oxford University Press.

Giuliani, R. and Bratton, W. (1994) *Reclaiming the Public Spaces of New York*. New York: New York City Police Department.

Goldthorpe, J. (ed.) (1984) *Order and Conflict in Contemporary Capitalism*. Oxford: Oxford University Press.

Gould, P. (1998) *The Unfinished Revolution: How the Modernisers Saved the Labour Party*. London: Little, Brown.

Green, D. (2003) Lock 'em up: if only we'd nick America's solution, *The Times*, 2 September: 16.

Greenberg, D. (2002) Striking out in democracy, *Punishment and Society*, 4(2): 237–52.

Greenberg, D.F. (2001) Novus Ordo Saeclorum? A commentary on Downes and Beckett and Western, *Punishment and Society*, 3(1): 81–93.

Greenberg, S. (1995) Reconstructing the democratic vision, in W.D. Burnham (ed.) *The American Prospect Reader in American Politics*. Chatham, NJ: Chatham House Press.

Greene, J. (1999) Zero-Tolerance: a case study of police policies and practices in New York City, *Crime and Delinquency*, 45(2): 171–87.

Greene, J. (2001) Bailing out private jails, *The American Prospect*, 12(16), 10 September, at http://www.prospect.org/print/V12/16/greene-ju.html

Griffiths, W. (1997) Zero tolerance: a view from London, in N. Dennis (ed.) *Zero Tolerance: Policing a Free Society*. London: Institute for Economic Affairs.

Harvey, D. (2000) *Spaces of Hope*. Berkeley, CA: University of California Press.

Hayes, B. (1998) Applying Bratton to Britain: the need for sensible compromise, in M. Weatheritt (ed.) *Zero Tolerance: What Does It Mean and Is It Right for Policing in Britain?* London: The Police Foundation.

Hewitt, P. and Gould, P. (1993) Lessons from America: learning from success – Labour and Clinton's New Democrats, *Renewal*, 1(1): 45–51.

Hill, M. (1997) *The Policy Process in the Modern State*, 3rd edn. London: Prentice Hall/ Harvester Wheatsheaf.

Home Affairs Committee (1987) *Contract Provision of Prisons*, Fourth Report, Session 1986–87. London: HMSO.

Home Affairs Committee (1997) *The Management of the Prison Service (Public and Private)*, Volume 1, Second Report, Session 1996–97. London: HMSO.

Home Affairs Committee (1998) *Alternatives to Prison Sentences: Minutes of Evidence*, Third Report. London: HMSO.

Home Office (1988a) *Private Sector Involvement in the Remand System*, Cm 434. London: HMSO.

Home Office (1988b) *Punishment, Custody and the Community*, London: HMSO.

Home Office (1990) *Crime, Justice and Protecting the Public: The Government's Proposals for Legislation*, Cm 965. London: HMSO.

Home Office (1996) *Protecting the Public*. London: HMSO.

Home Office (2003a) *Building Safer Communities Together*. London: HMSO.

Home Office (2003b) *Respect and Responsibility: Taking a Stand against Anti-Social Behaviour*. London: HMSO.

Home Office (2004) *Reducing Crime, Changing Lives: The Government's Response to the Carter Report*. London: HMSO.

Home Office (2005) *Sentencing Statistics 2003, England and Wales*. Home Office Statistical Bulletin 05/05, London: HMSO.

Hulme, R. (2000) Post-compulsory education in England and Wales, in D. Dolowitz with R. Hulme, M. Nellis and F. O'Neill (eds) *Policy Transfer and British Social Policy: Learning from the USA?* Buckingham: Open University Press.

Inkeles, A. (1981) Convergence and divergence in industrial societies, in M. Attir, B. Holzner and Z. Suda (eds) *Directions of Change*. Boulder, CO: Westview Press.

Jenkins, P. (1987) *Mrs Thatcher's Revolution: The Ending of the Socialist Era*. London: Cape.

Johnston, L. (1991) *The Rebirth of Private Policing*. London/New York: Routledge.

Johnstone, G. (ed.) (2003) *A Restorative Justice Reader: Texts, Sources, Context*. Cullompton: Willan.

Jones, T. (2003) The governance and accountability of policing, in T. Newburn (ed.) *Handbook of Policing*. Cullompton: Willan.

Jones, T. and Newburn, T. (2002a) Learning from Uncle Sam? Exploring US influences on British crime control policy, *Governance*, 15(1): 97–119.

Jones, T. and Newburn, T. (2002b) Policy convergence and crime control in the USA and UK: streams of influence and levels of impact, *Criminal Justice*, 2(2): 173–203.

Jones, T. and Newburn, T. (2002c) The transformation of policing? Understanding current trends in policing systems, *British Journal of Criminology*, 42(1): 129–46.

Jones, T. and Newburn, T. (2005) Comparative criminal justice policy-making in the US and UK: the case of private prisons, *British Journal of Criminology*, 45(1): 58–80.

Jones, T. and Newburn, T. (2006) Three strikes and you're out: exploring symbol and substance in American and British crime control politics, *British Journal of Criminology*, 46(5): 781–802.

Jones, T., Newburn, T. and Smith, D.J. (1994) *Democracy and Policing*. London: Policy Studies Institute.

Karmen, A. (2001) *New York Murder Mystery: The True Story Behind the Crime Crash of the 1990s*. New York: New York University Press.

Kelling, G.L. (1998) The evolution of Broken Windows, in M. Weatheritt (ed.) *Zero Tolerance: What Does It Mean and Is It Right for Policing in Britain?* London: The Police Foundation.

Kelling, G.L. and Coles, C.M. (1996) *Fixing Broken Windows: Restoring Order and Reducing Crime in Our Communities*. New York: Simon and Schuster.

Kennedy, J. (2000) Monstrous offenders and the search for solidarity through modern punishment, *Hastings Law Journal*, 51: 829–980.

Kerr, C. (1983) *The Future of Industrial Societies: Convergence or Continuing Diversity?* Cambridge, MA: Harvard University Press.

Kerr, C., Dunlop, J., Harbison, F. and Myers, C. (1973) *Industrialism and Industrial Man*. Harmondsworth: Penguin.

King, D. and Wickham-Jones, M. (1999) From Clinton to Blair: the Democratic (Party) origins of welfare to work, *The Political Quarterly*, 70(1): 62–74.

King, R. and Mauer, M. (2001) *Ageing Behind Bars: 'Three Strikes' Seven Years Later*. Washington, DC: The Sentencing Project.

Kingdon, J.W. (1995) *Agendas, Alternatives, and Public Policies*, 2nd edn. New York: HarperCollins.

Labour Party (1996) *Tackling the Causes of Crime*. London: Labour Party.

Labour Party (1997) *New Labour: Because Britain Deserves Better* (General Election Manifesto). London: Labour Party.

Lacey, N. (2003) Principles, politics and criminal justice, in L. Zedner and A. Ashworth (eds) *The Criminological Foundations of Penal Policy: Essays in Honour of Roger Hood*. Oxford: Clarendon Press.

Le Grand, J. (1998) The Third Way begins with CORA, *New Statesman*, 6 March.

Levi-Faur, D. and Jordana, J. (2005) Regulatory capitalism: policy irritants and convergent divergence, *The Annals*, 598: 191–7.

Levitt, S. (1996) The effects of prison population size on crime rates: evidence from prison overcrowding legislation, *The Quarterly Journal of Economics*, 111(2): 319–51.

Lilly, J.R. and Knepper, P. (1992) An international perspective on the privatization of corrections, *Howard Journal*, 31(3): 174–91.

Lindblom, C. (1959) The science of muddling through, *Public Administration Review*, 19(2): 79–88.

Lipset, S.M. (1996) *American Exceptionalism: A Double-Edged Sword*. New York/London: W.W. Norton.

Lustgarten, L. (1986) *The Governance of Police*. London: Sweet and Maxwell.

McConville, S. (1981) *A History of English Prison Administration*. London: Routledge and Kegan Paul.

McDonald, D. (1994) Public imprisonment by private means, *British Journal of Criminology*, 34(Special Issue): 29–48.

McDonald, D., Fournier, E., Russell-Einhorn, M. and Crawford, S. (1998) *Private Prisons in the United States: An Assessment of Current Practice*. Cambridge, MA: Abt Associates.

McLaughlin, E. and Muncie, J. (2001) *The Sage Dictionary of Criminology*. London: Sage Publications.

Mair, G. (1997) Community penalties and the probation service, in M. Maguire, R. Morgan and R. Reiner (eds) *The Oxford Handbook of Criminology*, 2nd edn. Oxford: Clarendon.

Mair, G. and Mortimer, E. (1996) *Curfew Orders and Electronic Monitoring*, Home Office Research Study No. 163. London: Home Office.

Majone, G. (ed.) (1996) *Regulating Europe*. London: Routledge.

Maple, J. (1999) *Crime Fighter*. New York: Doubleday.

Marsh, D. and Rhodes, R.A.W. (1992) *Policy Networks in British Government*. Oxford: Clarendon Press.

Marshall, P.F. and Vaillancourt, M.A. (1993) *Changing the Landscape, Ending Violence, Achieving Equality: Final Report*. Ottawa: Canadian Panel on Violence Against Women.

Mattera, P. and Khan, M. (2001) *Jail Breaks: Economic Development Subsidies Given to Private Prisons*. Washington, DC: Good Jobs First.

Mauer, M. (1999a) *Race to Incarcerate*. New York: The New Press.

Mauer, M. (1999b) *Americans Behind Bars: The International Use of Incarceration 1992–93*. Washington, DC: The Sentencing Project.

Melossi, D. (2004) The cultural embeddedness of social control: reflections on the comparison of Italian and North-American cultures concerning punishment, in T. Newburn and R. Sparks (eds) *Criminal Justice and Political Cultures*. Cullompton: Willan.

Michael, A. (ed.) (1997) *Tough on Crime and Tough on Causes: A Collection of Essays*, discussion paper 33, London: The Fabian Society.

Mintrom, M. (1997) Policy entrepreneurs and the diffusion of innovation, *American Journal of Political Science*, 41: 738–70.

Monk, R. (1998) Policing New York City: a view from the Inspectorate of Constabulary, in M. Weatheritt (ed.) *Zero Tolerance: What Does It Mean and Is It Right for Policing in Britain?* London: The Police Foundation.

Moore, M.H. (1988) What sort of ideas become public ideas?, in R. Reich (ed.) *The Power of Public Ideas*. Cambridge, MA: Harvard University Press.

Moore, M.H. (2003) Sizing up Compstat: an important administrative innovation in policing, *Criminology and Public Policy*, 2(3): 469–94.

Morgan, R. (2002) Imprisonment, in M. Maguire, R. Morgan and R. Reiner (eds) *The Oxford Handbook of* Criminology, 3rd edn. Oxford: Oxford University Press.

Murray, C. (1997) *Does Prison Work?* London: Institute of Economic Affairs.

National Institute of Justice (1999) Keeping track of electronic monitoring, *National Law Enforcement and Corrections Technology Center Bulletin*. Washington, DC: National Institute of Justice.

Nellis, M. (2000) Law and order: the electronic monitoring of offenders, in D. Dolowitz *et al.* (eds) *Policy Transfer and British Social Policy*. Buckingham: Oxford University Press.

Nelson, B. (1996) Public policy and administration: an overview, in R. Goodin and H.-D. Klingemann (eds) *A New Handbook of Political Science*. Oxford: Oxford University Press.

Newburn, T. (1992) *Permission and Regulation: Law and Morals in Post-war Britain*. London: Routledge.

Newburn, T. (1998) Tackling youth crime and reforming youth justice: the origins and nature of New Labour policy, *Policy Studies*, 19(3/4): 199–214.

Newburn, T. (2002) Atlantic crossings: 'policy transfer' and crime control in the USA and Britain, *Punishment and Society*, 4(2): 165–94.

Newburn, T. (2006) Contrasts in intolerance: cultures of control in the United States and Britain, in T. Newburn, and P. Rock (eds) *The Politics of Crime Control: Essays in Honour of David Downes*. Oxford: Clarendon Press.

Newburn, T. and Jones, T. (2005) Symbolic politics and penal policy: the long shadow of Willie Horton, *Crime, Media, Culture*, 1(1): 72–87.

Newburn, T. and Jones, T. (forthcoming) Zero tolerance: reflections on the development of a crime control concept, *Theoretical Criminology*.

Newburn, T. and Sparks, R. (2004a) Criminal justice and political cultures, in T. Newburn and R. Sparks (eds) *Criminal Justice and Political Cultures*. Cullompton: Willan.

Newburn, T. and Sparks, R. (2004b) *Criminal Justice and Political Cultures: National and International Dimensions of Crime Control*. Cullompton: Willan.

Newman, J. (2001) *Modernising Governance: New Labour, Policy and Society*. London: Sage Publications.

O'Malley, P. (2004) Globalising risk? Distinguishing styles of 'neoliberal' criminal justice in Australia and the USA, in T. Newburn and R. Sparks (eds) *Criminal Justice and Political Cultures: National and International Dimensions of Crime Control*. Cullompton: Willan.

O'Neill, F. (2000) The internal market and the reform of the NHS, in D. Dolowitz *et al.* (eds) *Policy Transfer and British Social Policy: Learning from the USA?* Buckingham: Open University Press.

Orr, J. (1997) Strathclyde's Spotlight Initiative, in N. Dennis (ed.) *Zero Tolerance: Policing a Free Society*. London: Institute for Economic Affairs.

Page, E. (2003) Europeanization and the persistence of administrative systems, in J. Hayward and A. Menon (eds) *Governing Europe*. Oxford: Oxford University Press.

Pakes, F.J. (2004) The politics of discontent: the emergence of a new criminal justice discourse in the Netherlands, *Howard Journal of Criminal Justice*, 43(3): 284–98.

Peck, J. and Theodore, N. (2001) Exporting Workfare/importing Welfare-to-Work: exploring the politics of Third Way policy transfer, *Political Geography*, 20(4): 427–60.

Pells, R. (1997) *Not Like Us: How Europeans Have Loved, Hated and Transformed American Culture since World War II*. New York: Basic Books.

Penal Affairs Consortium (1996) *Protecting the Public: Comments on the White Paper of April 1996*. London: Penal Affairs Consortium.

Pollard, C. (1997) Zero tolerance: short-term fix, long-term liability?, in N. Dennis (ed.) *Zero Tolerance: Policing a Free Society*. London: Institute for Economic Affairs.

Pollitt, C. (2001) Convergence: the useful myth?, *Public Administration*, 79(4): 933–47.

Poveda, T. (2000) American exceptionalism and the death penalty, *Social Justice*, 27(2): 252–67.

President's Commission on Privatization (1988) *Privatization: Toward More Effective Government*. Washington, DC: The White House.

Prison Reform Trust (1994) *Privatization and Market Testing in the Prison Service*. London: Prison Reform Trust.

Prison Reform Trust (1996a) *Truth in Sentencing*. London: Prison Reform Trust.

Prison Reform Trust (1996b) *Automatic Life Sentences: The Californian Experience*. London: Prison Reform Trust.

Prison Reform Trust (1997) *The Effect of American Sentencing Policy Changes on the Courts, Prisons and Crime*. London: Prison Reform Trust.

Prison Reform Trust (2005) *Private Punishment: Who Profits?* London: Prison Reform Trust.

Punch, M., Hoogenboom, B. and Williamson, T. (2005) Paradigm lost: the Dutch dilemma, *Australia and New Zealand Journal of Criminology*, 38(2): 268–81.

Pyle, D. (1995) *Cutting the Costs of Crime: The Economics of Crime and Criminal Justice*. London: Institute for Economic Affairs.

Radaelli, C. (2000) Policy transfer in the European Union, *Governance*, 13(1): 25–43.

Rawnsley, A. (2000) *Servants of the People*. London: Penguin.

Reiner, R. (1991) *Chief Constables*. Oxford: Oxford University Press.

Reitz, K. (2001) The disassembly and reassembly of US sentencing practices, in

M. Tonry and R. Frase (eds) *Sentencing and Sanctions in Western Countries*. Oxford: Oxford University Press.

Rentoul, J. (1995) *Tony Blair*. London: Little, Brown and Co.

Rhodes, J. (1997) *Understanding Governance*. Buckingham: Open University Press.

Richardson, F. (1999) The electronic tagging of offenders: trials in England, *Howard Journal*, 38(2): 158–72.

Roberts, J. and Stalans, L. (1998) Crime, criminal justice and public opinion, in M. Tonry (ed.) *The Handbook of Crime and Punishment*. New York: Oxford University Press.

Rock, P. (1990) *Helping Victims of Crime: The Home Office and the Rise of Victim Support in England and Wales*. Oxford: Clarendon.

Rock, P. (1995) The opening stages of criminal justice policy-making, *British Journal of Criminology*, 35(1): 1–16.

Rock, P. (1998) *After Homicide: Practical and Political Responses to Bereavement*. Oxford: Clarendon Press.

Rock, P. (2004) *Constructing Victims' Rights*. Oxford: Clarendon Press.

Rodgers, D.T. (1998) *Atlantic Crossings: Social Politics in a Progressive Age*. Cambridge, MA: Belknap Press of Harvard University Press.

Rose, R. (1993) *Lesson-drawing in Public Policy: A Guide to Learning Across Time and Space*. Chatham, NJ: Chatham House Publishers.

Rosen, J. (2000) Why Patrick Dorismond didn't have to die: excessive force, *The New Republic*, April.

Rothman, D.J. (1995) More of the same: American criminal justice policies in the 1990s, in T.G. Blomberg and S. Cohen (eds) *Punishment and Social Control: Essays in Honor of Sheldon L. Messinger*. New York: Aldine de Gruyter.

Rutherford, A. (1990) British penal policy and the idea of prison privatization, in D.C. McDonald (ed.) *Private Prisons and the Public Interest*. New Brunswick: Rutgers University Press.

Rutherford, A. (2000) An elephant on the doorstep: criminal policy without crime in New Labour's Britain, in P. Green and A. Rutherford (eds) *Criminal Policy in Transition*. Oxford: Hart.

Ryan, M. (1996) Private prisons: contexts, performance and issues, *European Journal on Criminal Policy and Research*, 4(3): 92–107.

Ryan, M. and Ward, T. (1989) *Privatization and the Penal System: The American Experience and the Debate in Britain*. Milton Keynes: Open University Press.

Sarabi, B. (2000) *ALEC in the House: Corporate Bias in Criminal Justice Legislation*. Portland, OR: Western Prison Project.

Sarabi, B. and Bender, E. (2000) *The Prison Payoff: The Role of Politics and Private Prisons in the Incarceration Boom*. Portland, OR: Western Prison Project.

Savage, S., Charman, S. and Cope, S. (2000) The policy-making context: who shapes policing policy?, in F. Leishman *et al.* (eds) *Core Issues in Policing*. Harlow: Longman.

Schiller, H. (1992) *Mass Communications and American Empire*, 2nd edn. Boulder, CO: Westview Press.

Schiraldi, V., Colburn, J. and Lotke, R. (2004) *Three Strikes and You're Out: An Examination of the Impact of Three Strike Laws Ten Years After Their Enactment*, Justice Policy Institute Policy Brief. Washington, DC: Justice Policy Institute.

Sentencing Project (2002) *Prison Privatization and the Use of Incarceration*. Washington, DC: The Sentencing Project.

Silverman, E. (1999) *NYPD Battles Crime: Innovative Strategies in Policing*. Boston, MA: Northeastern University Press.

Smith, A. (2004) Policy transfer and the development of UK climate policy. *Policy and Politics*, 32(1): 79–93.

Smith, J.A. (1991) *The Idea Brokers: Think Tanks and the Rise of the New Policy Elite*. New York: The Free Press.

Sopel, J. (1995) *Tony Blair: The Moderniser*. London: Michael Joseph.

Spelman, W. (2000) The limited importance of prison expansion, in A. Blumstein and J. Wallman (eds) *The Crime Drop in America*. New York: Cambridge University Press.

Squires, P. and Stephen, D. (2005) *Rougher Justice: Anti Social Behaviour and Young People*. Cullompton: Willan.

Stenson, K. and Edwards, A. (2004) Policy transfer in local crime control: beyond naïve emulation, in T. Newburn and R. Sparks (eds) *Criminal Justice and Political Cultures: National and International Dimensions of Crime Control*. Cullompton: Willan.

Stone, D. (1988) *Policy Paradoxes and Political Reason*. Glenview, IL: Scott Foresman and Company.

Stone, D. (1996) *Capturing the Political Imagination: Think Tanks and the Policy Process*. London/Portland, OR: Frank Cass.

Stone, D. (1999) Learning lessons and transferring policies across time, space and disciplines, *Politics*, 19(1): 51–9.

Stone, D. (2000) Non-governmental policy transfer: the strategies of independent policy institutes, *Governance*, 13(1): 45–70.

Surette, R. (1996) News from nowhere, policy to follow: media and the social construction of 'three strikes and you're out', in D. Shichor and D.K. Sechrest (eds) *Three Strikes and You're Out: Vengeance as Public Policy*. Thousand Oaks, CA: Sage Publications.

Thomas, D.A. (1998) The Crime (Sentences) Act 1997, *Criminal Law Review* (January): 83–92.

Tonry, M. (1999a) Why are US incarceration rates so high?, *Overcrowded Times*, 1 (June): 8–16.

Tonry, M. (1999b) Parochialism in US sentencing policy, *Crime and Delinquency*, 45(1): 48–65.

Tonry, M. (2001) Symbol, substance and severity in western penal policies, *Punishment and Society*, 3(4): 517–36.

Tonry, M. (2004a) *Punishment and Politics: Evidence and Emulation in the Making of English Crime Control Policy*. Cullompton: Willan.

Tonry, M. (2004b) *Thinking about Crime: Sense and Sensibility in American Penal Culture*. New York: Oxford University Press.

Travis, A. (1993) Doubt cast on Major's crime fight, *Guardian*, 15 October.

Travis, A. (2000) Courts fight shy of 'three strikes', *Guardian*, 27 December.

United States Department of Justice (2001) *Prisoners in 2000*. Washington, DC: US Department of Justice.

United States General Accounting Office (1998) *Truth in Sentencing: Availability of Federal Grants Influenced Laws in Some States*. Washington, DC: US General Accounting Office.

Vitello, M. (1997) Three strikes: can we return to rationality?, *Journal of Criminal Law and Criminology*, 87(2): 395–481.

Wacquant, L. (1999a) America as social dystopia: the politics of urban disintegration, or the French uses of the 'American Model', in P. Bourdieu *et al.* (eds) *The Weight of the World: Social Suffering in Contemporary Society*. Cambridge: Polity Press.

Wacquant, L. (1999b) How penal common sense comes to Europeans: notes on the transatlantic diffusion of the neoliberal doxa, *European Societies*, 1(3): 319–52.

Wacquant, L. (1999c) *Les Prisons de la Misère*. Paris: Editions Raisons d'agir.

Walker, J. (1969) The diffusion of innovations among American states, *American Political Science Review*, 63: 880–99.

Walker, N. (2000) *Policing in a Changing Constitutional Order*. London: Sweet and Maxwell.

Walker, R. (1998) The Americanization of British welfare: a case study of policy transfer, *Focus*, 19(3): 32–40.

Weatheritt, M. (ed.) (1998) *Zero Tolerance Policing: What Does It Mean and Is It Right for Policing in Britain?* London: The Police Foundation.

White, P. and Cullen, C. (2000) *Projections of Long-term Trends in the Prison Population to 2007* (No. 2/00). London: Home Office.

Whitfield, D. (1997) *Tackling the Tag*. Winchester: Waterside Press.

Whitman, J.Q. (2003) *Harsh Justice: Criminal Punishment and the Widening Divide between America and Europe*. New York: Oxford University Press.

Whitman, J.Q. (2005) Response to Garland, *Punishment and Society* 7(4): 389–96.

Wilensky, H. (1975) *The Welfare State and Equality: Structure and Ideological Roots of Public Expenditures*. Berkeley, CA: University of California Press.

Wilson, J.Q. and Kelling, G.L. (1982) Broken windows, *Atlantic Monthly* (March): 29–38.

Windlesham, D. (1993) *Responses to Crime*. Oxford: Clarendon Press.

Windlesham, D. (1998) *Politics, Punishment, and Populism*. Oxford: Oxford University Press.

Windlesham, D. (2001) *Dispensing Justice: Responses to Crime* (Vol. 4). Oxford: Oxford University Press.

Wolman, H. (1992) Understanding cross-national policy transfers: the case of Britain and the United States, *Governance*, 5(1): 27–45.

Young, H. (1991) *One of Us: A Biography of Margaret Thatcher*. London: Macmillan.

Young, J. (2003) Winning the fight against crime? New Labour, populism and lost opportunities, in R. Matthews and J. Young (eds) *The New Politics of Crime and Punishment*. Cullompton: Willan.

Young, P. (1987) *The Prison Cell: The Start of a Better Approach to Prison Management*. London: Adam Smith Institute.

Zedner, L. (2002) Dangers of dystopias in penal theory. *Oxford Journal of Legal Studies*, 22(2): 341–66.

Zimring, F.E. (2002) Entrepreneurs of punishment: the legacy of privatization, *Punishment and Society*, 4(3): 321–44.

Zimring, F.E. (2003) *The Contradictions of American Capital Punishment*. New York: Oxford University Press.

Zimring, F.E. (2005) Path dependence, culture and state-level execution policy: a reply to Garland, *Punishment and Society*, 7(4): 377–84.

Zimring, F.E. and Hawkins, G. (1997) *Crime is Not the Problem: Lethal Violence in America*. New York: Oxford University Press.

Zimring, F.E., Hawkins, G. and Kamin, S. (2001) *Punishment and Democracy: Three Strikes and You're Out in California*. New York: Oxford University Press.

Index